ON THE TRAIL OF THE MAYA EXPLORER

Tracing the Epic Journey of John Lloyd Stephens

STEVE GLASSMAN

THE UNIVERSITY OF ALABAMA PRESS
Tuscaloosa and London

To Raphael Barousse and Sally Duncan

Library of Congress Cataloging-in-Publication Data

Glassman, Steve.
On the trail of the Maya explorer : tracing the epic journey of
John Lloyd Stephens / Steve Glassman.
p. cm.
Includes bibliographical references and index.
ISBN 0-8173-1303-6 (cloth : alk. paper)
1. Mayas—Antiquities. 2. Maya architecture. 3. Stephens, John Lloyd, 1805–1852—
Journeys—Central America. 4. Central America—Description and travel.
5. Central America—Antiquities. I. Title.
F1435 .G555 2003
917.2804′4—dc21
2003004094

British Library Cataloguing-in-Publication Data available

Contents

Illustrations

Maps

Acknowledgments

A multidisciplinary work such as this could not have been written without a great deal of assistance. I want to thank heartily each of the following. First, thanks go to Robert Smith, former chair of the Spanish Department and professor emeritus at Stetson University. One of Bob's colleagues told me that of all his professional acquaintances, he felt Bob knew the most about Central and South America. Bob's perceptive comments on all phases of this manuscript—ethnological, archaeological, and historical, with particular emphasis on travel writing—supported that opinion. Speaking of that ever so technical field of Maya archaeology, Michael Smyth of Rollins College read appropriate parts of the manuscript and guided me through the extremely tortuous and ever shifting paths of Maya studies. Thanks also to F. Kent Reilly III, Department of Anthropology, Southwest Texas State University, and my particular gratitude goes out to Edward H. Moseley, Emeritus Director and Professor, Capstone International Center, University of Alabama, for his many instructive and useful comments, almost all of which found their way into the final document. Naturally, any mistakes or misconceptions that have crept into the manuscript are due to my deficiencies rather than the excellent advice tendered.

Equal thanks go to a whole slew of nonacademics who significantly guided or supported this effort. First, let me cite Randy Attwood, without whom this book may have died aborning. Randy found an interested editor and motivated me to complete the book when my attention had turned to other projects. The assistance of Raphael Barousse and Sally Duncan are noted in the text. Sally's help was multifaceted; at some point she did everything but write the book. I would like specifically to acknowledge Raphael for introducing me to Stephens. Thanks go Jorge Sanchez Perez and Pepe Aranda in Campeche, Mexico. Kitty Moore and Chip and Stephanie Davis and many other Embry-Riddle Aeronautical University (ERAU) students who accompanied me at various times to Mesoamerica must be mentioned. In particular, I have to acknowledge the students who made teaching at the University College of Belize instructive and enjoyable, Fernando Tzib, Lucy Zuniga, Diana Jones, Elizabeth Weatherington, Gertrudis, Emilio, Annamarie, Egbert Higinio, Salome among many others. Thanks also to Maurice "Socky" O'Sullivan, my collaborator on so many other projects. To ERAU Communications student, Ryan Delane, my gratitude for initiating me into the mysteries of digital photography. Also, thanks to John Wilton for the superb maps, with assistance from Sally Duncan.

For financial assistance I am grateful to the Fulbright program's Senior Scholarship and Embry-Riddle Aeronautical University's Vice-President's and Dean's funds for their aid. To my chairs at ERAU Nancy Parker and Bob Oxley go my heartfelt appreciation. In particular, Bob provided support at many crucial junctures. Others at ERAU who have been helpful in the completion of this project are Lynn Prine (the online reference whiz), Jane Deighan, Christine Poucher, Kathleen Citro, Ann Magaha, and Mary Van Buren.

ON THE TRAIL OF THE MAYA EXPLORER

JOHN LLOYD STEPHENS (1805–1852)

Introduction

The John Lloyd Stephens Tour Guide

In October 1839, John Lloyd Stephens climbed on a mule and began the arduous ascent of the Mico Mountains in eastern Guatemala. According to Stephens, Central America at that time was an obscure land filled with "volcanoes and earthquakes, torn and distracted by civil war," and with not much to offer a young man seeking fame and fortune.

Stephens's mule-back expedition was arguably the most important, from the point of view of the arts and sciences, undertaken by a lone American until then. His scientific achievement was the discovery of the lost civilization of the ancient Maya. The artistic upshot of the expedition was the first nonfiction international best-seller produced by an American.

I made the acquaintance of John Lloyd Stephens in Esquipulas, Guatemala, when a monk lent me a Dover reprint of Stephens's *Incidents of Travel in Central America, Chiapas and Yucatan.* As it happened, Stephens and I stayed at the same place in Esquipulas, the monastery attached to the gargantuan basilica built in 1747 to house the figure of the miracle-working Black Christ, the most revered shrine of Central America. Stephens was greatly impressed with the basilica; he likened it to the Church of the Holy Sepulcher in Jerusalem. I was taken with the other things Stephens had to say about the place—for instance, that in good years eighty thousand pilgrims braved the roads of Central America to celebrate the Black Christ's feast days in January.

It was downright eerie to read a book written in the first half of the nineteenth century that described the place with such telling accuracy almost a century and a half later. Just as importantly, Stephens's book made a similar

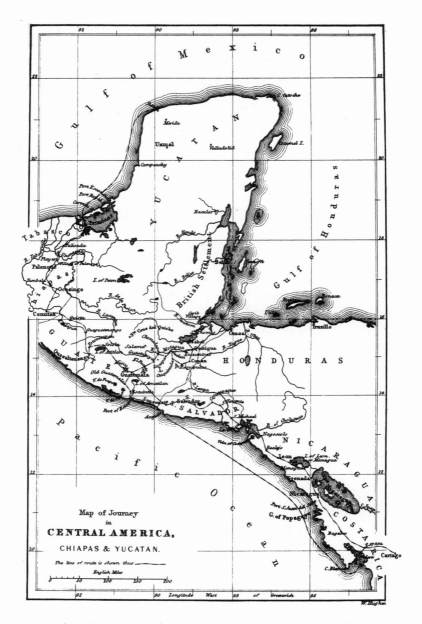

Map of Stephens's journey found in his *Incidents of Travel in Central America, Chiapas and Yucatan.*

hit with his contemporaries. In the first three months after publication, his *Incidents of Travel* sold twenty thousand copies, an astronomical figure in those days. Today, professional antiquarians call Stephens the Father of American Archaeology.[1] At a time when the preferred explanation for Mesoamerican ruins was that they were the work of Atlantans or migrant Egyptians, Stephens made a good commonsense assessment of the ancient ruins he found. What he said about the Maya, a term he was the first to apply more or less as we understand it today, still holds up remarkably well.

Had the great Mayanists of the early and mid–twentieth century, Sylvanus Morley and J. Eric Thompson, paid closer attention to Stephens, they could have avoided one of the more embarrassing intellectual blunders of our time. Morley and Thompson claimed the Maya were a peaceful and peace-loving people ruled by priest-kings devoted to mathematical and astronomical studies. Modern scholarship—notably the breaking of the Maya hieroglyphic code—has shown, as Stephens predicted so many years ago, that the Maya were pretty much like other peoples (only a little more blood-sated).[2] For instance, Harvard archaeologist William Fash notes, "Ironically, today's scholars have come to realize the wisdom of many of Stephens's original interpretations. Stephens correctly surmised that Copán and the other Maya ruins were the remains of indigenous New World peoples, that the human portraits on the monuments represented 'deified kings and heroes.' He also correctly guessed that the writing system recorded the history of the kings and their cities. However, many of Stephens's contemporaries and successors, caught up in the romanticism of the era, proposed far less reasonable reconstructions."[3]

Given all this, you are probably asking yourself, why have I not heard of this fellow (assuming, of course, that you have not)? If you have not heard of Stephens, you are in abundant company. There have been few serious essays written by literary professionals on Stephens in recent years, and half (of the four) strive to introduce him to the reading and critical public with a general biography and a few pithy quotes from his work. Two such articles are Richard Preston's "America's Egypt: John Lloyd Stephens and the Discovery of the Maya," which appeared in the Princeton University Library *Chronicle*, and Richard O'Mara's "The American Traveller," published in the *Virginia Quarterly Review*. The abstract of the latter says, "O'Mara profiles American travel writer John Lloyd Stephens and discusses some of his works." This provides an idea of the low level of critical discussion and exhibits the nearly supine literary profile Stephens cuts in O'Mara's eyes; interestingly, the *VQR* is a creative journal, not a critical publication. In the past thirty-nine years, the Modern Language Association Bibliography, which indexes essays from all major and most minor critical sources in the English-speaking world, lists only *two* entries about John Lloyd Stephens. Neither study is devoted solely to Stephens.[4] At the other end of the spectrum, a survey of anthologies of American literature used in freshman and sophomore courses turned up not so much as his name in the table of contents.

Nonetheless, three of Stephens's four books are in print—all three, for instance, are on the shelf at the local Barnes & Noble. His masterpiece, *Incidents of Travel in Central America, Chiapas and Yucatan* is available in two editions, one from the Smithsonian Institution Press and the other a Dover reprint. The most ambitious secondary work on Stephens is Victor Wolfgang von Hagen's biography, *Maya Explorer: John Lloyd Stephens and the Lost Cities of Central America and Yucatán,* which was written at the behest of Van Wyck Brooks shortly after World War II, and which has stayed in print sporadically through the years.

There is something incredibly romantic about a person who dies in oblivion and then long afterward is recognized as one of the great writers of the age (in point of fact, Stephens's work was forgotten some time after his death). Just about everybody knows the story of Herman Melville, Stephens's near-contemporary and admirer. Melville passed on thinking himself a wretched failure; his literary renaissance came four decades after his death. In recent years, the career of Zora Neale Hurston, who died in a poor-folks home and was buried in a potter's field, has traced a similar trajectory. Stephens's fortunes somehow seem more romantic than those two writers, because Melville, Hurston, and others such as Malcolm Lowry, have been restored by the literary establishment. Stephens, on the other hand, maintains a reputation as a classic writer by word of mouth (with some help from Central American historians and archaeologists who study him assiduously).

John Lloyd Stephens has fascinated—no, obsessed—me for the more than twenty years that have passed since I first made his acquaintance in that room of musty books in the basilica at Esquipulas, Guatemala. A few years ago, *National Geographic* did a spread on something called the Ruta Maya or the Maya route, a proposed trail through Central America for the serious amateur Mayanist. The route traces a path through Belize, Honduras, Guatemala, and lower Mexico. The bureaus of tourism in those countries readily took up the cry of the Mundo Maya, and today slick promotional material inveigling the modern traveler can be found in practically any travel agency in North America. And following that trail, or parts of it, are hundreds of thousands of tourists every year. Is it any surprise that the Ruta Maya was blazed by John Lloyd Stephens—on the back of a mule—in his epoch-making journey long ago? Indeed, although he may have missed a few of the more obscure sites on the modern route, the indefatigable Stephens visited others that still have not been studied by modern archaeologists.

To me, all this meant a book about Stephens was simply crying to be done, and Lady Fortuna had tapped me on the shoulder and insisted I be the one to do it (or so I felt). But what kind of book? A biography was not suited to my interests. Although by profession I teach literature and creative writing, I was not interested in doing a textual or any other kind of analysis of Stephens. While I was trying to sort out exactly the kind of treatment this material would get, I had more or less retraced the route of Stephens's Central American journey in piecemeal fashion. That was when I hit on the sort of book I'm offering here, what might be called a split-view travel book—partly from Stephens's perspective and partly from that of a modern traveler.

Of all places in the world, Central America must rank as one of the most eligible for Stephens's 160-year-old tour guide. For instance, even today in good years about eighty thousand pilgrims converge on Esquipulas for the feast days in January, the same figure Stephens reported.[5] Likewise, the startling air of surrealism Stephens ascribed to the sudden appearance of the colossal basilica of Esquipulas in a remote mountain valley mirrored my own feelings, although in Stephens's time, when the way into the valley was on mule back, the effect must have been even more stupendous.

Stephens's book makes for an effective tour guide for the rest of Central America and lower Mexico. For one thing, it is historically accurate. For another, his observations of the local folk are on target. His descriptions often make a transcendent leap clearly recognizable more than a century and a half later. The questions ballooning in the reader's mind might be, "If all that is true, what is the need for this book, which might be styled a travel book about a travel book? Why not just go down to your local bookseller and buy a copy of Stephens's *Incidents of Travel in Central America*, which you have assured me may be found there?"

First of all, do by all means acquire a copy of Stephens's book (do not forget there are two volumes—watch out for condensed versions). You might even purchase the companion volume written the following year and devoted only to the Yucatán. (From time to time I cite from the latter work but by and large I confine my itinerary and commentary to the earlier one.) However, despite the lucidity of Stephens's prose, whether you are a general reader or a literary professional casting around for a topic for a dissertation or a critical article, you will no doubt find that Stephens lacks something in the way of context. As it happened, Stephens was wandering through Central America at a time when the political infrastructure of the modern state was forming—or perhaps it would be more accurate to say misforming. He witnessed a key clash between the forces of Central American union (the Liberals) and disunion (the Conservatives) in something approaching a definitive battle. That the Conservatives came out on top is evidenced by the political fragmentation still seen on the isthmus. But it is not so clear that the state of peonage or near-peonage of much of the area's Indian population is due to the return of the Liberals in the latter part of the nineteenth century. Even a cursory understanding of Maya archaeology will show that John Lloyd Stephens was dead-on accurate in his surmises about the remarkable ruins he found moldering in the jungles. What is not apparent are the dogleg twists the course of archaeology took to return to many of the basic positions Stephens chartered in his narrative.

On the one hand, the book I offer here can be regarded as a halfway refuge. Enough of Stephens's prose is presented to give a feel for his literary abilities and accomplishments. On the other hand, a smattering and in some cases even a bit more than a smattering of background is provided to help assimilate the material. I also provide my own view as a traveler on Stephens's trail. All this is given in a nonjargonistic and nontechnical way (for the good reason that I am not an archaeologist or historian), readily accessible to the average reader.[6] In short, the book I offer gives the chairbound tourist some of the advantages of the Central American traveler who goes around with Stephens's *Incidents of Travel* in hand, of whom there are many.

Questions nag about Stephens. Why were his books so successful on publication? Why did he as a literary and historical figure fall into total eclipse, like the Maya cities he studied, for so long? And, finally, just what is the literary merit of his work? Does he deserve higher praise and more study?

So why were his books successful? There are two parts to the answer. The first is political. Stephens was not only a bred-to-the-bone New Yorker, he was also a Knickerbocker in the sense of being a member in good standing of the Knickerbocker literary establishment. Early in his career his family believed that he was squandering his law degree and ruining his life chances by hanging out in the Astor House bookstore discussing literature and politics. For once, this leisurely avocation paid off. New York, then as now, was the center of the literary industry in the country. And Stephens, wittingly or unwittingly, happened to ingratiate himself to the nascent literary elite. Had his Maya narratives been as pedestrian as the several other Central American travel narratives by Americans of the time, Stephens's books would still have received a hearty reception upon publication.

Stephens's work had great strengths. The first-person narrator is a regular go-ahead American. He is enterprising, industrious, cocky, good-humored, friendly, adventurous, a bit brash, inventive, and irreverent. Better yet, he was seeking after lost cities, which at the time was a hot topic. Just a generation before, the British and the French—Napoleon Bonaparte at the head of the French troops—clashed before the mighty pyramids of Cheops. The prize the leading countries of Europe sought was not some far off, over-populated desert, but the prestige and grandeur of ancient Egypt. Jean François Champollion, the linguist who deciphered the Rosetta stone, unearthed by French troops, was considered one of the great minds of the age for his intellectual triumph. Suddenly, Americans had a literary production that showed that they too were making their mark in antiquities. Or at least one of them, a John Lloyd Stephens of New York, was doing on his own what formerly European nation-states had been required to accomplish, that is, to bankroll an expedition to uncover lost cities of incomparable artistic and historical merit.

Even today, the mystique would be irresistible. In Stephens's day, it was a juggernaut. But there was much more in Stephens's narrative than just the ruins of a lost civilization to excite the passions of the romantically inclined. A second civilization was going to ruin in the fastness of the Central American isthmus. The Spanish had erected great buildings for government and especially for religion. For three centuries they had ruled with an iron hand—and now they too were gone, not claiming a single square foot of territory on the American continent. The reading public ate all this up.

Stephens's prose deserves special note. He wrote in a conversational style that 160 years later seems remarkably fresh and crisp. On occasion, he did not scruple to use fragments. His style established an intimate rapport with the reader with no trace of the irksome "dear-reader" familiarity common at the time. With a good pruning here and there, his writing could stand up to the very best nonfiction of today.

Given these formidable strengths, it is not surprising that Stephens's Central American book (which ran to about nine hundred pages, the equivalent of three fat modern novels) shot right to the top of the best-seller list. The puzzle is that it fell off the horizontal best-seller list, the one that stands the test of time.

To a great extent the answer to the puzzle boils down to a shift in literary tastes. After the Civil War, Americans had new subjects to occupy them—the faded glories of the old South, and the winning of the West among them. Stephens's books, published more than two decades before, no longer beguiled the always-fickle readership. This fact alone should not have completely proscribed a work with real claim as a literary classic (indeed, some of Stephens's works stayed in print to the 1880s). It was the swing of the country's literary center from New York to Boston that sealed Stephens's literary fate.

The phrase "banned in Boston" was the unhappy lot of many books that did not meet that city's literary establishment's criteria of good breeding as well as good reading. Even New England's own greatest thinker, Emerson, had difficulty breaking into the Boston literary elite because his ideas were too wild and unpredictable. Thoreau never made the grade. The New Yorker Herman Melville produced the greatest American novel in the nineteenth century without stirring a flicker of interest in the establishment. Therefore, it is no surprise that the bluenose Boston literary elite did not fall all over itself to keep alive the works of the irrepressible Stephens, who delighted in titillating his readers with glimpses of nude females, tales of crashing funerals, and going on and on about rock piles in obscure and now uninteresting lands.

Even worse for Stephens's reputation—and for him personally—was that he perished in 1852 (at the early age of forty-seven). By and by, his books went out of print. The Panama Railroad Company, which he led as president, was succeeded by the Panama Canal. Although his death was front-page news in New York, fifty years afterward, Stephens was completely forgotten. Van Wyck Brooks tried mightily to resurrect his reputation in the 1940s. As noted above, he set Victor Wolfgang von Hagen to the task of a Stephens biography. In 1949, Rutgers University Press brought out an edition of Stephens's *Incidents of Travel in the Yucatan*. Almost two decades later Dover republished the Central American book; those and other of his titles have stayed in print in many editions ever since.

To date, Van Wyck Brooks is still the critic who has done the most to promote Stephens. According to Brooks,

There was something extremely attractive in the character of John Lloyd Stephens, the frankness and manliness of feeling that one found in his books, traits that Poe noted in his review, together with the author's freshness of manner and his freedom and sound feeling and good sense. He had travelled through Egypt and Arabia alone with wild tribesmen, beyond the reach of any help, well knowing that everything depended on his coolness and discretion, while he had an infectious feeling of awe, a sense of the sublime that made his account of these travels singularly impressive. Thousands of years rolled through his mind as he gazed on the relics of faded kingdoms, recalling their mysterious uses and the men who built them and the poets, historians and warriors who had looked upon them with a wonder like his own in ages past. . . . in style, in the quality of his imagination, in his sombre sense of the flight of time, Stephens was one of the few great writers of travel, and he presently found his best account among the ruins of Central America. In his own way, John Lloyd Stephens, like so many other artists and writers, was one of the discoverers, in the [eighteen] forties, of the American scene. He revealed, at least in part, the visible past of a Pan America that was scarcely as yet aware of its own existence.[7]

In his youth Brooks wrote literary criticism with a firebrand. In mid-career he suffered a breakdown, going for the best part of a decade mentally incapacitated. The "third" Brooks was the discoverer of Stephens and a promoter of nineteenth-century American literature not until then highly regarded. As the venerable critic Malcolm Cowley said, Brooks's studies caused "a revolutionary change in our judgment of the American past," and a "radical change in our vision of the future."[8] But Cowley's quote gives only half the story. The later Brooks marched out of step with the experimentation of modernists, the likes of Joyce and Faulkner, and even more so with the writers and critics of the post–World War II era. There was a tinge of politics. Brooks seemed to many of his former admirers as "assum[ing] the role of laureate of American chauvinism."[9] The upshot of all this was the blunting of interest in Stephens's writing as serious literature. So despite the good work Brooks and von Hagen accomplished on Stephens's behalf, serious literary critics looked elsewhere.

Stephens had the misfortune to be born in a country where travel writing is rarely taken seriously. Had he been born in a state with an overseas empire, his name today would be as well known as the African explorers and adventurers Livingstone, Stanley, Speke and Grant, and Richard Burton are outside their homelands. In America the few travel books that managed to make it into the canon are the work of individuals known for something else. For instance, Mark Twain's *Roughing It* and *Innocents Abroad* and Washington Irving's travel chronicles were produced by professional writers whose names everyone knows. At almost the same level of recognition are Francis Parkman, who wrote the classic *The Oregon Trail,* and Richard Henry Dana, who did *Two Years before the Mast.* Parkman was a famous Harvard historian who became tragically crippled after a youthful adventure among the Sioux, which he details in his great work. Dana was a nationally infamous abolitionist and social reformer. By contrast, the greatest American travel writer of the eighteenth century, and perhaps the most influential American travel writer ever from a purely literary standpoint, was William Bartram. His *Travels* affected the British romantic poets in a large way. Nevertheless, his book, published in the 1790s with a press run of about a thousand copies, did not see a second printing in the United States until the 1920s.

Given the great strengths in Stephens's work, namely his deft balancing of various narrative strains, the accuracy of his archaeological surmises, the poignancy of his ethnological observation, the great value of his work to area studies, and above all the pellucid quality of his prose—never forgetting that he has been widely read and admired in the post–World War II period—I contend that John Lloyd Stephens's is one of the most powerful voices of nineteenth-century American letters. To put it in bolder terms, I assert he is an "unknown" literary great.

In Stephens's day, nonfiction prose was a literary curiosity. Real literature included only poetry, fiction, drama, and the essay. In our own age, nonfiction prose (including travel writing) has come into its own. It may be the leading literary form. The inevitable reevaluation of the nonfiction narrative of the past couple of centuries will be the tide that lifts Stephens to his rightful place in American literature. Until a goodly number of critics study Stephens's corpus closely, engage in a discourse, and come to a consensual judgment, it can be said, without fear of hyperbole, that Stephens's work stands on an equal footing with the travel writing of any nineteenth-century American, whether it be Parkman, Dana, Irving, or Twain.

1 / Landfall in Belize

From the quarterdeck of the English brig *Mary Ann* in October 1839, John Lloyd Stephens took his first sighting of the Central American isthmus, which he called in his endearingly idiosyncratic way, *Balize.** The colony was a little nail paring of land controlled by the British, appearing like *Venice and Alexandria to rise out of the water. A range of white houses extended a mile along the shore, terminated at one end by the Government House, and at the other by the barracks, and intersected by the river Balize, the bridge across which formed a picturesque object. While the fort on a little island at the mouth of the river, the spire of a Gothic church behind the Government House, and groves of coconut trees, which at the distance reminded us of the palm trees of Egypt, gave it an appearance of beauty. Four ships, sundry schooners, bungoes, canoes and a steamboat were riding at anchor in the harbor. Alongside the vessels were rafts of mahogany. Far out a negro was paddling a log of the same costly timber, and the government dory which boarded us when we came to anchor was made of the trunk of a mahogany tree.*[1]

The first task confronting the newly appointed U.S. minister to Spanish Central America—on a confidential mission to see a treaty with the central government ratified—was finding himself a room for the night. Throwing aside the dignity of his office, the five-foot, nine-inch Stephens, with sun-bleached reddish hair and searchlight eyes that matched the aquamarine of the Caribbean, slogged across the bridge over Haulover Creek to the low dives

*Stephens's quotes will be given in italics.

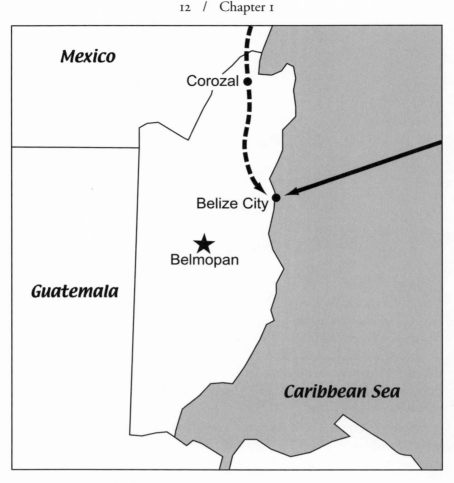

Landfall in Belize
Solid line indicates Stephens's arrival in Belize in October 1839 aboard the British brig *Mary Ann*. Dashed line indicates land route into Belize by author in December of 1991. Geographical locations and routes are approximate.

near the barracks. Although never one to stand on ceremony, it was only recently that the thirty-three-year-old Stephens had any particular reason to regard himself as a man of propriety. He started off as an underachiever.

After graduating from Columbia College and Tapping Reeves's law school in 1824, Stephens hung out in coffeehouses discussing books and politics rather than attending to his family's New York hardware business.[2] In season, he stumped for populist Jacksonian Democrats, but after a particularly vociferous campaign he came down with a case of strep throat. His voice was gone;

no more speeches. The prescribed cure was a change of climate. In 1834, at the age of twenty-nine, Stephens was packed off to Europe. His family's strategy worked: his interests evolved. He took up antiquities, and rumors of ancient ruins in Central America caught his fancy. Most authorities, on racial grounds, believed that Native Americans were incapable of high culture. Stephens determined to find out. Two enormous stumbling blocks lay in his way. The first, finances, was neatly solved when letters penned to friends found their way into literary magazines, and Harper & Sons tendered a book contract. In a few months he produced a manuscript with the ungainly title of *Incidents of Travel in Egypt, Arabia, Petraea, and the Holy Land.* It and the sequel did impressively well at the booksellers.

The book's popularity was due, in part, to the exotic places Stephens had ventured. But partly too it was due to the character of the author. He typified the kind of person Americans already believed themselves to be. He was adventurous, friendly, intelligent but without pretension—slogging through the muddy streets of the former alluvial swamp that was Belize did not bother him at all—and clean-cut in his way, showing a healthy, even clinical interest in the opposite sex.

The second stumbling-block problem was much harder to solve. Spanish Central America was embroiled in a fratricidal civil war, not a place for even the most intrepid traveler. When the newly appointed American minister to Central America, William Legget, a New York journalist with political connections died, Stephens applied for the post. Those speeches for the Democratic Party in New York were not forgotten. In the fall of 1839, Stephens had the appointment as American minister and was off to Central America.

I pushed my light pickup relentlessly for a solid week. Now, on New Year's Eve 1991, I had made Belize City, my first time in the capital of this Central American republic. In every other place where I had followed Stephens's trail, I could look through the pages of his *Incidents of Travel in Central America, Chiapas and Yucatan* and see a template of the modern place. But Belize City was different. The streets of the town swarmed with humanity—as Stephens had reported—but everything else had changed. The groves of coconut trees Stephens had seen from the deck of the *Mary Ann* were gone. In fact, hardly anything green was visible. Weathered frame houses stood shoulder to shoulder at four or more stories along narrow serpentine lanes. My little truck crept along Freetown Road then got snarled among bodies and traffic in Cinderella Plaza, a gravel-paved court hemmed in by dilapidated buildings. I was expecting a paradise but instead found something considerably more urban, even inner-urban.

A tall, rangy Rasta, sporting dreadlocks—hair and beard reaching to his waist—marched, hands and elbows flying, down the street. On spotting me his eyes flared like a guttering lamp. In an instant he changed course, leaped to my window, and poked his head into the cab. "Hey, mon, don't you remember me?" he screamed, dealing me what I would learn was one of the street hustler's standard ploys. "You can spare a little change for your old friend. How about, say, twenty dollars?"

The car in front of me jolted ahead. I let out the clutch. A policeman in a snappy Sam Browne belt motioned me onto a bridge. Suddenly, for the first time since entering Belize, I got that funny sense of parallax vision as in an old rangefinder camera when you fiddle with the tuning knob and the images sync up. *The bridge, the market-place and the streets and stores were thronged,* John Lloyd Stephens had written of the scene. In Stephens's time, as now, old women in hats haggled with street vendors, and gangs of urchins jostled in the crowds. Long ago, elderly men chatted with cronies on corners, girls strolled, and the old-time equivalent of Rasta-guys strutted shirtless, although I imagine reggae was not blaring from every street corner.

My Ford Ranger poked along Albert Street, the city swarming with life all around. From the curb, a vendor offered a small paper bag of salt-dusted Indian jujubes—tropical fruit, the size and color of large olives and tasting oddly like miniature Granny Smith apples. A half-mile farther down the street I left-turned at the paint-peeling, derelict-looking Mopan Hotel, a Belize institution frequented by scholars and serious travelers, and parked parallel to the Caribbean.

The apartment I had rented by long distance was situated just fifteen paces from the sea and not far from where the *Mary Ann,* with Stephens aboard, rode at anchor exactly 152 years, two months, and one day earlier. Two blocks to my right in a coconut palm grove—finally there were some trees—loomed Government House, a large frame building that looked as though it was the same one Stephens viewed from the *Mary Ann.* The steeple of the Anglican cathedral, which was indeed the same edifice Stephens took in, rose above the roofs of neighboring houses. It is claimed that slaves built the church with bricks brought as ballast from England. Across the channel lay the district still named for old Fort George; its main street was Barracks Road, intersected by Fort Street. Just as in Stephens's day, various fishing boats and lighters were moored in the bay.

Stephens's perambulations about Belize fetched him—in lieu of a room—a friendly invitation to enter a house, where customs stranger than any he had encountered in the Levant, along the Nile, or in the frozen wastes of Russia and Poland embarrassed him. His host, a merchant, was indulging in a "second breakfast," something Stephens found disgusting. But it was the social customs, as Stephens put it, "that some of my countrymen might find particularly strange."[3] At table sat the merchant, his wife, two British officers, and two mulattos—or Creoles, as they are known today. A place was made for the American minister between the Creoles.

Of the six thousand inhabitants of Belize, two-thirds were Creoles. The town—Stephens reported—seemed entirely in possession of blacks. Stephens *could not help remarking that the frock was their only article of* [female] *dress, and that it was the fashion of these ladies to drop this considerably off from the right shoulder, and to carry the skirt in the left hand, and raise it to any height necessary for crossing puddles.*[4] Good democrat as well as Democrat, Stephens took the seat between the two men of color without batting an eye. He noted that before he had been an hour in Belize he had learned that *the great work of practical amalgamation, the subject of so much angry controversy at home, had been going on quietly for generations* in Belize.

In the meantime, lodging had been found. Stephens sloshed through the flooded streets to a vacant house, way over on the wrong side of the river. A large puddle had to be cleared by a jump, made all the more difficult by the kippered fish and eggs he had enjoyed with his new friends. Fortunately, the house sat on piles two feet above the ground; underneath stood water nearly a foot deep. The yard, notwithstanding the mud and water, swarmed with little children.

On the way back to my new digs on the Southern Foreshore from a grocery run, I crossed a wrong bridge over a canal and ended up in the area of town called Mesopotamia, which was served by Tigris and Euphrates Avenues. I passed blocks of houses, like the one Stephens rented, up on piers with the grounds flooded by recent heavy rains, the last gasp of the rainy season. A woman in gum boots was hanging clothes on the line while her children splashed in the water in the yard, much as Stephens had described so many years before.

Stephens spent three days and two nights in Belize City. *The next day we had to make preparations for our journey into the interior, besides which we had an opportunity of seeing a little of Balize.* I spent a semester as a Fulbright lecturer at the University College of Belize. And like Stephens, I spent time learning about and seeing the country. The fact sheet published by the U.S. State Department's Bureau of Public Affairs described Belize as a cough-drop-shaped nation roughly the size and shape of Vermont, lodged between Mexico on the north and Guatemala on the west and south.[5] The Caribbean Sea bordered it on the east. It had achieved independence from Britain barely ten years before, on September 21, 1981, and had only been officially called Belize again for the past twenty years, being known as British Honduras for most of the nineteenth and twentieth centuries. Fewer than two hundred thousand persons inhabited the country. The most interesting fact was that neighboring Guatemala claimed Belize in its entirety as its twenty-third department.

The Honduras Almanac, which assumes to be the chronicler of this settlement, throws a romance around its early history by ascribing its origin to a Scotch buccaneer named Wallace. The fame of the wealth of the New World, and the return of the Spanish galleons laden with the riches of Mexico and Peru, brought upon the coast of America hordes of adventurers—to call them by no harsher name— from England and France, of whom Wallace, one of the most noted and daring, found refuge and security behind the keys and reefs which protect the harbor of Belize. Strengthened by an alliance with the Indians of the Mosquito shore [of Nicaragua and Honduras] *for the purpose of cutting mahogany, he set the Spaniards at defiance. Ever since the territory of Belize has been the subject of negotiation and contest. To this day the people of Central America claim it as their own.*[6]

Modern scholars generally agree with Stephens that the corruption of the surname of pirate Peter Wallace—known as "Ballis" to the Spanish— accounts for the origin of the country's name, which in Stephens's time was officially known as the Settlement of Belize in the Bay of Honduras. Wallace's colony was not the only pirate's lair along the Gulf of Mexico and Caribbean coasts. English-speaking enclaves existed as far north as Campeche in Mexico and south to Nicaragua. Wallace's crew was operating as early as 1638. After 1667, when the European powers agreed to suppress piracy, the pirates, so-called Baymen, settled down and started to extract logwood from the interior. Logwood is a small tree that was the principal source of yellow dye in the days before artificial coloring. The work was not difficult. The money was good. The life was rough. According to a shipwrecked mariner forced to live among the Baymen in 1720, they were "generally a rude drunken Crew, some of which [had] been Pirates." He said he had "little Comfort living among these Crew of ungovernable Wretches, where was little else to be heard but Blasphemy, Cursing and Swearing."[7]

The 1670 Godolphin Treaty affirmed English rights to lands already occupied in the Caribbean. Unfortunately for the Baymen, the treaty did not spell out which specific territories were included. On at least four occasions, in 1717, 1730, 1754, and 1779, Spanish attacks forced the abandonment of the colony. But the Baymen returned each time, often reinforced by settlers from more exposed locations, such as Campeche in 1717 and Nicaragua's Mosquito Coast in 1787. Finally worn down, the Spanish gave the British the right to cut wood in the northern two-thirds of present-day Belize while the Spanish formally retained sovereignty to the land. Plantation agriculture and local government were prohibited, although the principal men continued their once-a-year legislative council, called the Public Meeting.[8]

Not surprisingly, Stephens, a lawyer himself, was amused by the legal apparatus devised by the Public Meeting. *The court consists of seven judges, five of whom were in their places. One of them, Mr. Walker, invited me to one of the vacant seats. I objected, on the ground that my costume was not becoming so dignified a position. He insisted, and I took my seat, in a roundabout jacket, upon a chair exceedingly comfortable for the administration of justice. As there is no bar to prepare men for the bench, the judges of course are not lawyers. Of the five then sitting, two were merchants, one a mahogany cutter, and the mulatto, second to none of the others in characters or qualifications, a doctor. There was no absence of litigation. I remarked that regularly the merits of the case were so clearly brought out, that, when it was committed to the jury, there was no question about the verdict.*[9]

Stephens took a particular interest in the black populace of the colony. He enumerated its population, four thousand, and its type and condition of employment: *in gangs as mahogany cutters* and *that their condition was always better than that of plantation slaves. Even before the act for general abolition throughout the British dominions* [in 1838], *they were actually free.*[10] Stephens appears to have represented the perquisites of the Creole population of Belize as greater than the historical record warrants. For instance, the British superintendent had to insist the white population allow a Creole representative be seated at the Public Meeting (presumably the doctor Stephens sat the bench with) under the threat of penalty.[11]

Stephens's seeming exaggeration may be due to his own liberal sentiments or simply to his desire to shock his American readers—and most likely both. In any case, Stephens visited what he termed *the negro school* [which] *stood in the rear of the Government House. The boys' department consisted of about two hundred, from three to fifteen years of age.*[12] Other outings included a boat trip in the governor's pit-pan, discussed below, and a horseback ride with

Mr. Walker. *Immediately beyond the suburbs we entered upon an uncultivated country, low and flat, but very rich. We passed a racecourse, now disused and grown over. Between it and the inhabited part of Central America is a wilderness, unbroken even by an Indian path.*[13] In this passage the romantic Stephens, who obsessed on the wild state of the country, is at odds with Stephens the progressive, who was in favor of development. His paean to the fertility of the country was, no doubt, the obligatory boilerplate the local chamber of commerce types expected as payment for their hospitality. However, Stephens could not keep from being bemused by the fate of the *great Central American agricultural association, formed for the building of cities, raising the price of land, accommodating emigrants, and improvement generally. On the rich plains of the province of Vera Paz they had established the site of New Liverpool, which only wanted houses and a population to become a city. On the wheel of the steamboat, the last remnant of the stock in trade* [of the company], *was a brass circular plate, on which, in strange juxtaposition, were the words, "Vera Paz," "London."*[14]

Belize is now a more polyglot community than it was in Stephens's time. Maya refugees from the War of the Castes in the Yucatán in the second half of the nineteenth century spilled over the border and populated the northern and western part of the country. Immigrants from the British dominions arrived later, and the wholly European segment of the populace shrank to 1 percent or so. In *The Making of Belize: Globalization in the Margins,* Anne Sutherland says, "Today most articles on Belize begin with a description of the diverse ethnic groups living there, thus emphasizing Belize as a successful multicultural nation with a strong tolerance of diversity." She then quotes from a grammar school text, "Our population is made up of Creoles, Mestizoes, Garifuna, Maya, Mennonites; and people with Arab, East Indian, Chinese, European, British or other ancestry, and any number of combinations."[15]

During my months waiting to resume Stephens's trail, I gave lectures at the University College of Belize and collected images of Belizean multiculturalism at work—just as I'm sure Stephens would have done. Here are some narrative snapshots that stuck in my mind, a combination of British this and African that, with a generous measure of the Latin, the cosmopolitan, and the provincial:

Item: Postmen or rather post boys delivered mail on bicycles in fiercely white, pressed shirts. They stopped at the curb and rang their bicycle bells until you answered the door.

Item: Just as memorable were the names of things. Pickstock Street, Princess Margaret Boulevard, and Euphrates Avenue. Business establishments also had names that are not easy to forget: Smiling Meats, Brad's Chinese Restau-rant, Vasquez' Gift Shop and Saloon—and my favorite in this line, Myrtle's Saloon and Vegetables.

Item: From noon until 1:30 or so, all activity in Belize ground to a halt as everyone went home for lunch. Even the largest department store–supermarket pulled down its shutters.

Item: The East Indians wearing turbans and saris, and the Maya Indians dressed in embroidered *huipiles* added to the colorful mosaic of Belize City. An even larger minority was the Garifuna, a mixture of Carib Indians and Africans. And then there were the Mennonites in old-fashioned sunbonnets or bib overalls.

Item: A coffin maker could be seen plying his trade daily in an open-air shop on Freetown Road. Across the street his caskets were on outdoor display for passersby to admire.

Item: Bottled soft drinks were served with a straw. Only the most vulgar clod would drink straight from the bottle in Belize.

As you can perhaps gather, there was not a great deal to do in Belize City, which only numbered about fifty thousand souls. But I managed to while away the months, teaching, writing, and poking around the country. Before I knew it, it was Easter. I had a week off, enough time to make the trek to Punta Gorda, Stephens's other stop in the country.

2 / Punta Gorda and the Making of a Maya Explorer

Among the things I whiled away my time with during those days in Belize was speculating on how an intelligent young man with a professional education in the New York of a century and a half ago—a man who like his city and country, possessed untold prospects—became a seeker after lost cities, a job description that on the face of it offered little chance of artistic or scientific success.

For starters, as I learned by dipping into von Hagen's biography, Stephens began with a classical education.[1] Before being admitted to Columbia College at the age of thirteen in 1818, he had to show proficiency in Greek and Latin as well as an intimate acquaintance with Cicero, Caesar, Virgil, Homer, and Xenophon, among others. For Stephens, this curriculum was to prove eminently practical. After receiving his law degree, in 1824, he embarked on a grand tour of the North American continent, first venturing to Illinois, which was then called the Northwest. When well outside his family's reach, he slipped away to the more exotic—and forbidden—cities of the Frenchified South, St. Louis and New Orleans, hives of tropical disease and, even more terrifying, foreign blandishments.

Back in New York, although officially practicing law out of an office at 67 Wall Street, young Stephens showed all the earmarks of a person infected with a weird southern malady. He spent more time in coffeehouses than he did pursuing a livelihood. He even indulged the classic dodge of the literary idler, obtaining an M.A. from Columbia in 1828. Most of the work he produced came in the form of speeches, as noted earlier, for that damnable—

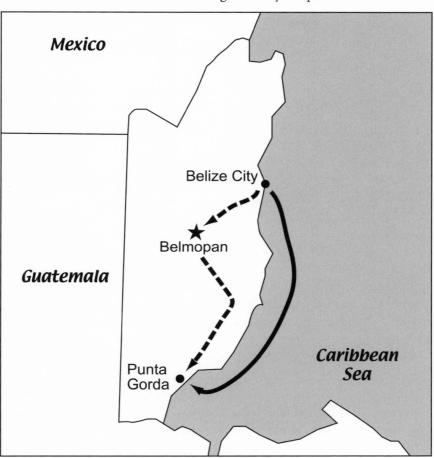

Journey to Punta Gorda
Stephens's journey to Punta Gorda aboard the steamboat *Vera Paz* indicated by solid line. Land route by author in March 1992 shown by dashed line.

from his family's point of view—populist Democrat, Andrew Jackson. Then in 1834 came the famous case of the strep throat, and Stephens's indulgent family packed him off to Europe with funds enough to support him like a gentleman for more than two years.

As yet, Stephens showed no particular interest in archaeology. True, somewhere he had read Constantin de Volney's *Ruins,* one of the inspirational texts of its age. And yes, ruined cities were then to Americans, who had new cities to build, something like dinosaurs today, a hot sexy topic. Jean François

Champollion had recently captured the attention of the world with his translation of the Rosetta stone. But Stephens, perhaps following the dictates of his literary education, wended his way from Paris to Rome then tracked the chapters of *The Iliad* from Greece to Troy in Anatolia. It was in Turkey's Smyrna that he acquired a taste for the Levantine—in the way of the Sultan's harem. "I never saw such beauty, such eyes, dark and rolling. And they walk too as if conscious of their high pretensions under that enchanting turban charged with the whole artillery of their charms."

But not even then did he turn toward the great archaeological fields of Egypt. Rather, he headed north to the Ukraine, being the first American, he believed, to visit Kiev. As an American who had cut his teeth on the doctrine of free speech, he looked aghast at the czar's secret police. By the same token he was ashamed to admit "the most odious feature of that despotic government found a parallel in ours. I do not hesitate to say that slavery stands as a dark blot upon our national character." From Russia, he traveled from Poland to Paris where he found a volume that, given his earlier tour of the known ruins of Greece and Anatolia, fired his imagination. It recounted a voyage to the lost city of Petra in the Sinai. Forthwith, Stephens obtained passage, not to America, but to Egypt.

With a homemade copy of the Stars and Stripes, Stephens sailed a chartered felucca up the Nile. He had first read of Egypt in Herodotus and other Greek texts at Columbia. In his time little modern commentary had been written on the great monuments. A thousand miles upriver he sailed, to the first cataract. The pyramids of Memphis and the great statuary of Thebes and Luxor worked a spell. So did the beauty of young Nubian women, one of whose costume he purchased to sate the anthropological curiosity of an Italian friend. "She was not more than sixteen, with a sweet and mild face, and a figure even the finest lady might be proud to exhibit in its native beauty. Every limb charmingly rounded and every muscle finely developed. It would have been a burning shame to put such a figure into a frock, petticoat, and the other etceteras of a lady's dress. I began to bargain for her costume. One of the elements of beauty is said to be simplicity. It was impossible to be more simple, without going back to the fig leaf. I thought nothing of seeing women all but naked, but I did feel somewhat delicate in attempting to buy the few inches that constituted the young girl's wardrobe." But Stephens overcame his scruples, for his own hand plucked the girl's breechclout from her loins.

A little tomfoolery on the Nile, bankrolled by the deep pockets of his merchant-prince father, made for an easy adventure; crossing the Bedouin-controlled Sinai to Petra proved the real test. No infidels were allowed to enter the city, which had been rediscovered by Europeans little more than twenty years earlier. The first European to have ferreted out the secret of the place was a German Arabist by the name of Ulrich Seetzen. Traveling incognito in the desert, Seetzen had been spurred on by Bedouin talk of a great lost city. Unfortunately, his disguise was seen through and he was killed. Donning burnoose, robe, red morocco slippers, blue sash, and a pair of pistols, Stephens became Abdel Hasis, a supposed Turkish merchant. He outfitted a caravan, which took the pilgrim's route from Cairo across dusty Suez to the Sinai. By the sixth day his water gave out. Stephens (a.k.a. Abdel Hasis) was saved from perishing by the fortunate sighting of a lone date palm. Some fast work with a shovel opened a well.

This trek tempered Stephens as a traveler. Interminable haggling was required to conclude an arrangement with El Alouin, a local warlord, to conduct him to Petra. After numerous pleas for more baksheesh, Stephens consented to a payment of five hundred piasters to enter the lost city. Otherwise, El Alouin warned, they would have to fight their way in. "The precise danger I had to fear," Stephens wrote, "was that he would get my money piecemeal and when we came among the Bedouins, he would go off and leave me to their mercy." Not easily defeated, Stephens achieved his goal of reaching Petra, a city carved from the living rock. The Greek, Roman, and endemic architectural styles, unknown and unseen for millennia worked a spell on him. As von Hagen says, "Stephens was lost for words." Even better, he was the first American to visit the place.

Napoleon, another whose early fortunes were largely forged in the crucible of Egypt, is claimed to have said of a commander, "I do not care how good a general he is. Does the man have luck?" Luck Stephens definitely had, as a young man at any rate. Like many who stand at the beginning of the great academic disciplines—Descartes in modern philosophy or Newton in physics and mathematics—Stephens had the good fortune to be a gentleman savant. He had the inherited means to allow him to pursue what appeared to be a not-for-profit hobby and the education and broad background needed to assimilate what he saw. But the heavens had not finished smiling on him. In those days the way from Cairo to New York ran through London.

In that city he met a remarkable Englishman, one whose tenure in the Levant far exceeded Stephens's. Among the many impressive entries on the Britisher's résumé was a stint as an instructor of architecture in Mehmet Ali's university in Cairo. This fellow, Frederick Catherwood by name, six years older than Stephens and of lower-middle-class background, had succeeded, in the early mid–nineteenth century, in the still difficult task of making his way in the world as an artist. More importantly, his best work had been done among the classical ruins of Rome, Greece, and especially Egypt, where he had sketched a detailed plan of the entire ruin of Thebes. According to von Hagen, he may very well have been the greatest, albeit unsung, archaeological artist in the world at the time. At the moment, Catherwood had returned to England to recruit his health and his purse. To that end he was working on four panoramas of Near Eastern scenes when Stephens encountered him in Leicester Square.

He showed Stephens two books. One was by a Spanish military officer. The other was written by a Count Waldeck. Both purported to describe pyramid ruins at a place called Palenque. Other texts too, such as an article published by a Colonel Galindo claiming ruins at the Central American site of Copán, came to their attention. Stephens was of middling height, sociable, gregarious, almost garrulous. Catherwood was taller, stouter, and more reticent, almost self-effacing. In spite of their personality differences, they hit it off. Stephens invited Catherwood to come to New York while he tried to figure a way to talk his indulgent family into financing yet another archaeological expedition, this time to find truly lost cities in the tropical fastness of his own continent. The Maya explorer had been forged in embryo.

While Catherwood set up shop at 4 Wall Street, two more lucky strikes fell Stephens's way, bolts that would actually put him in the field. The first was the fortuitous timing of his return, just before the election campaign for Jackson's successor to the White House, Martin Van Buren, the Democratic Party's candidate. Stephens took to the hustings to stump for "Little Van." The second lucky hit involved an obscure area of American foreign policy. At that time, in the 1830s, the United States did not maintain very friendly relations with Great Britain. A whole slew of friction points brooded between the two countries; the most important from the point of view of a budding author was the lack of copyright protection. American publishers simply bought a copy of a British book and reprinted it. Annoying as this practice was to British writers—many such as Dickens gave their American cousins a good tongue-lashing on account of it—it also inhibited the development of local writers. Why pay royalties, which custom at the time prescribed at the whopping rate of 50 percent, to new writers when the tried and true English article could be had gratis? Nevertheless, like many other hopeful young men, Stephens sat down to write his memoirs. Not only did Harper and Brothers, the country's largest publisher, assent to publish them, sales of *Incidents of Travel in Egypt, Arabia Petraea, and the Holy Land* went through the roof. The American public showed itself willing to pay for tales of lost cities—and Stephens's spicy anecdotes—and unwittingly bankrolled his and Catherwood's expedition to Central America.

This tortuous path brought Stephens (and Catherwood) to Belize as his first step to find an undiscovered New World civilization. His next stop after leaving Belize City was Punta Gorda, to which I traveled during Easter Break of 1992. He took a steamboat. I sailed my Ford Ranger up the Western Highway. In Stephens's day, there was only *one road opened, and there* [were] *no wheel-carriages in Belize. From want of roads, a residence there is more confining than living on an island.* The highways of Central America, as bad as they sometimes are, are the single greatest improvement since the Maya explorer's time. He would no doubt have been astonished by the asphalt throughway that vaguely paralleled the Belize River, on which he took a pleasure excursion.

His pitpan, an elaborate dugout canoe constructed of a forty-foot mahogany log, was *manned by eight negro soldiers, who sat two on a seat, with paddles six feet long, and two stood up behind with paddles as steersmen. A few touches of the paddles gave brisk way to the pit-pan. We passed rapidly the whole length of the town. All the idle negroes hurried to the bridge to cheer us. This excited our African boatmen, who, with a wild chant that reminded us of the songs of the Nubian boatmen on the Nile, swept under the bridge, and hurried us into the still expanse of a majestic river. Before the cheering of the negroes died away we were in as perfect a solitude as if removed thousands of miles from human habitation. The Belize River, coming from sources even yet but little known to civilized man, was then in its fullness. On each side was a dense, unbroken forest; the banks were overflowed; the trees seemed to grow out of the water. The sources of the river were occupied by the aboriginal owners.*[2]

I camped for the night at the Jaguar Sanctuary, a huge county-sized preserve obtained from a logging concession after the better grades of wood had been cut out. It was located some seventy miles south of Belize City, and seven miles off the unpaved Southern Highway into the rain forest at the foot of the Maya Mountains. From a few miles above the Jaguar Sanctuary to Punta Gorda, the highway was unpaved. I had a certain anxiety about hieing my vehicle across the miles and miles of dirt road along a stretch of the Caribbean coast where up to 120 inches of rain fell annually. This worry became almost a phobia when I thought about crossing Guatemala's Petén, my next step, at the beginning of the rainy season. But now it was only April, the driest month of the year. My anxieties were for naught. The country resembled a desert. Every time a truck passed, which fortunately was not often, volumes of red dirt were vented through the windows. And dust was constantly sucked up through the slits in the wagon bed and circulated into the cab via the split window. It settled like scarlet snow everywhere, on the dashboard and steering column, on the tabs on the radio and the louvers of the ventilating system. It even drifted in places, a regular blizzard of red dust in the parching dry heat. To make things even more uncomfortable, the vehicle vibrated like a tramp freighter from the poorly graded roadbed. Finally, after three hours of shuddering and rattling, Punta Gorda hove in sight.

Steamboats have destroyed some of the most pleasant illusions of my life . . . under the clatter of a steam-engine. It struck at the root of all the romance connected with the adventures of Columbus to follow in his track, accompanied by the clamor of the same panting monster. Nevertheless, it was very pleasant. We sat down under an awning. The sun was intensely hot, but we were sheltered and had a refreshing breeze. The coast assumed an appearance of grandeur and beauty that realized my ideas of tropical regions. There was a dense forest to the water's edge.

In Stephens's day five hundred souls inhabited Punta Gorda. As his steamboat approached, he saw an opening in the woods, which he likened to a clearing in the Great American Forest of the eastern states. The opening was *but a speck on the great line of coast; on both sides were primeval trees.* He landed at the foot of a bank about twenty feet high and *came at once, under a burning sun, into all the richness of tropical vegetation. Besides cotton and rice, the cohune, banana, cocoanut, pineapple, orange, lemon, and plantain with many other fruits which we did not know even by name, were growing with such luxuriance that at first their very fragrance was oppressive.* The houses extended along the shore at some distance from one another, and Stephens *was exceedingly struck with the great progress made in civilization by these descendants of cannibals, the fiercest of all the Indian tribes whom the Spaniards encountered.*

Stephens confused the Black Caribs of Punta Gorda with the Red Caribs, the Indian tribe of northern South America and the Lesser Antilles, who gave us the root word for "Caribbean"—and also for "cannibal." Africans got together with the Caribs on Saint Vincent Island and produced a race known in Stephens's time as the Black Caribs and nowadays as Garifuna. Subsequently the Garifuna rose against the British and were banished to Spanish Honduras from which, ironically, many fled after the initial turbulence of the civil war caused by the breakup of the Kingdom of Guatemala.

Stephens was traveling with an Irish priest. After inspecting—as his curiosity compelled him—every house in the community, he returned to view the priest performing his religious duties. But he got more than he bargained for. The priest had no Spanish. His acolyte Augustín, who was Stephens's servant, spoke only French and Spanish. Stephens took a stab at rendering the Irish priest's English into French for Augustín, who in turn questioned the supplicants. It was hot and the crush of eager petitioners made the going difficult. A baby was presented for baptizing and the good-looking young gringo was honored as the godfather. Stephens, a bachelor with an eye for the girls, did not want any confusion about the child's paternity. He demurred. But *the room was crowded, the doors choked up, and by this time the padre, with his Latin and English, and French and Spanish, was in a profuse perspiration, and somewhat confused. I thought myself clear, til a few moments afterward, a child was passed along for me to take in my arms.* To his relief, Stephens learned that the child at least was the one with a legal father standing by. *Still I most ungallantly avoided receiving the baby. On going away, however, the woman intercepted me and, thrusting forward the child, called me compadre; so that without knowing it, I became Godfather to a Carib child. I can only hope that in due season it will multiply the name and make it respectable among the Caribs.*[3]

More than 150 years later, in 1992, Punta Gorda was still a pleasant town, and also still much as Stephens had described it. The clearing in the forest had been enlarged substantially. In fact there was hardly a large tree to be seen. The houses nowadays are contemporary Belizean dwellings, two-story frame structures with corrugated roofs but, as Stephens described, each was centered on its own lot, many yards from the neighboring house, thus giving the town a suburban air in stark contrast to Belize City, which could well be the most urban small city in the world. The local folks still maintain their Catholicism. At an intersection, I had to wait for a makeshift procession to pass. Eight or ten Garifuna, mostly early middle-aged women, were parading an effigy of Judas—tricked out in hospital scrubs—hanging from a gibbet. The procession broke into a wild and wondrous litany in Garifuna every few hundred paces. The Garifuna language harbors elements from West Indian, Spanish, English, and French. But mostly it is African. The chant stirred the blood.

Finally in P.G. (as the town is locally styled), I went down to the wharf where Stephens could hypothetically be said to have landed and gazed across the Caribbean to Livingston, Guatemala, twenty-five or so miles away. I pined for the beauty of the Río Dulce that Stephens had waxed poetic on, but it would still be a few more weeks before I attained it. Then I found a fruit vendor and gave her a couple of bucks to watch my truck. I unracked my bicycle and headed along the black sand beaches of the Caribbean to Cattle Landing, which was the center of the Confederate settlement in British Honduras after the U.S. Civil War.

As many as seven thousand disgruntled southerners are estimated to have visited the colony. British colonial officials regarded them warily. The examples of Texas and Nicaragua, where southern expatriates came supposedly seeking only a home but ended up trying to overthrow the local governments, were never far from mind. Although exempted from local taxes and import duties for three years, the ex-Confederates were granted only limited civil rights. Plantations devoted to cotton sprung up like mushrooms—to blacken and wither just about as quickly as mushrooms in the inclement tropical climate. Not only was the climate hostile, but the labor situation was not to the southerners' liking. Slavery—as noted earlier—had been abolished in the colony before Stephens arrived, more than a quarter century before the Civil War.

The former "Southroons" imported East Indian laborers, whom, far from the eye of British authorities, they treated much like their field hands in the old South. Their "coolies" planted bananas. The crop prospered, but transportation was too irregular to make cultivation of a perishable fruit profitable. Finally, sugar was tried, and it worked. Today, sugar is Belize's leading export. The industry was started by those old Confederates, namely a gentleman named Price who imported the technology from the sugar fields and mills of Louisiana. But few of the ex-Confederates had the stomach or the capital to prosper in the new country. By 1870, only 250 Confederates were permanent residents of British Honduras, and of that figure, only seventy spent the end of their days there. An identifiable southern expatriate colony existed in the Punta Gorda area until the 1930s.[4] Gradually the members became assimilated into the Creole population of the country. The attorney general in office, Glenn Godfrey, traced his ancestry to those Confederates. Of the two major political parties, his is the less enamored of United States policy. No doubt, his ancestors would be pleased.

Returning to Belize City, I picked up a Maya hitchhiker who invited me in to take a look at his house. I was astonished to find the man's abode was almost identical to those Stephens described in Punta Gorda. *The houses were built of poles about an inch thick, set upright in the ground, tied together with bark strings, and thatched with cohune* [palm] *leaves. Some had partitions and bedsteads made of the same materials; in every house was a grass hammock and a figure of the virgin or some tutelary saint.*[5] The stick walls of my hitchhiker's house held up a thatch roof. Grass hammocks hung along the supporting walls, and there were religious pictures in evidence. The main difference was that the floor and the first four feet of my friend's house was poured concrete. With this discovery of a small parallel with Stephens, I cranked up the Ranger and drove back to Belize City.

3 / Back on the Trail

After leaving Punta Gorda, Stephens's steamboat coasted twenty-five miles south to Livingston, Guatemala, and then up the Río Dulce to Lake Izabal, Guatemala's principal port of entry for the Atlantic at that time. The mileage covered by this voyage is not great, perhaps forty-five miles or less—by boat. The land route, the only one available to me, required a couple of hundred extremely circuitous miles. And they promised to be very hard miles, almost entirely on dirt roads through Guatemala's outback province of Petén, one of the wildest places left in North America.

An excursion to the great Maya site of Tikal in the Petén some weeks earlier had shown the road to Punta Gorda to be a Sunday promenade by comparison. I had driven on the center ground between concrete-hard ruts plowed by eighteen-wheelers in the previous rainy season. But now it was late May, and the rains were expected again in earnest at any time. Rumor had it that regular rains were already falling in the south, and I wanted to pass that road before it was softened by monsoon downpours and churned into peanut butter again. The attitude of most locals, including the Americans at the embassy, was that the road was the least of one's worries about the Petén.

In the border town of San Ignacio in western Belize, where my duties took me every other week, I would regularly be entertained with tales of robbery by bandits. There was the infamous case where the bus driver was shot in the head in order to bring the bus to a stop. The passengers, after lining up, were forced to hand over their valuables. A heavyset woman with a diamond on her finger could not slip off her ring. A bandit pulled out his knife and was on

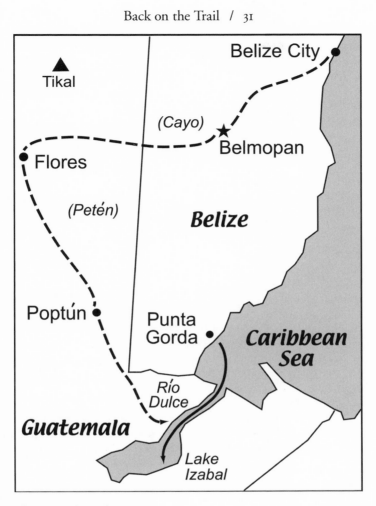

The Río Dulce at last
Stephens's journey from Punta Gorda, Belize, on the steamboat *Vera Paz* to Livingston, Guatemala, up the Río Dulce to Lake Izabal, shown by solid line.

Land route by author from Belize City to Lake Izabal via Flores, Guatemala, indicated by dashed line.

the point of hacking off her finger when another of the passengers produced some oil and shucked the ring from her hand.

Whenever I asked anyone in authority about these crimes—travel agents who regularly sent tourists overland to Tikal, border officials when I stopped at the frontier to change money, or to drink some of the better and cheaper

Gallo beer—would agree that, yes, there had been *bandidos* operating here. But they would claim the bandidos had been dispatched, always, it seemed in a multiple of two. Two weeks, two months, two years ago, the bandidos were captured, and killed. Usually—in an attempt to convince you of the pacific nature of the place—the grisly end of the bad guys would be described in loving detail. You would be told, for example, that their heads had been cut off and laid on their own doorsteps. Then there were the guerrillas operating in the area. The nicer ones had the interesting habit, according to one guidebook, of making Americans take off their clothes and, standing jay-bird naked, repeat Communist mottoes in Spanish. Jonno, a Peace Corps volunteer, had striven to get together with me for several weeks. Finally he sent his girlfriend over with his message. Do not cross the Petén. Do not go to Guatemala. It was too dangerous.

Stephens ended up staying in Belize City—not in the vacant house with the children swarming in the mud puddles—but just down the street from me at Government House. His host was her majesty's representative, Colonel Archibald MacDonald, whom Stephens proclaimed one of the most military-looking men he had ever seen.[1] MacDonald was a veteran of the wars spawned by the French Revolution, being blooded in the Spanish Peninsular campaign and decorated at Waterloo. However, MacDonald's most demanding job was that of supervisor to the Belize settlement. The first supervisor, Colonel Edward Despard, was appointed in 1784. Within five years the mahogany cutters demanded and received his ouster. (Not satisfied that his political savvy had been adequately tested in Belize, Despard returned to Britain and intrigued against the crown. He made history by becoming the last man drawn and quartered in England.[2]) In 1816, Superintendent George Arthur was still having difficulty with the Public Meeting crowd, or what he called the "monopoly on the part of the monied [mahogany] cutters."[3]

From the portrait that Stephens paints, MacDonald was fully capable of handling the Baymen and erstwhile pirates who now engaged chiefly in mahogany cutting. He was also perfectly capable of looking out for her majesty's strategic interests. Only one country posed a serious threat to British dominance in the West Indies at the time, and it was the one Stephens represented, the United States. Twice in MacDonald's life the two countries had been at war. Although at peace now, a half-dozen flash points threatened to flare into conflict. There had already been minor border incidents in Maine, gunfire had even been exchanged in the so-called Aroostook War.[4] More importantly, both countries claimed the northwestern territories of Oregon, Washington, and British Columbia. The British were alarmed by the rapid American expansion westward. Recently Texas had been separated from Mexico. It seemed there was little Great Britain could do to prevent the acquisition of the Mexican territories directly adjacent to the western states (which would happen after the Mexican War, less than ten years later in the late 1840s). But access to the Pacific Coast territories by way of the isthmus of Central America was a different matter. MacDonald was to do his bit to give the British Empire control of these important routes. Shortly after Stephens's visit, he occupied the Bay Islands of Honduras. Somewhat later, MacDonald dispatched an aide to the Mosquito Coast of Nicaragua to help keep it a British protectorate. Most decisively, he not only claimed Greytown, Nicaragua—at the head of navigation of the only water route across the isthmus—but he also tried to prevent American access. In short, Central America was one of the major strategic choke points in the world, and MacDonald in the years to come did what he could to try to swing it into the British orbit and to deny it to the Americans.

It was against this backdrop that John Lloyd Stephens, travel writer-cum-antiquarian-cum-political diplomat, wandered into the British den at Government House. Stephens tells us that MacDonald, the battle-scarred veteran, was waiting for him at the gate. And MacDonald had assembled the best men in the colony to meet the young American diplomat. There was the pious Mr. Newport, chaplain and pastor; and the intellectual Mr. Walker, *secretary of government, and holding besides such list of offices as would make the greatest pluralist among us feel insignificant.*[5] And there were other gentlemen from the civil and military sectors present as well. *Before rising, Colonel MacDonald like a loyal subject proposed the health of the Queen.* Then standing, MacDonald toasted, *"The health of Mr. Van Buren, President of the United States," accompanying it with a warm and generous sentiment, and the earnest hope of strong and perpetual friendship between England and the United States.*

Stephens thought, *Cursed be the hand that attempts to break* the friendship between the two countries. Even though warm with emotion and *not used to taking the President and the American people* on his shoulders, Stephens answered MacDonald's toasts *as well as he could.* Stephens modestly wrote that his *invitation to Government House was the fruit of his official character,* but he went on to add that he could not *help flattering himself that some portion of the kindness shown him was the result of personal acquaintance.* Among other schemes the old lion tried to foist upon Stephens was this one: if danger threatened in Guatemala, Stephens was to assemble the Europeans, hang out the Stars and Stripes and send word to MacDonald, who would charge to the rescue. Stephens wrote, *I knew these were not words of mere courtesy and in the* [distracted] *state of the country to which I was going, felt the value of such a friend at hand.*[6]

On a deeper level, Stephens was no more taken in by MacDonald than the latter was hoodwinked by him. The secret mission with which Stephens had been entrusted by the secretary of state was to complete a treaty with the confederation of Spanish-speaking Central American states. This treaty was to give special rights of navigation and transit to citizens of both countries, which of course was of no particular importance to Central Americans but vital to North Americans wanting to get to the West Coast. Given British suspicions of American intentions in the region, the urgency the State Department showed by dispatching a special agent—Stephens—to press for ratification of the treaty, and Stephens's private curiosity about the proposed trans-isthmus canal across Nicaragua, Stephens was obviously blowing a bit of diplomatic smoke.[7]

When Stephens arrived at Palenque in Chiapas, Mexico, he found yet another token of Colonel MacDonald's good fellowship. He learned then that MacDonald had dispatched Mr. Walker, the great pluralist, to steal a march on him. Walker was detailed to report on the ruins in lower Mexico. Stephens calmly recorded this fact, not seeming the least hurt by this duplicity, and no doubt he was not. Nor need Stephens have been much concerned about Walker's expedition to Palenque; he claimed the ruins were the work of migrant Egyptians. Walker's theories elicited such little interest that it was not until the 1960s that any scholarly notice was paid them.[8] MacDonald had to do what his government expected of him, as did Stephens. However, that did not mean they could not be professional and, so far as possible, even personal friends.

Stephens, full of the warmth of MacDonald's wine, boarded the dory that stroked across the bay to the steamboat that would bear him to Guatemala. Flags ran up in his honor at the fort, the courthouse, and Government House. A salute of thirteen guns and a cannon was fired from the fort, and the soldiers presented arms. A government schooner at anchor lowered and raised her ensign, and when Stephens mounted the British steamboat, the captain, with hat in hand, told him that he had instructions to place the boat at Stephens's disposal. How did he bear up under these honors, Stephens asked rhetorically.

He was a novice, he wrote, to having flags dipped and guns fired to honor his presence, *but I endeavored to behave as if I had been brought up to it.*[9]

When my Ranger rolled over the Hawkesworth Bridge into San Ignacio in western Belize, I could not suppress a pang of premature nostalgia. Belize, as an English-speaking, multicultural democracy, had been a familiar and friendly place. Its problems (street crime, drugs, illegal immigration) were familiar. Even the anti-Yankee panel of the mural on the retaining wall just beyond the bridge looked friendly, or at least familiar.

Guatemala's claims to Belize rested on a very thin reed. As noted earlier, the Spanish, though jealous of the British settlers, had never planted anything resembling a settlement in the area. Both Mexico and Guatemala laid general claim to the territory in postcolonial days, a claim that Mexico repudiated in 1892 and Guatemala ceded in an 1859 treaty. Thirty years later, Guatemalan government officials developed the notion that the agreement was invalid because the British never built a road to Guatemala City—which the Guatemalans claimed was promised in the treaty. The British cleverly, or so they thought at the time, outmaneuvered the Guatemalans in the nineteenth century by producing selected and misleading documents from their extensive archives; the Guatemalans, having lost many of their own documents, were unable to counter British arguments. Although the British were able to evade Guatemalan demands to build the road, this strategy caused much trouble later on. The matter seemed quietly forgotten until revived by Guatemalan strongman General Jorge Ubico in the 1930s. Subsequent right-wing despots used this dispute to whip up patriotic fervor in times of crisis. Troops had been massed on the border from time to time, and the Guatemalan claim came to be the major obstacle to granting British Honduras independence.[10]

Talks between Britain and Guatemala concerning the sovereignty of Belize stalled in the mid-1960s. President Lyndon Johnson offered his good services. The American mediator, Beuthal Webster, proposed that Guatemala be given control of Belize's defense, internal security, and external affairs, all supported by the United States delegation to the United Nations. Wily Belizean politician George Price took advantage of the situation by claiming that the United States offered Belize to Guatemala as the reward for its help with the Bay of Pigs. Price demanded independence with external guarantees from Britain. Thirty years later, the United States was still the butt of the San Ignacio mural, apostrophizing one of LBJ's lesser foreign policy fiascos.[11] In 1992, George Price was prime minister of Belize. Not surprisingly, given his political shrewdness, in the intervening years Price had continuously occupied high offices in the colonial and independent government. In 1992, British forces were still in the country because a lasting peace had yet not been signed with Guatemala.

Shortly I was into savanna terrain reminiscent of the Midwest or England, if you overlooked the occasional sign warning of vampire bats and the odd Maya ruin, such as Xunantunich, separated from the highway by the clear and swiftly flowing Mopán River. But on the other side of the border brooded that *land of volcanoes and earthquakes, torn and distracted by civil war.*

Much too soon, or so I suddenly felt, the concrete cube that was the Guatemalan immigration post loomed in the windshield. A pleasant chap in army fatigues with a baseball cap and a huge shooting iron on his hip wished me "Buenos diás," and asked me to please park my vehicle elsewhere. I spent fifteen minutes inside, mostly waiting for a clerk to finish pecking away at the keyboard of an ancient Remington. Finally I was handed my papers and I got back in the truck, but suddenly the friendly fellow in fatigues with the big shooting iron asked to see my driver's license and papers, which he took back into the immigration building. Now the really long wait started. I went through the stages—impatience, anger, finally fear. Had there been a hitch?

In any case I had ample time on my hands to cogitate on the historical and sociopolitical forces operating in the region. In Stephens's day, in October 1839, all of what we think of as Central America—with the exception of Belize and Panama—was known as the United Provinces of Central America. The territory had been severed from Spain when Mexico achieved independence in 1821. Separation from Mexico occurred in 1823 and for roughly the next decade all of Central America enjoyed relative peace under one flag. Then in the 1830s, the pro-Church Conservative party, based chiefly in Guatemala, but with strong local support in Honduras and Nicaragua, began to rail at the corruption of the dominant anticlerical Liberal party. Civil war rumbled throughout the area, which threatened to sunder along the lines that today mark the boundaries of Costa Rica, El Salvador, Guatemala, Honduras, and Nicaragua.

In May 1992, when I applied for entrance to Guatemala, almost all of Central America was (some would say, still) on a war footing. In Guatemala, an extremely nasty guerrilla insurrection was going on chiefly in the Petén and the northern highlands. El Salvador was technically still at war, although the intensity of its civil conflict had greatly diminished from the high point in the 1980s. Honduras, though not officially at arms, had militarized during this period. In Nicaragua, the Sandinistas had been voted out of office barely two years before, in February 1990. Only Costa Rica, in Stephens's time as well as in 1992, had remained relatively aloof from conflict.

If the intervening century and a half had not been one of continuous civil strife, there certainly had been a distressful number of coups, countercoups, assassinations, and other sorts of political violence. Nor was the violence confined to politics. The leading cause of death (among men) in all these countries was homicide, which frequently outpaced traffic fatalities fivefold. How does one explain a level of violence that would put to shame even the most trigger-happy, gang-infested areas of North America?

Thomas P. Anderson, in his introduction to *Politics in Central America,* begins by noting that "much of Hispanic America is a death-oriented society. Poverty and malnutrition combine to insure a very high infant-mortality rate. Death becomes a constant and familiar companion. The church too," he adds, "is death oriented. The use of relics and even whole bodies of saints is common, while rural people still hold a festival for the passing of a 'little angel' (a child below the age of reason)."[12] Anderson could have added that the roots of this death fixation go back to the religion and politics of ancient Mesoamerica. The gods required suffering and even death to coax the sun up every morning and to keep the cosmos in proper working order. "Blood was the mortar of ancient Maya life," Michael Coe writes in the preface of Linda Schele and Mary Ellen Miller's *Blood of Kings;* the cover of the book shows a Maya king running a thorn rope through his tongue.[13] Captured kings would be tortured—sometimes for years—before being sacrificed. Their suffering was considered a duty and a privilege to help regulate the universe.

Anderson goes on to say, "Life being brief, the emphasis [for a Central American male] shifts from prolonging one's life to living and dying in a heroic manner. For most men, to die tamely, of some disgusting disease, is thus a disgrace, an unworthy death. The best death is that which gives one the chance to display one's manhood to the fullest. The *golpe de estado* (coup d'état) and the *cuartelazo* (barracks uprising) are not regarded as aberrations, but rather as normal parts of the political process."[14]

Ten minutes had winged by since the armed man in fatigues disappeared with my travel papers. With Anderson's comforting thoughts in mind, I decided it was time to go confront the problem. As I slid the door open, I noticed the man with my papers on the verandah chatting pleasantly with a friend. I made a curt gesture. He waved back and after a while he ambled over and asked me to open the capper on the back of my truck, which he did not bother to look into. He handed me the papers with a smile and wished me a good day—and he really seemed to mean it. He was just doing his job—in the macho way business was frequently conducted by guys in military uniforms in Central America.

The Ranger spun over the concrete bridge spanning the Mopán River and went from the pale shadow of the first world that Belize is into the village of Melchor de Mencos and the fourth world of Guatemala's Petén. Although hunkered on the Belizean border and practically disenfranchised from its own country by miles of very poor road, Melchor is no Jekyll-Hyde border town, like say Brownsville or Laredo, partly of its own country and partly that of the neighbor. There is something as palpably Guatemalan about the place as a military presence.

Women in colorful Indian blouses known as huipiles, chickens, dogs, goats, children running bare-assed, all hustled in the dust churned up from the road. In the swift-flowing river, girls of school age washed clothes. Rusty tin houses whitewashed with road dust baked in the sun. The market in the town center featured stall upon stall crammed with hundred-weight burlap bags of dried peppers and herbs, gigantic baskets of tomatoes, other vegetables, and exotic tropical fruits, along with everything else a local household could possibly use. In all of Belize City, with its vastly larger population, its drinkable tap water, flush toilets, and supermarkets, there was not a market to compare with the one in this Guatemalan village, isolated in the fastness of the Petén.

I accelerated briskly up a little hill. Suddenly I saw an obstruction ahead and slammed on the brakes. A load of Coke bottles lay piled in the lane before me. Those bottles represented a small fortune, given the deposit you were made to shell out when buying the drink. I carefully skirted that deadly, tire-puncturing heap, went around a bend, now a mile out of Melchor. Four men in tuxedos were standing in a ditch—in the blazing sun—playing a saxophone, a marimba, and an accordion. I would have bet there was not a regulation necktie in the entire town, let alone four tuxes lined up in a row. I have not a clue as to what all that was about. A knot of locals was half-mooned around the musicians. The audience, from its dress—not marrying or burying clothes—did not seem to know what was going on either. Welcome to Guatemala, the land of magical realism. I hit the accelerator.

Guatemala is slightly smaller than New York State. Although falling entirely within tropical latitudes, the climate over much of the country is quite temperate owing to the fact that about half lies at altitudes above three thousand feet. It is here that most of the population resides. In fact, Guatemala calls itself, with considerable justification, the land of eternal spring. Guatemala is the most populous country in Central America, with a 1992 population estimated at almost ten million—more than New York City. Approximately half the population is of mixed Indian and Spanish blood and the other half full Indian.[15] The gross domestic product in 1990 was $11 billion, with a per capita income of almost $1200. Nevertheless, some authorities reported that half the population actually brought in less than $80 a year. Perhaps the fact that about one telephone existed for every sixty-three residents gives the best view of the state of the wealth and modernization of the country.[16]

The weather of the uplands may be forever vernal, but not so the political climate. Strife and alternating periods of deceptive languor have characterized the country since Cortez's hand-picked lieutenant, Pedro de Alvarado, stormed the highlands and brought the Quiché, Mam, and Cakchíquel Maya—and ultimately the other twenty-one to twenty-eight Mayan linguistic groups in the country—under control in the sixteenth century. Alvarado immediately handed out fiefdoms known as *encomiendas* to his loyal conquistadores. These Indians would pay tribute in the way of spoils or labor. The conquerors provided religious instruction. This system bred a bone-deep contempt of the natives by those who claim kinship to the larger Europeanized culture. I once heard a Guatemalan say that it would be an insult to God to let an Indian worship in the same church with his family.[17] Interestingly, in Guatemala the difference between an Indian or *indio* and a so-called *ladino* has little to do with race, and much to do with the language spoken at home, the style of clothes worn, and whether one lives in an Indian village and submits to the authority of the communal system. Those who do not live in Indian villages call themselves ladinos.

Lesley Byrd Simpson explains how the encomienda adapted to the area: "Spain had gone through invasion and subjugation a number of times (by Goths, Arabs, and Moors), and was living in a social system erected upon the privileges of conquest. We call it the feudal system, the essence of which was a personal relationship between conqueror and conquered. The conqueror seized the land, defended it (when he could) from his marauding neighbors, levied tribute (feudal dues) on his vassals, protected them after a fashion, forced them to serve him, and permitted no one to bear arms but himself and his retainers. It is true, to be sure, that there has been a great deal of blending of the two races; but patterns of conduct do not necessarily follow changes in complexion. That is an Indian or mestizo landowner is indistinguishable from the white in his treatment of those who serve him, and that attitude has not changed perceptibly since the conquest."[18]

The encomienda system of the Conquest and post-Conquest periods was so abusive that the Spanish priests, Fray Bartolomé de Las Casas foremost among them, protested. Charles V agreed that the system was abusive. The practice of granting encomiendas was stopped. But Guatemala was far from Spain. Those already distributed were not disturbed, and the relationship between the *latino* overclass and Maya serf was established. Understanding this relationship is essential for comprehending modern Guatemalan politics. Indeed, a second relationship was also established, which has endured into the present, that of the Church as the protector of the Indians, insofar as they have protection.[19]

A brief overview of modern Guatemalan politics may help show the influence of the Conquest in the past couple of hundred years and establish the various benchmarks in the pendulum swings of Central American history. During the post-Independence turmoil of the 1820s and 1830s—the period prior to Stephens's arrival in the country—the established Church was able to thwart the progressive ideas of the Liberal Party only through the aid of an uprising of the Indian peasantry under the leadership of the Conservative José Rafael Carrera. Carrera, whom we will meet through Stephens's eyes, became the model Central American *caudillo,* or strongman. Even though he did not learn to sign his name until he became president of the republic (or so it is claimed by many, including Stephens), Carrera ruled for more than a quarter of century, until his death in 1865. He had the satisfaction of seeing all the Liberal legislation of the early republican era repudiated. Civil marriage, guarantees of constitutional rights, and so on, all went by the boards. If Carrera died happy in the belief that his people were safe from the perfidy of the Liberals, he was very much mistaken.[20]

He was succeeded in 1873 by Guatemala's second great caudillo, Justo Rufino Barrios, known as the Great Reformer. Among other things, Barrios extended the rail lines, brought electricity and telephone service to the capital, and established a national school system. As a good anticlerical Liberal, he stripped the Church of many of its prerogatives and expelled all religious orders except one missionary order. Barrios was a progressive in the Babbitt sense of the word. Above all else he wanted to promote industry and commerce. To do so, energy was needed and it was found in abundance in the labor of the Indians (who after all were a force of conservatism and backwardness). Barrios abolished the Indians' right to hold communal lands. Many of those lands were expropriated by a new class of coffee planter. And the Indians were compelled to work on the lands they once thought of as their own by the old gimmick of debt peonage: supplies were fronted out to an individual; the interest rate charged was high; the wages at which it was worked off were low. A man's debt passed on to his children. A low-cost, never-ending labor supply was Barrios's great legacy—and one that has caused profound grief for his country.[21]

Guatemala boasts four great social institutions: the landowners, the Church, the army, and, starting around Barrios's time, the foreign corporations, most notably perhaps the banana and utility companies. Until after the World War II, these entities divided up the spoils in an edgy balance. The military would enforce the laws at the behest of the landowners, the clergy, and the corporations generally at the expense of the Indians or the ladino proletariat. By mid–twentieth century, the military officers began to ask why relocate the Indians and let others have the land when they could keep it themselves? Similarly, why make the Indians work for free, or nearly for free, for someone else? Why not have them work on the military leaders' own estates? If a group of Indians or other laborers refused to work, obviously they were Communists and were dealt with summarily. In short, the military became the dominant class.[22]

With that broad context for the country as a whole in mind, let us take a look at the Petén, through which I was now passing. As the country's largest department, it encompasses more than a third of the total land area of Guatemala. Unlike much of the rest of Guatemala, the Petén is low and hot and humid, and very isolated. Also, unlike the rest of the country, it was, until very recently, almost uninhabited. Twelve hundred years ago the Petén boasted the most accomplished and richest settlements in the Americas, and it was here that the Maya astronomers and mathematicians perfected their studies. Their artists chiseled, painted, and drew objects that today fetch six and seven figures on the world's black markets. Then came the collapse, at about the beginning of the ninth century—one of the great riddles of history. For a while, a few hearty souls hung on, and then, finally, the centers became complete ghost towns, their great pyramids claimed by tropical vegetation.

For one thousand years the region lay as an unbroken jungle wilderness. Then James Adams and Charles Wrigley tumbled to the fact that the sap of the Petén's sapodilla tree, whose wood was used by Maya engineers for door lintels, could be flavored and sugared—and chewed. Chewing gum made Wrigley a multimillionaire and brought North Americans the Chicago Cubs baseball team. Central Americans learned the therapeutic effects of steady work habits, as a network of several thousand peasant farmers (campesinos) became bound to the company store by advances they were never able to work off. But by the middle of the twentieth century, even this modest boom had gone bust. As late as the 1970s, less than seventy thousand people inhabited this region, which is about the size of Vermont and New Hampshire combined and which a millennium earlier had been the cultural, political, and economic heart of the North America.[23]

Finally, about ten years before my 1992 journey, a bridge had been completed across the Río Dulce, the natural barrier to the Petén from mainland Guatemala. The Guatemalan equivalent of the opening of the Cherokee Strip ensued as land-hungry campesinos streamed in looking for homesteads. But the boomers found sooners in the way of insurgent guerrillas and the Guatemalan army in possession of the choice parcels of real estate. Undeterred, settlers poured in, ignoring the occasional battle between government and Communist forces, or even the much more common disappearance or murder of those suspected of being troublemakers. Longtime American resident Michael DeVine was considered one of the latter. He had been murdered in 1990 at Poptún, the second city of the Petén with a population of five thousand.

A few miles from the border the view out the window of my truck showed that the forest had been shaved back from the road for a few hundred yards. Cattle grazed peacefully, and beyond was pristine-looking scrub. The landscape did not look raped and plundered, and I had not seen much evidence of the Guatemalan army. Oops. Spoken too soon. Ten kilometers from the border a soldier stood in the road with his arm at a lazy three-quarter slant. I halted, and a swarm of green-clad, rifle-toting kids surrounded the pickup. Average age, fifteen. The leader, a stern-faced youth approaching twenty, demanded my passport and immigration papers, which he inspected carefully before motioning me out of the truck. No other cars were stopped on the road. Just me and this swarm. The horde of youngsters descended on the truck, pawing, prying, sometimes sniffing. After two or three minutes the lad in charge called the younger ones off. I was given my passport. I got in my truck and drove off.

Stephens's first encounter with the military authorities of the country at the port on Lake Izabal, though more cordial, was just as unsettling. *I next called on the commandant with my passport. A soldier about fourteen years old, with a bell-crowned straw hat falling over his eyes like an extinguisher upon a candle, was standing at the door as sentinel. The troops consisting of about thirty men and boys were drawn up in front, and a sergeant was smoking a cigar and drilling them. The uniform purported to be a white straw hat, cotton trousers and shirt outside, musket, and cartridge box. One particular uniformity was strictly observed, viz., all were barefooted. The commandant of this hopeful band was Don Juan Penol, a gentleman by birth and education, who with others of his family, had been banished by General Morazan, and sought refuge in the United States. His predecessor, who was an officer of Morazan, had been just driven out by the Carrera party, and Don Juan was but twenty days in his place. Senor Penol gave us a melancholy picture of the state of the country. A battle had just been fought near San Salvador, between General Morazan* [chief of the federal government] *and Ferrara* [leader of the Honduran breakaway faction] *in which* [Morazán] *was wounded, but Ferrara was routed and his troops cut to pieces. He feared Morazan was about to march upon Guatemala. He could only give us a passport to Guatemala City, which he said would not be respected by General Morazan* [or the federal forces].[24]

Morazan's [the Liberal leader] *rise into power was signalized by a persecution of the clergy. His friends say that it was the purification of a corrupt body. His enemies that it was a war against morality and religion. From the Archbishop of Guatemala down to the poorest friar, they were in danger.* As bad as the news of Morazán's putative ascendency might have seemed to the Irish padre, a day or so later Stephens received another bit of alarming intelligence. *He told us what seemed in better keeping with the scene, that Carrera had marched toward the San Salvador border. A battle was daily expected between him and Morazan.*[25]

A kilometer beyond the army guard post on the side of the road, a tall blonde in a white dress that could have been made out of a pocket handkerchief stood with thumb out. She had a lap dog on a lead. Her presence in that forsaken country was like a scene from the Miguel Angel Asturias novel *El Señor Presidente.* Asturias won the Nobel Prize in literature in 1967. He was the first Guatemalan to be awarded that most coveted of all prizes, but even more importantly he is generally credited as the father of magical realism, the literary movement which, as its name suggests, mixes the most outrageous events and images with a more or less pedestrian reportorial narrative.

Where was she going, I asked. I said I was heading for Flores.

"I was planning to catch a bus at the *cruces* to Poptún, but they say Flores is nice. I've even heard it said that the island city in Lake Petén Itzá should not be missed."

Ilsa and I exchanged bona fides. She told me she was a Finn and a Swedish-language journalist who had come to Central America on assignment and

Bust of Nobel Prize winner Miguel Angel Asturias,
the father of magic realism, located on a boulevard
in Zacapa, Guatemala.

stayed for an extended period of R&R. "Last time I spent the best part of a
year in southern Mexico. So far from god, so close to the United States, as
they say there."

We both laughed at that old chestnut.

Then we were talking about the American involvement in Guatemalan
politics. Nothing could give those poor people relief until the United States
quit arming the Guatemalan army, she observed.

But the United States did not give the Guatemalans any military support
at all from 1977 until democracy was restored in 1986, I pointed out, and darn
little even then.

There were secret appropriations, she intimated. And even if there were
not, American companies dominated the Guatemalan economy. They con-

spired to keep wages down and when the workers rose up they got the Guatemalan army to quash them.

I argued that foreign corporations were forces of enlightenment. They paid steady wages and demanded a relatively educated work force. Foreign-owned companies helped develop a middle class. A larger middle class, I conjectured, was less likely to put up with feudalism or the thuggish practices of the military dictatorship, which enforced that feudalistic order.

Ilsa raised her head as though to offer another objection but simply nodded. "Isn't that the cutoff to Poptún? Please stop your vehicle. I want to take the bus."[26]

You do not have to be a Swedish-language journalist to object to the influence of the United States in Central America. One of the more outspoken American critics has been Walter LaFeber. He—like my Swedish-language journalist—would not agree that the Conquest was the social institution most responsible for the contemporary problems in Central America. To him, as to Ilsa, American dependency is what has held Central America down.

LaFeber traces American attitudes and involvement in Central America back to the beginning of the nineteenth century. Attempts to establish an American presence in the area by the Polk and other administrations were thwarted by the British or internal U.S. politics. It was not until about 1890 that the United States got into the business of neocolonial control in earnest. That was when Congress began building the Great White Fleet. At the same time, U.S. entrepreneurs started to invest heavily in banana plantations and Central American securities, and to build up and ultimately control the area's transportation, communication, and utility infrastructure. The Spanish-American War of 1898 secured Cuba, Puerto Rico, and the Philippines for the United States. It also left no doubt about American imperial intentions worldwide.

Teddy Roosevelt adopted Central America and the Caribbean as a special province of American interest. The idea, according to LaFeber, was not to protect the canal that was being built through the isthmus, per se, but to secure the burgeoning economic interests of the United States in the area. One must not "overemphasize the role of Wall Street and underemphasize that of Washington. . . . North American investors and traders had created enormous U.S. economic leverage over the region between the 1870s and 1920s, and the State Department worked with them. In nearly every instance, the interests of the State Department and North American business coincided. When they did not, the business interest usually gave way, as indeed it had to do if a system was to be maintained."[27] By 1920 the U.S. Marines had been sent to Central America and the Caribbean countless times to ensure American hegemony.

Central American economies did not necessarily come easily to heel. Guatemala, in particular, had a thriving trade with European countries, especially Germany, until the 1930s. Strongman Jorge Ubico, in power from 1931 to 1944, took as his model the rising fascist leaders Hitler and Mussolini. Even today the toothbrush mustache can be seen pasted on the upper lip of latter-day Armasistas, who revere Carlos Castillo Armas, one of Ubico's strongman successors. Guatemala's most important crop, coffee, was shipped principally to Germany. Being a realist, Ubico bowed to State Department pressure when he appointed an American officer as head of the Guatemalan military academy. He even went so far as to confiscate the coffee estates of many German planters, some of whom were personal allies. By 1939, only 15 percent of Guatemalan coffee was heading to Germany. Most of the crop followed bananas north to the United States.

Ubico was overthrown in 1944. However, as we shall see later, the political "spring" his downfall brought was brief. By the mid-1950s, the military had taken full control of Guatemalan politics. Thirty years went by before their grip weakened. According to LeFeber's way of looking at things, U.S. interference was chiefly responsible for this course of affairs.

LeFeber's views on the extent of American influence on the internal social and political mechanisms of these states is by no means universally accepted by scholars. The example of Coca Cola in the mid-1970s may (or may not) help shed some light on the issue. The franchise was managed by a Texas lawyer by the name of John Trotter. When his employees threatened to unionize, three union secretaries as well as three other union personnel were murdered, presumably by forces directed by the military government (and with some connivance by Coke officials). Later, sixteen union workers were beaten and several hundred employees arrested. After the sixth murder, the union's twenty-seven-member executive committee was summoned into session. Government forces surrounded their meeting place and none of the twenty-seven was ever heard from again. It was assumed they were "disappeared" by being dropped from airplanes into the ocean. Just so Coca Cola did not get the wrong idea, the Guatemalan government promptly proceeded to sue the company for $300,000 in back taxes. Then, in an apparent attempt to make peace with the labor movement, the government raised the daily minimum wage, the bottlers becoming the highest paid of all workers at $4.12

a day. Seeing the handwriting on the wall, Trotter and associates sold their interests and left the country.[28]

Does the Coke incident stand as evidence for Ilsa's and LaFeber's view of Guatemala as an American neocolonial appendage? Or does it show the Guatemalans as their own masters in a topography altered by the immense economic and political leverage of the colossus to the north? The answer to that question is far beyond the scope of this puny work. But LaFeber does raise a point that anyone writing on Stephens must find intriguing. According to him, for the first time during the Polk years when Stephens was maneuvering in Panama, the United States got involved in the business of Central American adventuring. Not surprisingly, John Lloyd Stephens—many years after his archaeological exploration of Central America—was the man who negotiated the treaty with Colombia that LaFeber sees as this first projection of American influence onto the isthmus. In what other ways, one wonders, did the affable, self-effacing young American help change the face of Central America and forge the way for U.S. economic and political dominance in the years to come?

Every few miles or so there would be a hamlet of palapas (thatch houses with pole sides), complete with a hole-in-the-wall *tienda* (shop) advertising Rubio (meaning Blond as in light tobacco leaves) cigarettes and cold drinks, even though there were no electricity lines. Sprays of those intensely colored bougainvillea—lavender, orange, red—festooned the villages. The lawns seemed to be closely mowed, although cropped would probably be a truer description since grazing animals performed the yard work. The houses, though thatch, showed their origin in the term "ranch style," for these plain, rectangular boxes must surely have given the world this usage. Pride in ownership was reflected right down to the pole or stone fence that marked the boundaries of the rancho. Few builders bothered to include a gate large enough to drive a vehicle through.

The business of the hamlet was conducted on the road. Women carried bowls of lye-soaked corn on their heads. Down the dirt highway they went to a neighbor with a hand-crank mill who reduced the corn to dough for tortillas. Men chatted near the road at the tienda. Or they trundled along it, coming from their fields toting bundles of firewood for the hearth or *zacate* (forage) for their animals. Water bottles swung from their shoulders, as their machetes—like a knight's broadsword—dangled from their belts. Because it was the straightest, flattest spot around, children used the highway for a playground. Even the hamlet's critters picked it as the venue of choice on which to live (and sometimes die). Dogs copulated, chickens scratched, and horses and cattle foraged on the shoulder for whatever sustenance could be found.

Because Stephens traveled in a day when public lodging was unheard of, he bunked in the homes of folks very much like those I passed on the road. After *we showed them our watches, compass, sextant, chronometer, thermometer, telescope, the woman, with great discernment, said that we must be very rich, and had "muchos idees," "many ideas." They asked us about our wives, and we learned that our simple-minded host had two, one of whom lived at Hocatan, and that he passed a week alternately with each. We told him that in the North he would be imprisoned for life for such indulgences, to which he responded that ours was a barbarous country. The woman, although she thought a man ought to be content with one, said that it was not peccato or a crime to have two. But I heard them say, sotto voce, that we were "mas Christianos" or better Christians than they. In the morning we continued to astonish the people by our strange ways, particularly by brushing our teeth, an operation which, probably, they saw then for the first time.*[29]

But just as often the campesinos startled Stephens with the logic of their customs and manners: *Don Miguel and his wife were curious people. They slept with their heads at different ends of the bed, so that, in the unavoidable accompaniment of smoking, they could clear each other.*[30] Then there was the time Stephens *woke in the middle of the night to find a girl about seventeen sitting on the bed at the foot of his hammock. She had a piece of striped cotton tied around her waist, and falling below her knees. The rest of her dress was the same which nature bestows alike upon the belle of fashionable life and the poorest girl. At first I thought it was something I had conjured up in a dream. As I waked up perhaps I raised my head, for she gave a few quick puffs of her cigar, drew a cotton sheet over her head and shoulders and lay down to sleep. I endeavored to do the same.*[31]

In terms of physical requirements, the inhabitants of the Petén that I drove past did not live much differently from those Stephens encountered a century and a half earlier. *The people lived exclusively upon tortillas—flat cakes made of crushed Indian corn, and baked on a clay griddle—and black beans.*[32] A modern description of tortilla making would be nearly identical to the one Stephens gave. *At one end of the cocina was an elevation, on which stood a comal or griddle, resting on three stones, with a fire blazing under it. The daughter-in-law had before her an earthen vessel containing Indian corn soaked in lime-water to remove the husk. Placing a handful on an oblong stone curving inward, she mashed it with a stone roller into a thick paste. The girls took it as it was mashed, and patting it with their hands into flat cakes, laid them on the griddle to bake. This is re-*

"At one end of the cocina was an elevation, on which stood a comal or [clay] griddle, resting on three stones with a fire blazing under it," J. L. S. Photograph by Kirk Briggs.

peated for every meal, and a great part of the business of the women consists in making tortillas.[33]

The other staple of the diet was *the "national dish," frijoles, or black beans,* [which] *we "cottoned" to at once.*[34] Other comestibles the explorer commonly encountered were largely confined to eggs and the occasional chicken. As for potables, sometimes chocolate could be procured. *When Mr. Catherwood arrived the tortillas were smoking, and we stopped to breakfast. They gave us the only luxury they had, coffee made of parched corn, which in compliment to their kindness, we drank.*[35] Occasionally, the dining habits of the country provoked in Stephens some consternation. *Immediately the fire was rekindled in the cocina, the sound of the patting of hands gave notice of the making of tortillas, and in half an hour dinner was ready. Soon I was called in to supper, which consisted of fried beans, fried eggs, and tortillas. The beans and eggs were served on heavy silver dishes, and the tortillas were laid in a pile by my side. There was no plate, knife, fork or spoon. Fingers were made before forks. But bad habits make the latter, to a certain degree, necessary. Poultry, mutton, beef, and the like do not come amiss to fingers, but beans and fried eggs were puzzling. How I managed I will not publish. But from appearances afterward, the old lady could not have supposed that I had been at all at a loss.*[36]

One of the difficulties in traveling in a land without inns or hotels is finding the proper coin with which to repay one's hosts. Luckily for Stephens and Catherwood, the means came readily to hand, in the way of the local folks' application to them for medical assistance. Here's a sample of how Stephens practiced. *His wife, fortunately, was suffering from rheumatism of several years' standing. I say fortunately, but I speak only in reference to ourselves as medical men. The honor of the profession accidentally confided to our hands. I told her that if it had been a recent affliction, it would be more within the reach of art. But as it was a case of old standing, it required time, skill, watching of symptoms, and the effect of medicine from day to day. For the present, I advised her to take her feet out of a puddle of water in which she was standing, and promised to consult Mr. Catherwood, who was even a better medico than I, and to send her a liniment with which to bathe her neck.*[37]

As I approached Flores, my pickup slid past a vast army base, replete with monuments of ironic progress: an old jet fighter—collapsed and rusting in the weeds—and a gigantic gear wheel set on a concrete plinth and covered with pustules of rust. Then I was in the teeming precincts of Santa Elena, Flores's mainland twin city. From the activity and clamor—people afoot, on motor scooters, riding bicycles, in cars, with packs on their backs or baskets on their heads—you might think you had entered some great city. Outside the tourist realm, the blacktop was replaced by powdery gravel. All those wheels and feet raised an oppressive white chalky dust. I bounced down a street, worse than the road I had spent the morning bumping over, which shortly turned into a causeway leading out into Lake Petén Itzá. The water lilies—a regal species with scalloped leaves and an elegant white bloom held erect—had not yet folded. In the limpid lake water I could see the slender stem of the lilies all the way down to their roots. On an island (called *petén* in Mayan) in the near distance reposed Flores, the capital of this province since 1699 and the site of the ancient Itzá city of Tayasal, famed as the very last Maya city to fall to Spanish arms.[38] *We had an eager desire,* Stephens reported while in Belize, *to penetrate by* [the Belize River] *to the famous Lake of Petén, where the skeleton of the conquering Spaniard's horse was erected into a god by the astonished Indians.*[39]

Cortez had visited Tayasal as early as 1525. Legend has it he left the Indians a lame horse, for which he promised to come back. Luckily, for the Itzá,

Cortez did not make the return trip. Unfortunately, for the horse, it was treated like a god, and fed chicken, the flesh of other animals, and flowers. It died. The Itzá made a stone monument resembling the horse, which they called Tzimin Chac.[40]

There matters rested until 1696–97, when the Spanish painstakingly built a road to Tayasal. Over that road came 325 Spanish soldiers equipped with harquebuses and artillery and a baggage train of 120 muleteers, plus a goodly number of human porters. The Spanish Commander Ursúa had a galley built and outfitted on the shores of Lake Petén Itzá. A flotilla of Itzá war canoes challenged him. The ensuing battle left Ursúa and his forces in control of the island. The Itzá broke ranks, many—it was reported—drowned in their frenzy to escape to the far shore of the lake. The Spanish spent the next day destroying the Itzá idols—the process took eight full hours. About sundown, Ursúa chose the main temple, where there was fresh evidence of human sacrifice, as the place to hold Mass. Thus ended the last independent Maya nation. Interestingly, many claim that the most primitive and the wildest of all modern Maya, the Lacandón of Mexico's neighboring state of Chiapas, descended from the ruined civilization of Tayasal. Linguistic evidence shows this is not the case, but it does make for a romantic claim.[41]

After finding a hotel, I moseyed down the cobbled lane to a lakeside restaurant. While sipping a beer, I felt something tug on my toe. Checking my Nikes, I found a keel-billed toucan pecking away. The bird was surprisingly small, probably no more than twelve or thirteen inches long, but its beak was at least half its length. A dark-complexioned fellow in a vest sitting at the next table laughed. He went to the kitchen and came back with a finger banana, which he offered to the bird. The fowl ignored the fruit and pecked at *his* shoe.

"Ain't that a hell of a note?" the man said in perfect American English.

It turned out he had been born in Guatemala and was taken to Arkansas, near Hot Springs, when he was two years old. Did he know Bill Clinton? "No, but I knew his brother," he joshed. "And Bill lied. He did inhale." The fellow, Marcos, had returned to Guatemala five years before. Why? "Divorce," he said tersely.

His bread and butter came from guiding, hence the vest, the guide's badge of office. He said the kind of work he preferred was as a research specialist for scientists and institutions. Recently he had been hired by a curator at a world-renowned museum to conduct detailed studies of sites where anthropologists had unearthed significant finds. The finds had subsequently disappeared and the institution needed a site study. "You figure that out," he said, hinting broadly that reputable museums were acquiring artifacts underhandedly. Marcos knew all kinds of interesting stuff. For instance, he said the Maya had practiced silviculture with gumbo-limbo trees, which are fast growing but provide rather poor firewood. He said the healing sap of the gumbo-limbo, which is an easy tree to identify because of its reddish flaking bark—it is sometimes called the West Indian birch—could be applied to cuts and rashes such as poisonwood- or poison ivy–induced dermatitis. The bark, when steeped in a tea was good for colds. He claimed green begonia sap applied directly to the skin could cure skin ulcers. He learned this by studying with a Maya herbalist. When a pharmaceutical company investigated the herbalist's cures, it turned out that 40 percent were already known to have powers of the sort the elder claimed. Somehow it came out that Marcos led mule-back expeditions to remote sites such as El Mirador, almost on the Mexican border and which I had seen as a minor upthrusting of the jungle vegetation from the top of the Grand Pyramid at Calakmul in extreme southern Campeche, Mexico. El Mirador was a place I had a powerful desire to get to one day—before a four-lane highway led to the site. I asked idly of prices and we exchanged cards. I then fell to talking with others and might possibly never have thought of this fellow again had I not received an interesting letter from a woman in Texas some time later. "My brother left the United States after wrongly being accused on several charges. Now 14 years later, the USA embassy security forces arrested him as he went to meet a group of tourists at the airport. He was accused of murder . . . put on the Federal Marshal's 10 Most Wanted list and accused of selling drugs internationally."[42] From time to time I continue to receive letters from her, saying Marcos is now in prison in the United States.

The market, even more than the church or *ayuntamiento* (city hall), is the nerve center of a Central American village, and on my way out of town the next morning I made a point of driving through the local one. All the fruits of the countryside were displayed in bewildering profusion. Pineapples, passion fruit, papayas, bananas, avocados, huge burlap bags of plum tomatoes, peppers of all sorts, plus any number of unknown (to me) local fruits. The produce vendors were female and usually were dressed in colorful huipiles. Hand-operated machines were employed to wind the peel off oranges. One itinerant merchant had a loudspeaker set up—this in a stall of perhaps one hundred square feet, walls and ceiling made of plastic. He was blaring away, "Barato, diez quetzales," Cheap, ten quetzales. Stall upon stall was stuffed full of dry goods. Most of the products on sale, though, were geared to the frontier homestead: pack saddles, huge coils of rope, hand tools. Incongruously, just down the street from the open-air market stood a glassed-in building that did one-hour photo finishing catering to the needs of the other stalwart of the local economy, the upscale tourist who jetted in for a day, or overnight, visit to the ruins of Tikal.

On the outskirts of town I came upon a man who was offloading trash pulled by a trailer hitched to a spanking new Suzuki Samurai. Obviously I had arrived at the local landfill, in reality the side of the road. It could not be called a ditch because there was no ditch. The garbage all seemed to be plastic or tin cans, but several junked cars were also in evidence. A couple of *zopilotes,* or black vultures, were working over this unproductive-looking mess. In a few minutes my pickup was barreling down the dirt road to Poptún, sixty miles distant. In stark contrast to yesterday, the road here was wide and well-graded. I hit fifty miles an hour in the spots with nothing but miles and miles of gently rolling countryside, which looked as though it had been cleared in places and then abandoned to scrub-jungly undergrowth. Once I saw a grove of slash pine trees. Someone had cleared the tropical forest (with its wealth of valuable hardwood and medicinal species) and planted a stand of lowland Caribbean pine. Wild craboo (nance) trees were in bloom, adding a jot of color to the scrub.

In the middle of nowhere I was flagged to a halt. This checkpoint was staffed by a mustachioed sergeant in his late twenties or early thirties who offered his hand before he inspected my papers. Later, a bunch of red-painted logs in the road turned out to be another checkpoint, which I almost ran through. After I screeched to a halt a couple of teenagers demanded I get out of the pickup. While two youths who obviously could not read pretended to go through my papers, others who should have been in school picked over the stuff on the front seat and then demanded I open the back of the truck. I stood by the window and watched the kids in front. They went through everything, my backpack, styrofoam cooler, and the books and maps on the seat. When there was only one kid left in front I opened the back and they poked around in there a bit and then I was allowed to proceed.

About noon I hit Poptún, the town where the American DeVine had been killed two years before. It was widely believed his death was the work of a government-backed death squad. Investigations by then U.S. Representative Robert J. Torricelli of New Jersey and others established that the killer, a senior officer in the Guatemalan military, was a CIA "informant." Although there is no suggestion the CIA had a hand in DeVine's death, the agency continued to cooperate with the killer after the deed, and the agency seemed to think forcing those in the know into retirement was adequate punishment.[43] I was happy to buzz right through that town and head into the Maya Mountains. The home-on-the-range sky had morphed, as skies in the tropics, especially around mountains, tend to do. Rain splattered the windshield, and the strain of grinding up slopes intensified a slight hitch in the engine, which on the straightaways had hardly been noticeable. The road was washed out and rocky, with a lot of switchbacks. Despite the difficult driving, some of the vistas were spectacular.

In one spot though, the entire forest had been cleared down a mountain valley. Only grass and cohune palms, the signature trees of central Maya lowlands that resemble larger and statelier coconut palms, were left. The cohune's fronds are twenty feet or more in length, with a sort of feather-duster growth habit. A grove of them is a noble and stirring sight. In many other locations the clearing was just being undertaken and was far from picturesque. Hardly anything is as ugly as land-clearing operations, Central American style, which starts with the burning of the undergrowth and follows with the girdling of the larger trees. The dead trunks and scaffold branches stand like gaunt skeletons until they are toppled and disposed of for fuel.

The next checkpoint was the worst yet. I was ordered out of the pickup, and the adolescent soldiers really gave my stuff a going over. The chief indignity came when a fifteen-year-old boy got on the tailgate in muddy boots to look inside the truck. But I had nothing to gripe about compared to the treatment Stephens received at the hands of the local authorities. *I was half undressed, when the door suddenly burst open, and twenty-five or thirty men rushed in, the alcalde* [mayor]*, alguazils, soldiers, Indians and Mestitzoes, ragged and ferocious-looking fellows, and armed with staves of office, swords, clubs, muskets, and machetes, and carrying blazing pine sticks. At the head of them was a young officer of about twenty-eight or thirty, with a glazed hat and sword, and a knowing and wicked expression, whom we afterward understood to be a captain of one of Carrera's companies. The alcalde was evidently intoxicated, and said that he wished to see my passport again. I delivered it to him, and he handed it over to the young officer, who examined it, and said it was not valid. In the meantime, Mr. Catherwood and I dressed ourselves. I was not very familiar with the Spanish language, and through Augustin, explained my official character, and directed him particularly to the endorsements of Commandant Penol and General Cascara. He paid no regard to my explanations. But after a warm altercation, the young man said that we should not proceed on our journey, but must remain at Comotan* *until information could be sent to Chiquimula, and orders received from that place. We had no disposition to remain in such hands, threatened them with the consequences of throwing any obstructions in our way. I at length said that, rather than be detained there and lose time, I would abandon my journey to Copan altogether and return by the road on which I came. But both the officer and the alcalde said peremptorily that we should not leave Comotan.*

The young man then told me to give up my passport. I answered that the passport was given me by my own government. At length I told him again that I would not give up the passport. He answered insultingly that we should not go to Chiquimula or anywhere else. Neither forward nor backward. That we must stay where we were and must give up the passport. Finding arguments and remonstrances of no use, I placed the paper inside my vest, buttoned my coat tight across my breast, and told him he must get it by force. The officer with a gleam of satisfaction crossing his villainous face, responded that he would. I added that, whatever might be the immediate result, it would ultimately be fatal to them, to which he answered, with a sneer, that they would run the risk. During the whole time, the band of cowardly ruffians stood with their hands on their swords and machetes, and two assassin-looking scoundrels sat on a bench with muskets against their shoulders, and the muzzles pointed within three feet of my breast. At length Stephens was allowed to write a note to the local commander, an Italian. *Not to mince matters, Mr. Catherwood signed the note as Secretary, and having no official seal with me, we sealed it, unobserved by anybody, with a new American half dollar, and gave it to the alcalde. The eagle spread his wings, and stars glittered in the torchlight. All gathered round to examine it, and retired, locking us up in the cabildo, stationing twelve men at the door with swords, muskets, and machetes. At parting, the officer told the alcalde that, if we escaped during the night, his head should answer for it.*

The excitement over, Mr. C. and I were exhausted. We had made a beautiful beginning of our travels. But a month from home, and in the hands of men who would have been turned out of any decent state prison lest they should contaminate the boarders. A peep at our beautiful keepers did not reassure us. They were sitting under the shed, directly before the door, around a fire, their arms in reach, and smoking cigars. Their whole stock of wearing apparel was not worth a pair of old boots. With their rags, their arms, their dark faces reddened by the firelight, their appearance was ferocious. We opened a basket of wine with which Col. M'Donald had provided us, and drank his health.[44]

I topped off the tank at a lonely gas station in a lonely village. The attendant handcranked a generator to pump the gas. The southern sky boiled black with thunderheads. The road had deteriorated and I had to ford a fast gushing stream. Pulling up on the opposite bank, I lowered the tail gate, replete with the fifteen-year-old soldier's muddy footprints, and had a picnic lunch. While I sat contemplating the crud the folk of the Petén must live with on a day-to-day basis, a man in a pickup pulled out of the adjacent rancho, blocking the road. He popped out of his truck with a sly grin and in English offered to buy my canoe, which in the Belizean fashion he called a "dory." He had a plastic face, which though expressive, was also somehow unsettling. He said he had retired from the Guatemalan army; that revelation of course alarmed me. He said his name was Jorge Bubu, clown in Spanish. I complimented him politely on his rancho, and he invited me to have a look around. I thanked him, but said I had to move on. He said it was still a long way to Río Dulce, two and a half hours. He insisted I visit his place. His adamant stance only strengthened my resolve. I slammed the tailgate, slid into the cab and wheeled far off the muddy shoulder to get around his obstructing truck, waving as I went by. Whether the man was merely lonely, as a fellow out there had a perfect right to be, or was some sort of frontier road agent, I was not going to risk finding out.

The road turned to blacktop in about an hour, and in another half hour I arrived at Lake Izabal where Stephens had touched down in Spanish Central America. At the Hotel Izabal Tropical, a jungle lodge, I secured a boat and a room, both at somewhat more than the going rate. It did not matter. I was pleased just to be set to retrace the next morning Stephens's path down that most beautiful of waterways, the Río Dulce—and to be through with the Petén.

4 / The Río Dulce and the Mico Mountains, through Rain Forest and across Desert to Esquipulas

From the deck of the steamboat that bore Stephens from Punta Gorda, Belize, into Spanish Central America, he saw *on each side, rising perpendicularly from three to four hundred feet, a wall of living green. Trees grew from the water's edge, with dense, unbroken foliage to the top. Not a spot of bareness was to be seen. On both sides, from the tops of the highest trees, long tendrils descended to the water, as if to drink and carry life to the trunks that bore them.*[1]

The *lancha* I hired to take me from Lake Izabal backward toward the area just described was a dugout vessel thirty feet long and about forty-eight inches wide powered by a forty-horsepower Mariner engine. A thatch canopy shaded the seven or eight board seats that ran gunwale to gunwale. This canoe was just one of dozens of similar vessels, with hulls and superstructures daubed in bright, primary colors, that plied the waters moving local folks, cargo, or the occasional excursion party of Guatemalan tourists. These were linear descendants of the dugouts Stephens employed. Here is the description he gave of the governor's pitpan in Belize: *This is the same fashion of boat in which the Indians navigated the rivers of America before the Spaniards discovered it. Ours was about forty feet long, and six wide in the center, running to a point at both ends, and made from the trunk of a mahogany tree. Ten feet from the stern, and running forward, was a light wooden top, supported by fanciful stanchions, with curtains for protection against sun and rain. It had large cushioned seats, and was fitted up almost as neatly as the gondolas of Venice.*[2]

We motored by the *castillo*, a fortified castle complete with moat, built to repel pirates penetrating to Lake Izabal, the entrepôt of the Kingdom of Gua-

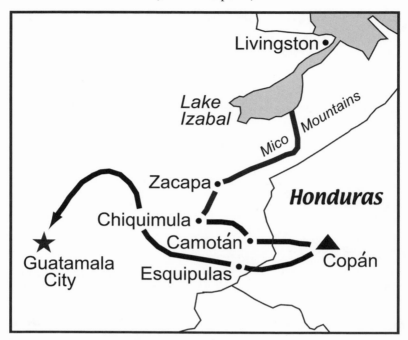

Through rain forest and across desert to Esquipulas
The solid line indicates Stephens's journey. He crossed the Mico Mountains and then followed the Motagua River until about Chiquimula, where he continued on to the Copán ruins across the border in Honduras. Stephens left Catherwood to finish his illustrations and headed for the capital at Guatemala City via Esquipulas.

Contemporary roadways approximate Stephens's journey. The author more or less paralleled Stephens's route until the turnoff to Copán. The author continued on to Esquipulas.

temala. Then we slipped under the Río Dulce bridge, one of those very high rainbow spans, looking shiny and modern and not the least out of place, given the jungle lodges, summer villas, and marinas stocked to overflowing with high-masted sailboats and sleek motor cruisers. How different from the wild conditions of thirteen years before, when the bridge was still under construction and the Petén frontier started on the north bank of the river. At that time there was nothing to see but shacks selling the crudest provisions and rude *comedores* (eateries) with food being prepared over open fires. I still have an image in my mind of a tough-looking hombre sitting in a little Japanese truck with two prostitutes in satin dresses, a memory that seemed to characterize the spot perfectly. Now the place looked like Lake Champlain.

Then the river narrowed, as Stephens related, and the banks rose until the passage was not much wider than the bluffs on either side. Like the Rock Islands of Palau in Micronesia, the vegetation grew right out of the limestone walls. There were some open bluff faces too sheer for the trees and vines to get their roots into. When I was a young man in the Peace Corps in Palau, I thought some miracle was required to sustain the forest vegetation on those soil-less Rock Islands. Now I took this similar situation in the gorge with equanimity, figuring the 120 inches of rainfall here nourished the plants and that most of the nutrients were contained in biomass as in the regular rain forest, meaning that every time a leaf fell to the rocky surface, roots immediately sucked its nutrients back into living tissue. Gumbo-limbo trunks and heart-shaped split philodendron leaves were easily distinguished amid the riot of jungle vegetation. In places I caught the aroma of the flowers from a white-blooming vine growing high up the slopes.

Sometimes we were so enclosed that it seemed as if the boat must drive in among the trees. Occasionally, in an angle of the turn, the wall sunk, and the sun struck in with scorching force, but in a moment we were again in the deepest shade. But all was as quiet as if man had never been known there before.[3]

An Indian village now squatted on the lip of Stephens's silent retreat. The structures were uniform, of pole and thatch. There bulked a chapel, a small, blocky concrete edifice with a massive false front that mimicked the mission style with formalized arches and bell tower. All this was smeared a bright green with hand-painted letters proclaiming it a Nazarene church, one of many fundamentalist sects stealing a march on the traditional Roman Catholicism hereabouts. In contrast to most of the villages of the Petén, power lines ran down the side of the mountain and into the village.

The Caribbean, or rather the section of it known as the Bay of Honduras, was calm as a pane of glass that morning. Manuel, the boatman, beached his canoe on black sand at Livingston where a dozen similar craft were strewn about. *On the right bank of the coast was one of the places I intended to visit. It was called by the familiar name of Livingston, in honor of the distinguished citizen of Louisiana whose criminal code was at that time introduced into Guatemala.*[4]

The distinguished Louisianan to whom Stephens refers was Edward Livingston (1766–1836), whose political proclivities Stephens shared and with whom he may have been acquainted, even though the legal reformer was forty years the explorer's senior.[5] As Stephens hints, the Livingston family is among the most respected names in the Union, one having signed the Declaration of

Independence, another overseeing the Louisiana Purchase negotiations, and a more recent one serving a short-lived term as Speaker-elect of the House of Representatives. Edward Livingston's political career was a study in adversity. He was born in New York ten years before the American Revolution. After three terms in the House of Representatives before the turn of the nineteenth century, he was elected mayor of New York City, but, unhappily, he soon went bankrupt thanks mainly to the peculation of a business partner. He went south and started over again in New Orleans in time to fight with Andrew Jackson.

Livingston's attempts to reform the penal code met with little success, but his political fortunes improved on Jackson's election. He was appointed Senator from Louisiana by the president, due to an election imbroglio, and later secretary of state and finally ambassador to France. While in Jackson's cabinet, he authored the Anti-Nullification Proclamation in response to South Carolina's threat to withdraw from the Union, one of the more important documents of state in the nation's history. The document was later widely cited as justification for going to war rather than letting the Union disintegrate. Livingston's penal code was printed in England and France. Author Victor Hugo and philosopher Jeremy Bentham praised it. The King of the Netherlands gave him a medal on account of it. Nevertheless, the fate of his penal code in Guatemala was no better than in his adopted state; it was repudiated by the Conservatives after they took power from Morazán's Liberals.

[Livingston, Guatemala] *was supposed so advantageous in position that* [it was expected to] *become the port of entry of Central America but these expectations were not realized. The bank was elevated about thirty feet above the water and rich and luxuriant as at Punta Gorda. The site of the intended city was occupied by another tribe of* [Black] *Caribs. Their leaf-thatched huts were ranged along the bank, shaded by groves of plantains and coconut trees. Canoes with sails set were lying on the water, and men and women were sitting under the trees gazing at us. It was a soft and sunny scene speaking peace and freedom from the tumults of a busy world.*[6]

As so often, Stephens's impressions still held a century and a half later. Livingston was a remarkably pleasant and colorful town. Because it is practically sea-locked, there were few cars. I saw only one in operation. The concrete streets that sharply dip and ascend because of the hilly nature of the place were really just broad sidewalks. The houses, small and of corrugated metal, bore paint as gay as Manuel's canoe. Many of the signs were in English, owing in part to the creolized version of English the black inhabitants still speak and partly to the backpack tourists that were the town's lifeblood.

After returning to my hotel on Lake Izabal, I sauntered the four kilometers to the market near the bridge. I bought a honeydew melon for one quetzal (20 cents), a pineapple for less than that, and an avocado for pennies, provisions for the trek to Esquipulas over the Mico Mountains the following day. I then strolled to the top of the bridge and was thrilled again by the beauty of the scene, with the waters of Lake Izabal spread before me and range upon range of rain-forest-clad mountains all around.

At eight o'clock Mr. C. and I mounted. In a few minutes we were in an unbroken forest. At every step the mules sank to their fetlocks in mud, and very soon we came to great puddles and mudholes. In an hour we reached the foot of the mountain. The ascent began precipitously [through] *a narrow gully, worn by the tracks of mules and the washing of mountain torrents. The sides were higher than our heads, and so narrow that we could barely pass through without touching. Our whole caravan moved singly through these narrow defiles, the muleteers scattered among them and on the bank above extricating the mules as they stuck fast raising them as they fell, arranging their cargoes, cursing, shouting and lashing them on. For five long hours we were dragged through mudholes, squeezed in gullies, knocked against trees and tumbled over roots. Every step required care and great physical exertion, and withal, I felt that our inglorious epitaph might be, "tossed over the head of a mule, brained by the trunk of a mahogany tree and buried in the mud of Mico Mountain."*[7]

I was impressed by the floodplain of the Río Dulce the first time I saw it, in part because of the bromeliads, big as birdhouses, that grew high up in the trees. There had been, more than a decade earlier, plenty of mahogany trees with their characteristic seed pods looking, interestingly, like a ruptured cucumber. This time I spied no mahogany, but I was impressed with the verdure of the pasture lands that had replaced them. After a quarter of an hour the climb up Mico Mountain began. It was raining on the mountain and I had to turn on the heat to defrost the windshield. In just a few minutes the potholed but asphalted and almost deserted road carried me over the top of the mountain that Stephens had accorded his worst one-day travel ever.

Not long afterward I came to the junction with the Atlantic Highway. Travelers had whispered of its splendor, notably a Guatemalan by the name of Juan Salazar, whom I had met on a plane a couple of months before. Señor Salazar was reading an English-language book about IBM, drove a BMW,

believed in foreign investment and democracy for his homeland, and was toting a Compaq laptop complete with printer and projector, which he had used
to give a presentation to Caterpillar Company officials in Miami. He was an
executive with the Guatemalan division. He told me I would be impressed
with the economic development I would see in Guatemala. Those absentee-
owned summer houses and sailboats on the Río Dulce amazed me, and this
highway was perhaps the most extravagant two-lane road I had ever driven.
Here and there huge Texaco and Esso truck-stop gas stations were going
up, replacing single-pump shacks—and not a military checkpoint in sight.
The road would zoom up and fall away to a vista Stephens waxed ecstatic
over. About lunchtime I turned off the trunk highway and headed toward
Quiriguá. The approach to the Maya site at Quiriguá goes through a vast
banana plantation, an old United Fruit Company grove.

*This is the great high road to the city of Guatemala, which has always been a
place of distinction in Spanish America. Almost all the travel and merchandise
from Europe passes over it. Our guide said that the reason it was so bad was
because it was traversed by so many mules. In some countries,* Stephens observed
dryly, *this would be a reason for making it better.*[8] Although he would have had
to eat his words had he seen the new Atlantic Highway, Stephens was right
about transportation being the bane of a poor, mountainous country. As
it happened the first cure for Central America's transportation woes—the
banana—turned out to be very bitter medicine indeed.

In the late nineteenth century a young engineer from Boston by the name
of Minor Keith ramrodded a railroad through the trackless wilderness of
Costa Rica's Caribbean coast. After completing the road and wangling for
himself a major interest in the line, he could not find enough freight to make
his possession pay. So Minor Keith decided to become a great gastronomic
benefactor to the industrial countries by founding the modern banana industry.

Although sometimes called a tree, a banana produces no wood and goes
from shoot peeping above ground to production of a stem—or bunch—of
fruit in a relatively short period of time, ranging from nine months to two
years. Horticulturists believe the banana was among the first fruits brought
into cultivation. More than five hundred varieties of edible bananas are known
to exist. The banana industry in the Americas grew up around one variety
called Gros Michel. Big Mike, as it was familiarly known by American banana
company employees, pushed up to twenty or more feet and produced huge
bunches of superlatively flavored fruit, which—when cut green—shipped
well. Unfortunately, Big Mike suffered from one fatal weakness, a susceptibility

to Panama Disease. That malady is a fungal disease related to the fusarium wilt that can quickly blight a backyard tomato patch. Fortunately for latter-day banana growers, the common Dwarf Cavendish variety—which was introduced to the world from Devonshire, England, of all places, by a horticultural devotee who recognized the stocky variety's potential as a potted plant—proved resistant to Panama Disease. The banana companies in the interval have bred larger, resistant varieties from the Dwarf Cavendish.[9]

Today, thanks to Minor Keith as much as anyone, we know the banana as a staple fruit. It would be hard to imagine a modern diet without this starchiest of fruits, loaded up with beneficial nutrients such as potassium. Unlike most other commercial fruits, the banana does not have natural protection in the way of a heavy rind, nor does it keep well. Minor Keith was not a man in a position to be fussy; the banana was the only commodity available. And it did possess a surpassing advantage, it could be cut green and it ripened into a tolerably good fruit many weeks later, thousands of miles away.

In time, the banana came to be known as the inflation-proof fruit because of its relatively low cost to northern consumers. Many Central Americans, too, were pleased by this turn of events. True, vast stretches of steaming lowland jungle came under the control of Keith and the few competitors able to buck him, but then those lands had been completely unused before the arrival of the banana industry.[10] In return, local folks were able to make use of (by paying through the nose) the rail network the fruit companies laid down throughout the isthmus, the first reliable, artificial system of transportation the area had seen since the days of the Maya.

Although the company provided some medical and educational benefits to its workers and paid them about three times the going wage, no source that I have consulted has had a complimentary thing to say about the United Fruit Company's business practices, especially in Guatemala.[11] Traveling foreigners were frequently thankful for the consideration employees showed them, while at the same time deploring the company's exploitation. For instance, the company tried every trick it could think of to prevent the completion of the first Atlantic Highway, running parallel to its own railroad from Puerto Barrios to the capital. Tensions came to a head in the early 1950s, less than ten years after a clique of army officers threw strongman Ubico out of office.

The trouble started when Captain Jacobo Arbenz Guzmán was elected president. Arbenz called himself the president of the people. During the election he had been supported by peasant groups, organized labor, and other left-wing entities, including the small communist party (PCG). To begin the difficult task of replacing feudalism with a modern capitalistic economy he encouraged state-owned enterprises to compete against the foreign electrical and rail monopolies. These practices did not go over well with United Fruit, which, it may be recalled, owned the rail line. But it was Arbenz's scheme for massive land reform that was his undoing. All unused public lands as well as uncultivated private lands of more than 90 hectares (225 acres) were to be open to homesteading by peasants. Compensation was to be at the tax value of the parcels. ("Land reform," my airplane friend Juan Salazar said, "is an idea that never works.")

The United Fruit Company objected. Everyone knew its 220,000 hectares of land, of which about only 15 percent were cultivated, were worth more than the tax value, which the company had bribed officials to grossly underappraise at $610,000. The government seized 160,000 hectares for redistribution. Compensation was generously set, from the government's point of view, at $1.2 million—to be paid in twenty-five years at 3 percent interest. United Fruit claimed the land was worth $15 million. It knew a communist plot when it saw one.

And United Fruit had its justifications. If Arbenz was not a communist, he had some very peculiar advisers. For instance, his wife was a member of the communist party, and his government was advised by a number of folks from the newly communized states in Europe. Fearing the military would not support him in case of a coup, Arbenz imported weapons from Czechoslovakia, which he hoped to distribute to the populace to form a people's militia. Despite these actions, most scholars judge Arbenz in the vein of a latter-day Barrios, a progressive (in Arbenz's case more labor oriented than Barrios) rather than a Marxist-Leninist revolutionary.

Nevertheless, Arbenz's political antenna was poorly tuned. Whether he liked it or not, he was in bed with the northern elephant, whose trainer at the moment was Senator Joseph McCarthy. And even if McCarthy and the accusations and counteraccusations over who "lost China" had not still lingered, there was the fact that John Foster Dulles, the secretary of state, and his brother and CIA director Allen Dulles were both Bostonians. Not only was United Fruit's home office in that city, but John Foster had also been one of the company's legal representatives in the 1930s; his brother had sat on the company's board as had another high officials in the State Department. Henry Cabot Lodge, the ambassador to the United Nations, was a stockholder, and the husband of President Eisenhower's personal secretary was the company's public relations chief.

The CIA was commissioned to go to work. In 1954 they pulled together a ragtag army numbering less than 150 troops. Finding a figurehead president was no cakewalk. The first candidate who was approached, Arbenz's opponent in the election, waffled. Finally a failed coup leader, Carlos Castillo Armas, agreed. A comic opera war ensued. Two of three mercenary-piloted planes crashed, but not before strafing the capital and sinking a British ship on the assumption it was a Russian freighter. Arbenz signaled the end by seeking asylum in the Mexican embassy. The United Fruit Company and Central America returned to the turn of the century.[12]

The United Fruit Company in Guatemala, though responsible for the restoration of Quiriguá, became a fading memory. In the early 1960s, while the company was still flush from its victory over Arbenz, a U.S. federal court deemed it a monopoly and mandated it divest itself of its holdings in Guatemala. On my first visit in the 1970s the banana plantation surrounding the Maya site had fallen into disrepair. Now the place was in excellent shape. Ditches, ten or more feet deep and lined with riprap, drained the fields, and the bunch-trolleys were in good condition. The banana plants towered fifteen or twenty feet, unlike so many contemporary banana groves with their runty Cavendish breeds.

At the entrance to the Quiriguá ruins, a youth sold me a huge hand of bananas. The things were the size of plantains. *Of one thing there is no doubt,* Stephens wrote of Quiriguá, which he himself never visited (Catherwood doubled back to survey it while Stephens was performing diplomatic duties elsewhere), *a large city once stood here. Its name is lost, its history unknown and no account of its existence has ever before been published. For centuries it has lain as completely buried as if covered with the lava of Vesuvius. Every traveler from Isabal to Guatemala City has passed within three hours of it. We ourselves had done the same and yet there it lay, like the rock-built city of Edom, unvisited, unsought and utterly unknown.*[13]

Even today the location of Quiriguá contributes enormously to the romantic impression you carry away. It is known for its stelae, or stone columnar monuments, that rise up to thirty-five feet. The detail on some, especially Stela D, is astonishing. But it was the tropical parklike setting—kept well-trimmed by machete-wielding campesinos—with a patch of rain forest on the perimeter and dotted here and there with gigantic tropical trees that moved me most. The rains had been falling here for some time, and there was that hot, lush, greenhouse feeling of the tropics in high rainy season. Although fiercely hot in the sun, the shade was black as a full-moon shadow. Any move-

Quiriguá, Guatemala.

ment would bring sweat, but under the tall trees in the open it was breezy and cool.

Modern archaeological investigation has shown that the city of Quiriguá dates to the early Classical period, circa A.D. 400. It is speculated that an elite ruler, nicknamed Tok Casper, from the great Maya city of Tikal in the Petén, colonized the site. The people of Tikal were probably drawn to the area because of the nearby jade quarries, one of the two locations of jade in the Maya realm, and also because of the strategic trading position; the site dominates the lower Motagua River, one of the very few navigable streams in the Maya area. The evidence for a Tikal colonization is suggested by the layout of the early buildings on the grounds, the structures and their building pattern much resembling the great Maya center's acropolis, among other things.[14]

The same impetus that saw Quiriguá colonized appears to have also been responsible for the installation at Copán in A.D. 426 of Yax K'k' Mo', whose descendants were to extend for at least sixteen rulers into the future. Copán lay just sixty miles, as the crow flew, over the mountains to the southeast. It is not yet clear when Quiriguá fell under Copán's suzerainty. Some evidence suggests domination could have occurred as early as A.D. 500. It is certain from an inscription on Altar L at Quiriguá that Smoke Imix, Copán's twelfth ruler, (A.D. 628 to 695), had subdued the site and presumably began to siphon off a share of its lucrative trade. In 725 Cauac Sky was installed in office through the grace of the Smoke Imix's successor at Copán, 18 Rabbit. By 738, Cauac Sky had captured the man who had put him in place and beheaded him in a public ceremony at Quiriguá. In celebration of this great feat, and bankrolled by the considerable resources in trade and jade now at his disposal, Cauac Sky set about designing the largest statuary plaza in the Maya world— along with the tallest monuments. All but two of the gigantic stelae are dedicated to him. He seems also to have claimed rulership of Copán. Whether that claim is braggadocio or rooted in fact has not yet been substantiated. What is known is that Cauac Sky's bold action paid off handsomely for him and his town. He remained in power in Quiriguá for sixty-five years. Quiriguá's glory days, however, ended with Cauac Sky. Not long after his death, the site was occupied and presumably conquered by non-Maya, perhaps militarized traders moving up the Motagua River. Within one hundred years, Quiriguá was abandoned and awaiting its rediscovery by Catherwood and Stephens one thousand years later.

When I pulled back onto the Atlantic Highway, the truck was running roughly. For the moment, my hopes were concentrated on just arriving at Esquipulas without incident. *At about three o'clock we entered Gualán. There was not a breath of air. The houses and the earth seemed to throw out heat. Gualán stands on a table of breccia rock, at the junction of two noble rivers, and is encircled by a belt of mountains. One principal street, the houses of one story, with piazzas in front, terminates in a plaza or public square, at the head of which stands a large church with a Gothic door. Before it, at a distance of ten or twelve yards, is a cross about twenty feet high. The population is about ten thousand, chiefly Mestizoes.*[15]

By coincidence, I also crossed the bridge over the Motagua into Gualán at about three. Unlike the clear streams of the Petén, this river was muddy, reflecting the arid region where it heads. Although just a few minutes driving time from Quiriguá and its lowland equatorial climate, the vegetation here is distinctly different, what geographers call tropical monsoon forest. The hills—or at least the areas not denuded—are clad in deciduous forest, and almost all of the trees' leaves lay on the ground, just as surely as though it were the winter solstice in Minnesota. The dry season in a monsoon climate is a sort of winter (although locally it is known as *verano,* or summer). Weeks, even months, can go by in the dry season without a drop of rain falling. Gualán gets the worst of the equatorial climate that lies close by, but which is blocked by the rain shadow of the mountains. The air was hot, humid, and gritty. It was much less pleasant than Quiriguá, although not so bad as the day Stephens arrived.

It was perhaps thirty minutes to Zacapa, but what a change in scenery. Mountains surround that town on all sides, but the forest had been left far behind. A few pine trees stood way up on top of ridges, but the valley was barren and scorched. The principal vegetation was organ-pipe cereus cactus. They were huge—a house could be hidden in a single clump—and covered with dust. Also, there were large aggregations of prickly pear cactus and gargantuan milkweeds. Oddly, the area seemed more populous than any I had yet traversed. Men, either alone or in groups, always carrying machetes, which here sported a billhook, sauntered along the road. Most toted something. All manner of conveyances were employed to help with the toting—handcarts, wheelbarrows, horse carts with wooden wheels, horse carts with auto tires, bicycles, the backs of horses or burros. The principal instrument, however, was each person's own back, with a little help from a tumpline around the forehead. The most common item carried was firewood. Pickup trucks were even loaded with the stuff. All the wood-gathering may have had something to do with the desiccation of the land, for I had heard from someone—probably my Benedictine monk friend Raphael, who first took me to Esquipulas long ago and whom I was to meet in Esquipulas—that in days gone by the region was moister and better forested. Stephens's impression, at the end of the rainy season, was quite different.

At four o'clock we had a distant view of the great plain of Zacapa, bounded on the opposite side by a triangular belt of mountains, at the foot of which stood the town. We descended and crossed the plain, which was green and well cultivated and, fording a stream, ascended a rugged bank and entered the town. It was by far the finest we had seen. The streets were regular, and the houses plastered and whitewashed, with large balconied windows and piazzas. We rode up to the house of Don Mariano Durante, one of the largest and best in the place, being about a hundred feet front, and having a corridor extending the whole length, paved with square stones. The door was opened by a respectable-looking St. Domingo negro, who told us, in French, that Senor Durante was not at home, but that the house was at our service. I was sitting at a table writing, when we heard the tramp of mules outside, and a gentleman entered, took off his sword and spurs, and laid his pistols upon the table. Supposing him to be a traveler like ourselves, we asked him to take a seat; and when supper was served, invited him to join us. It was not til bedtime that we found we were doing the honors to one of the masters of the house.

He must have thought us cool, but I flatter myself he had no reason to complain of any want of attention.[16]

A garrison and old railroad town, Zacapa exudes the kind of forlorn, dusty charm that needs a Graham Greene to do it justice. But it was the auto parts store, located right there on the highway, not the old frame railway depot or the cameos of girls in Sunday frocks being wooed by beardless youths in fatigue greens, which caught my more prosaic fancy. I asked the clerk in an open-air window, a young fellow in his twenties by the name of Roberto, if he had a distributor cap for my Ranger. He shook his head sadly. The nearest place it could be found would be Guatemala City, he informed me. Despair must have shown on my face because by gesture he gave me reason to hope. Shortly I was informed that Jim would check out my engine, if I would permit him to inspect it.

As though I would not. While Jim, who had spent some time in Anaheim, California, where he learned English and acquired his name, was having me rev the engine and go through the usual diagnostic monkeyshines, an aggregation of idlers—Néstor, Beto, and José—collected. I told them I had come from Belize. Jim said that Belize used to be Guatemalan territory, but the British were very strong and Guatemala could not take it back. Because I had just spent a semester among the Belizeans, my identification with those folks was strong. I took umbrage, but these fellows were so pleasant (not to mention working on my car) that I did not ask them, as I would have liked, when Guatemala had ever occupied a square foot of Belizean territory—the answer, as I think is clear from the discussion of Belizean history earlier, is never. After about forty-five minutes of mixed discussion and engine diagnostics, Jim acquired some emery paper and sanded the distributor cap. I took the truck out for a test spin. The engine purred like a cat. I came back, gave the okay sign and tried to press some money on Roberto and Jim. They refused to take anything. They would not even allow me to stand them to a round of drinks. As Stephens observed and as I had already seen many times, *The hospitality of Central America is in the country and the villages. Here I never knew it to fail.*[17]

At the military checkpoint on the outskirts of town, I was motioned right through. I hoped this meant my luck was changing—much as Guatemalans were hoping their political climate was finally changing. In a sense I owed my introduction to Stephens to the counterrevolution of 1954, the cataclysm from which much of modern Guatemalan history has flowed. The archbishop of Guatemala was an adamant opponent of Arbenz's reforms. He was thanked for his support by the restoration to the Church of many of the prerogatives stripped by the Liberal reforms of the Barrios regimes (1873–97) beginning eighty years earlier. I suppose this detente between state and Church was responsible for Father Raphael's American contingent of monks being allowed to enter the country. Unfortunately, there were many other, more immediate consequences of the CIA counterrevolution, not the least of which was reasserting latino hegemony and the submersion of the nascent Indian consciousness. This was forcibly shown by the summary execution of peasant and other liberal leaders in Arbenz's government. The toll, depending on the source consulted, ran from the hundreds to the thousands. Nor did the counterrevolution establish a stable government. The CIA pawn, Castillo Armas, was assassinated while in office. His successor, Ydígoras, was corrupt or repressive by turn. By 1960 young military officers—taking a page from Castro's book—headed for the hills, where, under the leadership of Yon Sosa and others, they mounted a guerrilla movement among the ladino populace in the departments of Izabal and Zacapa. Although their military actions were generally ineffective, they fired the first shots in a civil war that was still going on as my little pickup chugged up that mountain outside of Zacapa thirty-two years later.[18]

Few of the succession of presidents—military officers or military puppets such as Julio César Méndez Montenegro, who was compelled to give the military complete autonomy—were able to boast seeing their term of office expire. Miguel Ydígoras Fuentes was overthrown by Colonel Enrique Peralta Azurdia, who proved to be even more authoritarian than the man he replaced. Leftists struck back with urban terror, kidnapping wealthy Guatemalans. The government countered by organizing death squads—or acquiescing to death-squad activity by political organizations calling themselves the Movimiento Anticomunista Nacional Organizado or MANO, better known as "mano blanca" (the white hand), and another sponsored by the MLN (Spanish acronym for National Liberation Movement) political party, Armas's own, known as "the party of political violence." Any political activist from the center to the left—labor leader, intellectual, student, or peasant—was a potential target. Grisly torture frequently preceded death.[19]

In the countryside, Colonel Carlos Arana Osorio, the so-called Jackal of Zacapa, swept the guerrillas from that department with the advice of U.S. Green Berets, causing the death of thousands of innocent peasants. Urban leftists struck back by kidnapping and killing the German and American ambassadors. The two rural guerrilla movements merged. The Jackal of Zacapa assumed the office of president in 1970. The *New York Times* estimated two thousand had been murdered by the regime in his first six months in office. Within three years the total mounted to fifteen thousand. Arana's handpicked successor tried a new tack of moderation, but the devastating 1976 earthquake thwarted him. Throngs of homeless and unemployed demonstrated for relief. Instead they got a new wave of death-squad activity. All this spurred the nearly dormant rural insurgency.[20]

A novel and disturbing wrinkle—from the perspective of Guatemala City—was added. For the first time, Indians began to be recruited by a new irregular force, the Guerrilla Army of the Poor, operating in the western highlands. Suddenly, a political avenue was opened to the oppressed 50 percent of the population, one that for more than a hundred years had no political voice. The next election was probably stolen from former strongman-president Colonel Peralta by Fernando Romeo Lucas García. Three years later elements in the army, mostly young field-grade officers, ousted Lucas García and General José Efraín Ríos Montt was put in his place. Oddly a wave of optimism swept the land. Ríos Montt, an evangelical, was known to possess strong moral values. Unfortunately, the army-directed violence in the Petén and the highlands grew to even more staggering proportions, as did death-squad activity under Ríos Montt. The only good thing to be said about Ríos Montt was that the highwater mark in the country's militarism had been reached.

Now eleven years later, two more or less freely elected presidents had taken office. The first had fallen to the moral hazard of southern politicians; neither he nor his cohorts had been able to keep their hands out of the till. But my airplane friend, Juan Salazar, was hopeful for the newly elected regime. He thought ultimately democracy would be able to rein in the military because it was obvious to everyone that militarism had not worked.

The ascent out of Zacapa was very steep, a fifteen-hundred-foot climb at least, and, at the first sign of strain, the engine began to miss terribly. The temperature gauge shot up to 210, and then, almost at the top of the slope, a guy in fatigues with his helmet on, and a rifle slung over his shoulder, directed traffic to the shoulder of the road. The needle continued to edge up, and, just when I figured the game was lost, my papers were cursorily inspected and I was motioned on. The crest lay two hundred feet above. I slammed the shift lever into first. The Ranger crept toward the ridge line, the motor bucking and throbbing. Although higher and cooler up here in the pine trees, the countryside all around was brown and sere, looking as though it had been sprayed by a flame thrower.

Down in the valley, I came to the turnoff to the great Maya site of Copán. Here Stephens veered off to the ruin that was to make him famous, before continuing to Guatemala City. Sometime later, he set out from the capital on a swing through the lower Central American states. My present itinerary combined both these trips. My friend, Father Raphael, and I planned to weave through El Salvador, Honduras, Nicaragua, Costa Rica, and then come back to eastern Guatemala via Copán in Honduras. For the present, my main concern was simply arriving in Esquipulas without auto failure.

Then I was climbing again. I went past a sign pointing toward the village of San Jacinto, where Stephens was treated to the hospitality of the *cura,* the local priest, a man *above six feet, broad shouldered, and with a protuberance in front that required support to keep it from falling. But he had a heart as big as his body and as open as his wearing apparel.*[21] After making Stephens rest a day, he sent him on his way with *chocolate, bread, sausages and fowl, a box of cakes and confectionary and the whole side of an ox with merely the skin taken off and the ribs cracked.*[22]

Being a WASPish North American, Stephens had been prepared to look askance on the padres. But he was not long in the country before he observed that the life of the cura in an Indian village was *the life of labor and responsibility devoted faithfully to the people under his charge. Besides officiating in all the services of the church, visiting the sick and burying the dead, he was looked up to by every Indian in the village as a counselor, friend and father. The door of the convent was always open and Indians were constantly resorting to him.*[23]

As the Ranger pulled up the grade toward Esquipulas, I recalled years before meeting the then-cura of San Jacinto, a Louisianan by the name of Father Don Bahlinger. Unlike Stephens's portly pastor, Father Don, a Jesuit, was thin. with a nervous personality. He was attached to a group called Caritas. His sibling, a nun by the name of Barbara, headed up the mission, which was located in a very modest walled house at the base of a mountain. I was invited in and offered a glass of lemonade. An attractive French couple had just arrived to help with the work of Caritas. They were fresh and eager, equal to any challenge. Father Don and his sister's faces, though, were careworn and preoccupied. The lemonade had been squeezed from the fruit of their own tree—those lemons the only amenity in an otherwise impoverished and incredibly hot homestead. Even the hill behind their house was barren, a few pine trees way up on top showing like hair on a bald man's head. There was guarded talk in English of interference with their work by "them." The next time I asked after the Caritas mission I was not surprised to learn it had been abandoned, no doubt bringing great pleasure to "them." The "them," of course, were the members of the local power structure who saw themselves as the inheritors of the Spanish Conquest and who still believed the campesinos were theirs by divine right to do with as they pleased.

Near the top of another mountain, I was pulled over by soldiers who demanded my papers and conducted a cursory search. I figured the laboring engine would overheat and stall, but it faltered on. I was high above the Zacapa desert, but still the countryside had that scorched end-of-the-dry season aspect. My vision of Esquipulas was of a cool, green oasis. Reluctantly I had come to believe that Esquipulas too would be hot and dusty, when without knowing it I crossed the continental divide and found—most pleasantly—my presentiment wrong. *Descending, the clouds lifted, and I looked down upon an almost boundless plain, running from the foot of the Sierra and afar off saw, standing alone in the wilderness, the great church of Esquipulas, like the Church of the Holy Sepulchre in Jerusalem and the Caaba in Mecca, the holiest of temples. The view from this platform of the great plain and the high mountains around was magnificent. The church, rising in solitary grandeur in a region of wildness and desolation, seemed almost the work of enchantment, the great church of pilgrimage, the Holy Place of Central America. Every year on the fifteenth of January, pilgrims visit it even from Peru and Mexico, the latter being a journey not exceeded in hardship by the pilgrimage to Mecca. When there are no wars to make the roads unsafe, eighty thousand people have assembled among the mountains to barter and pay homage to "our Lord of Esquipulas." Late in the afternoon we entered the town and rode up to the convent. I was a little nervous, but could I have doubted the hospitality of a padre? The whole household of the cura turned out to assist, and in a few minutes the mules were munching corn in the yard, while I was installed in the seat of honor in the convent. It was by far the largest and best building in the place. The walls were three or four feet thick.*[24]

I too was a bit worried about how I would be received at Esquipulas. My friend, Father Raphael, was scheduled to arrive later in the evening from Louisiana, but Father Philip, the guest master, a cheerful man who sported an uncharacteristic-for-a-monk pompadour and cigarette holder, greeted me with a chortle. "Raphael told me to be on the lookout for you." He led me to a room in the monastery and advised me that soup would be on directly.

When I had first glimpsed Esquipulas in 1979, the monastery residential hall had just been built—no three foot masonry walls here. Freestanding and airy, designed by a Guatemalan, it resembled a tropical resort, with its potted-palm, Mexican-tiled atrium set on a campus of 20 acres of greenery, mostly

F. Catherwood.

ESQUIPULAS.

Catherwood's view of Esquipulas, Guatemala.

A modern view of Esquipulas. Photograph by Kirk Briggs.

citrus and tropical fruit. A couple of acres around the church were devoted to ornamental landscaping of the most lavish tropical greenery. The rooms (technically known as "cells") were snug but comfortable, thanks to the clever arrangement and the altitude. In the interval the building had become not seedy but a bit worn. The single bed, really just a shelf extending from the wall with a foam mattress, that had seemed so brilliantly designed thirteen years ago, now after having been slept on by hundreds of itinerants seemed claustrophobic and lumpy. At supper I had a similar feeling about the monks. That is, that they too were a bit worn.

My impression when I first saw the Benedictine priory at Esquipulas many years before was that it housed the happiest group of people I had ever been among. But then I had been there during a festival week. Prior Matthew had been celebrating the twenty-fifth anniversary of his ordination. Also, the monks were predominantly American and young and full of beans, and the language of discourse was English.

At supper, everyone seemed older and grayer, even though in truth the mean age had dropped considerably. The priory (satellite community of Raphael's stateside monastery) had become a full-fledged abbey. Most of the members of the community now were Latin American and quite young, as the novitiates broke bread with the regular members of the community. The common tongue was Spanish. As we sat down to supper that night, a workaday air in the refectory made the scene resemble an overgrown farmhouse kitchen right down to the religious pictures on the walls. Most of the young fellows seemed to have not a vocation so much as a career path that led to a square meal: hamburger with noodles, boiled sweet potatoes, string beans, home-baked rolls, home-made tortillas, and fresh milk still warm from the dairy on the grounds. Dessert was conspicuous by its absence. All this was prepared plainly and self-served by passing through a cafeteria-style line, which contained less food than an ordinary Thanksgiving table, to serve twenty-five to thirty full-grown men. Still, from the smiles and horseplay on the seminarian side of the horseshoe-shaped table, I got the impression these were pretty good pickings and that a vocation was considered a not-bad career choice, if you could get it, and providing that you did not fall victim to the leading occupational hazard of being hauled off by a death squad.

As for the older members of the community, their smiles were still there, but they quickly disappeared into a sort of vacant preoccupation. Even when they told of the Esquipulas II Peace Conference, when the monastery housed the heads of Central American states and for which Costa Rican president Oscar Arias garnered a Nobel Prize—if no peace for the countries of the isthmus—the expression on the monks' faces had after a brief smile looked careworn and drawn. Not even the retelling of the pope's visit to the abbey sometime later really animated them. All this was the result of thirteen years in the crucible of civil war.

Later, on the same porch overlooking the same courtyard Stephens may have sat when chatting with the cura of Esquipulas, Jesús María Guttiérrez, I talked with Father Charles Villere, a crusty octogenarian who Melvyn Douglas would have to play in the movie (or vice versa). He wore a beret and carried a cane. As a youth in the 1920s, Charles went to West Point. He flunked out of the academy on account of calculus (ironically when Raphael met him he was teaching math at the Benedictine seminary in Louisiana), joined up with the marines and served in Nicaragua and China. Around 1960 he led the contingent of American Benedictines to Esquipulas, an unenviable task, considering the authorities were not greatly in favor of gringos taking over a national icon. But successive Liberal governments had shot out all the local priests, and so it fell the lot of the monks from Louisiana to become stewards of the national shrine. Charles's Marine background served him in good stead, although it was a bit severe even for the Benedictines, who are known as being just a hair less rigorous than the Trappists.

I had accompanied the supposedly terminally ill Father Charles to Guatemala many years before, on what he believed was his last trip to his priory. A lucky diagnosis some years later showed that he had a rare disease called tropical sprue. This malady only seems to affect foreigners who have spent more than twelve years in the tropics. Recovering now, and considerably mellower, he had chosen to return to Guatemala for good. Father Charles was outspoken vis-à-vis local politics, something the other priests kept their counsel on. Yes, the economy seemed to be booming—for some—compared to stagnant times in days gone by. And yes, Guatemala was prosperous now, relatively. He positively beamed when he told me the banana plantation at Quiriguá was owned and managed by Guatemalans. And yes, the siege mentality had lifted some in the past couple of years. But no, the elections would not make any difference, he proclaimed. The human rights violations would continue, although he did grudge that at least they were not killing priests the way they used to.

Raphael arrived late in the evening, almost midnight. He found me reading in my guest monk's cell. "What's a woman with one leg shorter than the other called?" the corpulent, bald-headed, mean-mouthed, one-eyed Cajun dressed in baggy trousers and guayabera asked after the usual how-do-you-dos.

"Eileen (I lean)," he answered. "What's a Japanese woman with one leg shorter than the other called? Irene."

One of Raphael's favorite japes was to claim he and I were schoolmates, which was after a fashion true. After his twelve years at Esquipulas, he returned to the parent abbey near New Orleans, where it was decided to make him over into an English instructor for the seminary college. He was sent to graduate school, where we met. Because we were both older than most of our fresh-out-of-college classmates—even though Raphael was fifteen years my senior—we had a natural affinity, and then there was the fact that I was a bachelor, which Raphael assumed meant a celibate. He invited me for a visit to the abbey. It was always my feeling that he assumed should I like the lifestyle—and because he did he figured I would—that small matters such as lack of religious conviction could be worked around somehow. In fact, Raphael was so irreverent and nasty-tongued (and irascible), that for a time I suspected he may have been an unprofessed agnostic.

On our half-dozen previous sojourns in Central America and Mexico,

Author's sometime travel companion Raphael Barousse, Benedictine monk, at the Skull Rack at Chichén Itzá, Yucatán.

Raphael's favorite conversational opener was that I was writing a book on Stephens. Mostly, he used that gambit to embarrass me, but also to soften up an acquaintance (or perhaps an acquaintance of an acquaintance and sometimes total strangers) on whom we would drop in, generally, about mealtime. After the conversation had droned on long enough to bore even Central Americans, who specialize in drawn out, episodic discussions, he would insert that we were looking for a cheap place to eat. "We are simple people. We do not require much. A few beans, a little rice," he would repeat like a litany until the point was gotten and we were fed. "The table fare, these tortillas and beans," he would work in, once the food had been produced, "are excellent, but a little meat would be nice, and some beer too."

In short, it came in very handy to travel with a member of a mendicant (begging) order when you were a poor graduate student. Many a night my belly was filled or a bed had been procured, mostly in houses of religious people. As my fortunes improved, Raphael's style occasionally caused my toes to squirm uncomfortably in my Nikes, not to mention causing me to spend more time in many too many ecclesiastical retreats. Now, however, Raphael told me he had just passed a round birthday—his sixtieth—and that he could feel himself slowing down. Nevertheless, he was all fired up about our proposed trip to the southern Central American countries, places he had never had the chance to travel to for one reason or another.

The first order of business the next morning was putting the Ranger in tiptop shape. The proprietor of the auto-electric *taller* (shop), a middle-aged mestizo, was beside himself on seeing the long-departed Padre Rafael. They gave each other the *abrazo,* a sort of one armed hug, and then the shopman and his helpers went to work under the hood of the Ranger, still parked on the street. As they removed one of the spark-plug wires, the metal head fell out. The proprietor and his assistants grinned as though they had just solved a murder.

The temperature was pleasant, mountain resort weather, in the low 80s, as it usually is in Equipulas, which at three thousand feet partakes of the best features of both the *tierra templada,* or the temperate zone, and the *tierra caliente,* the lowland tropics—coconut and plumeria trees flourish there but apples and other northern fruits, grown in the surrounding mountains, can be bought in the market. Raphael and I hiked out to the aqueduct, some fifty feet high, of Roman arches constructed of brick. This immense and graceful structure, which would have cost hundreds of thousands of dollars to replace, carried water in one small rusty pipe about three inches wide from the mountains and was still, at that time, the town's chief source of the precious fluid. Gushing under the aqueduct *was a small stream, one of the sources of the great Lempa,* the principal river of El Salvador. *It was the first stream* [Stephens] *had seen which emptied into the Pacific Ocean, and* [he] *saluted it with reverence.*[25]

About Esquipulas itself, Stephens wrote: *The town consists of a population of about fifteen hundred Indians. There was one street nearly a mile long, with mud houses on each side. Most of the houses were shut, being occupied only during the time of the fair. At the head of this street, on elevated ground, stood the great church.*[26] The population of Esquipulas had grown sevenfold since Stephens's day. The mile-long street was still there, and some of the houses were still made in the daub-and-wattle style, but most were somewhat more substantial and had tile roofs. In one of the back streets we passed the former Bethlehemite convent. The physical structure was like an ordinary Spanish country house, with rooms along the wall, a *sala,* and a courtyard. The courtyard had been the abode of a Dodge Colt minibus, its wax and polish showing the nuns' pride in their vehicle. At our earlier visit, some thirteen years before, that Dodge Colt had only recently superseded four-legged conveyances as the nuns' chief mode of transportation.

I recalled with fondness Sister Paula, a Nicaraguan, dark complexioned, attractive, and full of spunk, and the mother superior, Sister Socorro, a Colombian, much more sober, but still not averse to Raphael's wheedling charm. Raphael had also recalled the wonderful memories he had shared with the nuns, of riding the circuit of outback mountain chapels, of bedding down in campesino huts, of eating peasant food. After the second pitcher of iced tea was offered to Raphael and me, and tumblers were extended, our problem was divulged. According to Raphael, our thirst was so great because we had spent the hot, dusty day tramping the streets in search of transportation. If a vehicle did not turn up he would not be able to show his favorite nephew and closest relative, Kirk (our travel companion on two journeys), and his old school chum, Steve, the one writing the book on Guatemala (Stephens had not entered the story yet), the splendors of the country. What a shame it would be for them to go back to *los Estados Unidos* (the United States) without having seen the wonders of Quiriguá and Lake Izabal and Cobán and elsewhere.

Nuns kept arriving, including Sister Victoria, who gave Raphael a chaste version of the abrazo. "Are you still teaching?" Raphael had asked.

"No, I help with a youth group called the *Cachorros*. We teach the pupils to do good deeds." She and others stayed to make suggestions about possible vehicles. Finally, spunky Sister Paula noted that their own Dodge Colt minibus was not spoken for during the time in question. Raphael demurred. He could not use the nuns' vehicle. Sister Paula insisted. She would take it upon herself to ask the mother superior. Well, all right, if she insisted, Raphael acceded. After a gracious hello, Sister Socorro, probably due to her long acquaintance with Raphael, had evidently tumbled to the fact that Raphael's one good eye was focused on their pride and joy—and had sequestered herself in her office. In the heat Sister fluttered to the office, in her flowing habit. She came back all abashed, or at least as far as the ebullient woman could ever be abashed. We could not borrow it. The car was needed bright and early on the third day. Raphael grinned. He had Sister Socorro, and she did not even know it. Another pitcher of iced tea and much coming and going was required before Sister Socorro emerged from her office to tell us all right we could use the vehicle, but we had to have the little van back and ready for use at the crack of dawn on the day after the day after tomorrow.

After we finished sharing these memories, I noticed a tear in Raphael's eye.

And I was batting my eyes to keep from following his example. The Bethle-hemite convent now stood vacant. The Colt minibus had burned there in the courtyard—all this just a couple years after we borrowed the vehicle. "About two in the morning," Raphael sobbed momentarily losing control of his voice, "a dozen men, in civilian clothes with handkerchiefs over their faces, poured over the low back wall and doused the minibus with gasoline and set it ablaze. Several nuns were beaten. One was wrapped in a sheet and thrown on the blaze. Miraculously, she escaped with minor injures. The cook, a laywoman, was severely hurt. Sister Victoria was hauled away by the squadron. Her body turned up several months later. Her offense was that she ran that youth group called the Cachorros, or Cubs. The military-police colonel in charge of the 'investigation' said at the time that it was probably an *autosecuestro,* a self-kidnapping, and that she would turn up some day. Talking out of the other side of his face, he also said that Sister Victoria had been seen giving food to a ragged man who looked suspiciously like a *rebelde* [rebel] and that she had brought her troubles on herself."

We skulked down a side street for several blocks and stopped in front of a newly built structure bearing the legend "casa de mi hermano" (house of my brother). Considering the dreary clouds hanging over us since our last stop, we debated the wisdom of looking through anything as depressing as an old folks home. Before we had the chance to skip out, the gate swung open and a pleasant woman in what looked like lay dress greeted us. She was in her forties with very fair skin, salt and pepper hair, and the most astonishing neon-blue eyes. She introduced herself as Sister Moira (pronounced Myra). She had a thick Irish brogue. There was no getting away now.

Sister Moira grabbed us by the ears and ushered us in as she apologized profusely for the filth and mess. The house was easily the most spotless domi-cile I had seen in Guatemala and perhaps any place else, redolent of soapsuds and disinfectant. Dour-faced Guatemalan women were turning mattresses up and going at the floor with maniacal vigor. Sister Moira explained in an imp-ish aside that she had been away for a couple of days. Her lay helpers had slacked off. She was now making them atone for their slovenliness.

There did not seem to be an ounce of meanness in Sister Moira, despite her castigation of the cleaning ladies. She wore an apron over her plain blue frock. Her hands darted under the apron then flitted out and fidgeted around. When she was talking, she would get up in your face and fix her gaze on you, electric-blue eyes widening like a cat's, and touch you with those flighty hands, which—matching her personality—were warm to the touch.

She explained that many years earlier a group of Esquipulans decided something should be done for the destitute old people sleeping in the town's doorways. Enter Sister Moira. Each room, which was designed for two beds, of her old folks home shared a bathroom with the room across the way, and both rooms also shared a very small courtyard. Sister Moira said these old folks who had slept on the streets or in crowded huts all their lives now sometimes objected when a third bed was put into their rooms.

In the day room she introduced us to her charges. All the men wore headgear of some sort, mostly tufted ski caps. The toothless old gentlemen in their stocking hats, all of them smiling, looked like refugees from the green room of a Snow White production. One fellow insisted on singing a song. He crouched and wailed away. Sister Moira threw up her hands in mock disgust at a racy part where he talked about going with a married woman. This got them all laughing. Sister Moira braced a hoary, hunched-over woman and told her to stand up straight. In an aside, she confided that the old woman was a hypochondriac and chronic naysayer. Sister Moira let us know she was bent on breaking her of her negativism. She gave a woman by the name of Marta short shrift because she was Protestant. She had tried to barter her off to the Protestant old folks home, but Marta would not leave. Another was called the Doll, because of her full head of tow hair and her ageless, unseamed face. Sister Moira found a little doll-like hat among the woman's possessions, fluffed it out, and pulled it onto the Doll's head to the woman's delight, and to the merriment of the other women.

A black butterfly fluttered by. Sister Moira let out a yelp, telling us that it meant one of her wards would die. Then she assured us that they all welcomed death because that meant they would go to heaven. The charges at the Protestant old folks home in a neighboring town, on the other hand, were saddened and disheartened by death. Several times on his sojourns Stephens met women he thought about settling down with on the spot. Sister Moira, if you overlook her religious vows, was such a person. One wonders how she came to give up a normal family life for the sort of routine she was leading in Guatemala, where she could be marked out for death for nothing more than what she was doing.

Our very last stop was at the poor box hanging by the door, which Sister Moira called our attention to most charmingly. On the street, Raphael remarked that her place was the only old folks home he had ever been in that did not have an overpowering stench of urine. I said it was the only one where everyone was smiling, everyone, that is, except the cleaning help, who clearly were in the doghouse.

Our next stop was the basilica. *The facade was rich with stucco ornaments and figures of saints larger than life. At each angle was a high tower and over the dome a spire, rearing aloft in the air the crown of that once proud power which wrested the greatest part of America from its rightful owners, ruled it for three centuries with a rod of iron, and now has not within it a foot of land or a subject to boast of.*

We entered the church by a lofty portal, rich in sculptured ornaments. Inside was a nave with two aisles, separated by rows of pilasters nine feet square, and a lofty dome, guarded by angels with expanded wings. On the walls were pictures, some drawn by artists of Guatemala and others that had been brought from Spain. And the recesses were filled with statues, some of which were admirably well executed. The pulpit was covered with gold leaf and the altar protected by an iron railing with a silver balustrade, ornamented by six silver pillars about two feet high and two angels standing as guardians on the steps. Rows of Indian women were kneeling around the altar, cleanly dressed, with white mantillas over their heads but without shoes or stockings. A few men stood up behind or leaned against the walls. In front of the altar, in a rich shrine, is an image of the Savior on the cross, "Our Lord of Esquipulas," to whom the church is consecrated, famed for its power of working miracles.[27]

In the 1500s the Spanish friars offered the locally famous sculptor Quirio Cataño—his residence is still pointed out in Antigua, Guatemala—100 *tostones* (50 ounces) of silver. The story Kelsey and Osbourne tell in their interesting but now dated book on Guatemala, is that "because the Indians, terrified by the cruelty of the Spaniards, believed all white men were evil and that Christ could not be a kind and charitable god if he were white, the priests commissioned Cataño to make the image of balsam wood whose dark color resembles the complexion of the Indians. Soon it was credited with miraculous powers, but not until after 1737, when the newly elected Bishop of Guatemala, Pardo de Figueroa, was cured there of a severe chronic ailment, did its fame as a miracle shrine become widespread. In gratitude, the bishop ordered the imposing *santuario* that now dominates the valley to be built to house the Black Christ. The temple was completed in 1758."[28] The cost of the building—it is said—was $3 million, not including labor, which the local Indians "donated," gratis.

The Black Christ of Esquipulas still draws about one million pilgrims a year, and to it miracles are still attributed. On entering the church, Raphael pointed out the crutches and similar implements adorning the walls, which had been abandoned by the afflicted after their miraculous cures. The gold and silver Stephens reported had either disappeared or had only been the same stamped tin I saw on the walls and ceiling. Pews had even been installed in the great church's nave since Stephens's time—and my own last visit two years before in 1990. The demographic profile of worshipers had expanded a bit. There were Maya from the highlands in their colorful huipiles, ladinos in street clothes, family groups of campesinos—the men in cowboy shirts and ten-gallon hats, the women lugging infants and toddlers—and there were a few wealthy dowagers, who had possibly roared down in their Mercedes or BMWs from Guatemala City for the afternoon. The changes were subtle. The color of choice for the women's mantillas was black rather than white (as Stephens reported), and most of the women now wore shoes. The men, many fewer, still stood in back holding up the walls, and almost all the supplicants had looks of incredible awe. The objective of a lifetime had been attained and they were not—as those of us from northern climes so frequently are in such cases—disappointed. Otherwise, here, as in much of Guatemala, things had not changed a great deal.

5 / Finding the Seat of Government or El Salvador, Honduras, Nicaragua, and Finally Costa Rica

Stephens's ostensible reason for going to Central America was to conclude a treaty for Peace, Amity, Commerce, and Navigation between his country and the Central American federation.[1] Before he could do so, he had a much more formidable task, which was finding a central government.[2] To locate the administration officially recognized by the United States, he had to leave the relative safety of Guatemala City and trek south and east to El Salvador and the other countries of lower Central America. A little history taken directly from Stephens may help to understand why finding the government was by no means a straightforward endeavor. These few words may also provide some insight into the mindset of contemporary Central America, which still seems to reel from the forces set in motion shortly after independence from Spain in 1821.

From the time of the conquest Guatemala had remained in a state of profound tranquility as a colony of Spain. The Indians submitted quietly to the authority of the whites, and all bowed to the divine right of the Romish Church. In the beginning of the [1800s] *a few scattering rays of light penetrated to the heart of the American continent* [in the example of the French Revolution and its aftermath and in the failed rebellion sparked by Father Hidalgo in Mexico], *and in 182[1] the Kingdom of Guatemala, as it was then called, declared its independence of Spain. After a short union with Mexico, it constituted itself a republic under the name of the United States of Central America. By the articles of agreement the confederacy was composed of five states, viz., Guatemala, San Salvador, Honduras, Nicaragua, and Costa Rica.*

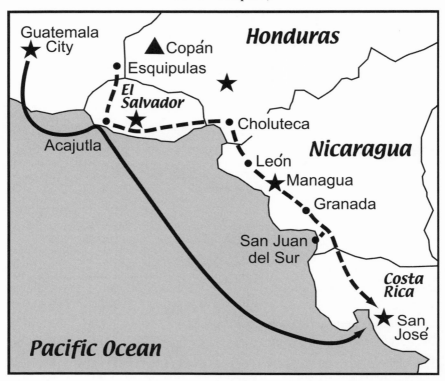

El Salvador, Honduras, Nicaragua, and Costa Rica
Stephens's route started in Guatemala City and made for the Pacific coast of Guatemala, where he shipped aboard the *Cosmopolitia*. The vessel's first and only port of call, other than Stephens's destination of Costa Rica, was Acajutla, then the principal seaport of El Salvador. Stephens went inland to Sonsonate then resumed the sea voyage to Costa Rica.

Leaving from Esquipulas in Guatemala, the author made his way to Santa Ana in El Salvador then retraced Stephens's route to the Pacific. He then paralleled the Pacific coast all the way to San José, Costa Rica, visiting many of the sites Stephens stopped at on his return trip north by land.

A line of demarcation was at once drawn between the Conservative (or Aristo-cratic) and the Liberal (or Democratic) parties. The Conservative Party consisted of a few leading families, which, by reason of certain privileges of monopoly for importations under the old Spanish government, assumed the tone of nobles, sustained by the priests and friars, and the religious feeling of the country. The [for-mer] were composed of men of intellect and energy, who threw off the yoke of the Romish Church, and, in the first enthusiasm of emancipated minds, tore away at once the black mantle of superstition, thrown like a funeral pall, over the genius of the people. The Conservatives wished to preserve the usages of the colonial system and resisted every innovation and every attack, direct and indirect, upon the privileges of the Church, and their own prejudices and interests.[3]

These factions dated to the War of Spanish Succession, 1701–14, when the Bourbons replaced the Habsburgs on the Spanish throne. The Conservatives were the holders of royal concessions, or those benefiting from maintaining the economic status quo, principally large landowners. The Liberals were the supporters of the Bourbons who opened trade (slightly); the anticlericalism, shown by the Bourbon expulsion of the Jesuits, intensified over time. These party divisions, in countries without an internal political structure or well developed national identities, were the only vestiges of a political infrastructure in Central America. In some cases, Liberal-Conservative bickering formed the base of political discourse until the last quarter of the twentieth century.[4] We will see in the upshot that Stephens's definitions of the parties could use some fine tuning. Many Liberals could by no means be categorized as democratic, and the Conservatives had Indians and other elements that were far from aristocratic.

The Liberals, ardent, and cherishing brilliant schemes of reform, aimed at an instantaneous change in popular feelings and customs, and considered every moment lost that did not establish some new theory or sweep away some old abuse. The Conservatives forgot that civilization is a jealous divinity, which does not admit of partition and cannot remain stationary. The Liberals forgot that civilization requires a harmony of intelligence, of customs, and of laws. At the third session of Congress the parties came to an open rupture.

About the same time religious fanaticism swept the state, and the Liberal party was crushed in Guatemala. But the state of San Salvador, from the beginning the leader in Liberal principles, was prompt in its efforts of vengeance, and on the sixteenth of March 1827, its army appeared within the outer gates of Guatemala City, threatening the destruction of the capital. But religious fanaticism was too strong. The friars headed mobs of women, who, with drawn knives, swore destruction to all who attempted to overturn their religion, and the San Salvadoreans were defeated and driven back. For two years the parties were at open war. In 1829 the troops of San Salvador, under General Morazan, who had now become the head of the Liberal Party, again marched upon Guatemala City and, after three days' fighting, entered it in triumph. All the leaders of the Conservative Party were banished or fled, the convents were broken up, the institution of friars abolished, the friars themselves put on board vessels and shipped out of the country, and the archbishop, anticipating banishment, or perhaps fearing a worse fate, sought safety in flight.

In 1831 General Morazan was elected president of the republic. At the expiration of the term he was reelected. For eight years the Liberal Party had the complete ascendancy. During the latter part of his term, however, there was great discontent, particularly on account of forced loans and exactions for the support of government, or, as the Conservatives said, to gratify the rapacity of unscrupulous and profligate office holders. The Church party was always on the alert. Some of the exiles in the United States and Mexico, and on the frontier, some in penury, ventured to return, and these not being molested, others soon followed. There was but one side to politics in Guatemala. Both parties have a beautiful way of producing unanimity of opinion, by driving out of the country all who do not agree with them. Seeing its chance had come, the Conservative Party gained control of Guatemala and declared that country independent of the Federation.

The Conservative party, only six months in power [in the state of Guatemala when Stephens arrived], *and still surprised at being there, was fluttering between arrogance and fear. In May preceding my arrival* [in El Salvador] *the term of the president, senators and deputies* [of the larger Central American Federation] *had expired, and no elections had been held to supply their places. The vice-president, who had been elected during an unexpired term, was the only existing officer of the federal government* which, while still claiming to be the legitimate government of the entire isthmus, could claim military control of only three states: El Salvador, its base, Honduras (thanks to General Morazán's recent defeat of Ferrara's forces), and Quetzaltenango, a department of Guatemala that had been accorded the status of statehood after attempting to secede and form union with Mexico. *Virtually, then the states stood "three and three." Where was my government?* Because the mission Stephens had been sent to execute required a central power and, in particular, a government in control of Nicaragua, Stephens set off to find such a government. As a pretext for our own sojourn south, we were set to follow in his steps, or at least as close to his steps as was practicable given the evolution of transport a century and a half later.

I woke the next morning with violent headache and pain in all my bones. Nevertheless we started at daylight and rode til five o'clock. The sun and heat increased the pain in my head and I was in great suffering.[5] That was how Stephens began his trip from Guatemala to the lower states of Central America. For my part, it was all I could do to haul myself out of bed, thanks to several bowls of very greasy popcorn I had indulged in the evening before. We got on the road about nine and had not cleared the outskirts of Esquipulas when we were pulled over at a military checkpoint. We were made to exit the vehicle, which was searched—the seventh time since entering Guatemala. At the turnoff to El Salvador, up the mountain several miles and at the side road that goes to Quetzaltepeque, a cop signaled us to the shoulder. When I flashed my U.S. passport, he immediately waved us on.

Raphael said, "That American passport is the ticket. We'll just wave our U.S. papers under their noses and zip right through the next checkpoint."

That theory was put to the acid test two kilometers up the road. A military jeep was parked under a tree on a rise. An adolescent in army fatigues with a shoulder-slung Uzi motioned us over. We shook our U.S. passports in his face. Totally unimpressed, he thumbed us out of the Ranger. Two soldiers descended on Raphael on the passenger side. While the unbearded youth examined my papers, his lips moved. I glared at him with a look just short of contempt, my feeling—taking a cue from Stephens—being you had to handle these fellows from a position of strength. Raphael's theory was that you should conciliate them. I could hear him on the other side of the vehicle entreating them earnestly in Spanish. The words "padre" and "Esquipulas" drifted over.

My interlocutor tried to walk off with my papers. I thrust out my hand and he gave the papers back to me, although reluctantly, and poked his head in the cab. He opened the flap on my backpack, eyeballed the insides, looked under the seat, flipped the seat forward, and insisted the hood be raised. In the meantime, another guy wanted the key to open the camper. I raised a finger, indicating I would be with him as soon as the first soldier finished with me. Between these two, I completely lost track of what was going on with Raphael. Finally, I got the hood down and the driver door closed and the soldiers descended on the wagon box, where they fiddled interminably with the camping gear and luggage. After too long a time, a twenty-something lieutenant bestirred himself from his roost under a tree. He gestured with his hand, and we were allowed to go on.

Back on the road, I asked Raphael, "What were you doing with those guys that took so long?"

"They forced me to spreadeagle against the truck. They patted me down."

"So much for the flashing-the-U.S.-passport strategy."

"Yeah, I guess we can scratch that one, all right."

To add to the indignity, as we descended from the mountains the landscape became dry and brown and the air incredibly hot. Then, as unpromising as

the landscape seemed, a pair of blue-headed motmots, one of the most spectacular birds of the neotropics, arced above the road as we approached the
El Salvadoran border. They flashed their racket-like tails. They were the first
motmots I had seen in my months in Central America. It was a beautiful sight
and helped steel me for the always-trying border crossing.

I went immediately to the Government House where I requested a passport [or
visa as we would say today]. *The secretary of state objected, on the ground that
none could be made out on that day. There were several clerks in the office, and I
urged my pressing necessity. After an unpleasant parley, one was given me, but
without assigning me any official character. I pointed out the omission, and put
into his hands my passport from my own government, reminded him that I had
been arrested and imprisoned once and wished to know definitively whether he
would give me such a passport as I had a right to ask for. After much hesitation
and with a very bad grace, he interlined before the official title the words con el
caracter. This attempt to embarrass my movements excited a feeling of indignation
I did not attempt to conceal.*[6] Or, in other words, Stephens experienced a pretty
ordinary border-crossing transaction in Central America.

Unaccountably, we breezed through Guatemalan immigration, customs,
automotive control, and *fumigación*. At the latter station, we were told we
could pay a dollar to have the truck sprayed against the international trans-
mission of insects, or two dollars and not have it sprayed. Had it not been for
the middle-aged, nicely dressed man in guayabera, slacks, and shell-rim spec-
tacles standing nonchalantly by the road, as though waiting for his wife or
chauffeur, holding a leash that led to a small-dog harness enclosing a very
plump and contented Norwegian rat, you might not even know you were in
an area of the world where the rules were made up out of thin air on the spot.

The El Salvadoran border checkpoint was a modernistic concrete structure,
large, cavernous, and airy. It was reminiscent of a modern air terminal, glaringly out of place considering the aggregation of ramshackle tin huts on the
Guatemalan side and the civil war this country was in the final throes of. A
young boy by the name of Wilber showed us the first place to go. The official
behind the counter checked our El Salvadoran visas, efficiently stamped our
passports, and said we were free to go. So much for a warning I had received
back in Belize from a British expat that it would take two hours to cross the
El Salvadoran border. They did not even bother checking the vehicle's papers.
Wait a minute, that was too good to be true. "Can we go even if we have a
vehicle?" Raphael asked.

"Oh, you have *un carro*," the fellow said and pointed to a corner, where we found a young man in uniform who was either drunk or feeble-minded. When we showed him our documents, he tried to copy the information off the registration and passports. Failing, he would chuck the paper and start again. We were detained by his incompetence a quarter-hour; then it was on to more stops in an interminable number of offices.

While Wilber, our *coyotero,* as we learned border guides were called, went off in search of a customs cop, supposedly our next stop, I skipped ahead to a second-story office and a pleasant young woman in a blue police uniform wearing the suggestion of a smile on her face. Because she was the first amiable person I had seen all day, I flashed her a grin. Immediately, her face clouded over with a bureaucratic frown. I required, she told me coolly, a clearance from the customs police first.

When I got back to the truck, Wilber had returned and so had a customs cop who, affecting an air, sent Wilber off looking for another officer. This cop was tall for a Central American. He had a Castilian face, complete with a hook nose and a strong chin and an extremely light complexion. Although in his late twenties, he had already developed that cop/bus driver look, fat belly and skinny butt. And he walked with the arrogant cop's cob-up-the-rear swagger.

"You know what he wants," Raphael said.

"He's nuts if he thinks I'm going to tender a bribe in a notorious police state where I've never been before and have no idea how things work," I said.

So instead of getting a sawbuck he got Raphael working his version of the con on him. Raphael sidled over, offered him a cigarette, and then launched into a monologue. As a result, the cop seemed to acquiesce to Raphael's entreaty. He strutted over to the Ranger, Raphael motormouthing behind him. The cop ordered all the gear offloaded, then he pawed through everything, paying no particular attention to the items that would likely contain contraband. He went through the cab and took two books out of my backpack, one an Elmore Leonard novel with a glitzy foil cover, and the other a Frommer tour guide, both in English, not a word of which he understood. *(Literary in his tastes,* as Stephens noted about a wayfarer, *he asked if we had any books: he said their being in English made no difference—books were good things.)*[7] He tucked those books under his arm like a fullback and made me raise the hood. I asked if I could reload the gear. Also, could I please have my books back. The books were reluctantly handed over, but he said no to allowing the gear to be stowed again in the truck. I set up my camp chair and settled in. After more than an hour an older policeman came up and told our cop to sign off on the papers, which he did, but only after ostentatiously checking the ID number of the vehicle against the registration.

Evidently, this guy had overdone it even by El Salvadoran border standards. When I approached the woman at the next station, she was again smiling—and also seemed a bit apologetic. But, as with Stephens, her colleague had *excited a feeling of indignation I did not attempt to conceal,* and I'm afraid I left the border in a not-very-charitable mood.

The Guatemalan side had not looked like territory anyone would go to the trouble of fighting for—mountainous, arid, sparsely populated, and hot. That went double for the El Salvadoran side, which looked even more bleak and desolate, thanks to the campesinos' custom of burning off the plots in preparation for the rainy season.

El Salvador is the smallest country in Spanish Central America, being about the size of Massachusetts. More importantly, its population is approximately the same as that densely populated North American industrial state, with a late 1980s estimate of 5.5 million people, only about a million of whom lived in the capital city of San Salvador.[8] The denser population on this side of the Guatemalan frontier was shown by the great number of campesinos out in the blazing sun, strolling along the road or working in the fields.

Before independence in 1823, El Salvador's history was similar to Guatemala's—but less so. Because El Salvador lacked easy to acquire riches, namely precious metals, the Spanish did not greatly bother with the territory, parceling the country out in encomiendas to the most loyal or aggressive conquistadors, and then pretty much forgetting about it. For a brief period after the break with Spain, El Salvador was a hotbed of political activity. It was, as Stephens noted, always the most Liberal—in the sense of Liberal party—state in Central America, and therefore the one most in favor of unification of all the states of the isthmus. When Morazán was driven out of Guatemala in the late 1830s, as Stephens also noted, he made his headquarters in El Salvador in a futile effort to pull the United Provinces together.[9]

For one hundred years the Liberal State, as the rule of the Liberal party is deemed, rolled prosperously on, buoyed by the introduction of coffee in the last quarter of the nineteenth century. Few of the Liberal heads of state finished their terms of office, but this was deemed as no great consequence. For instance, Andrés Valle, elected in 1876, was shunted aside by forces from Guatemala when that country's great Liberal, the elder Barrios, tried to reunite the isthmus by force of arms. Although Barrios himself was ultimately killed in this adventure, his hand-picked Salvadoran replacement for Valle,

Rafael Zaldívar, was elected president twice in his own right. He, too, was overthrown by a would-be president-dictator, Francisco Menéndez, who himself fell victim to his army commander, Carlos Erzeta, who had him shot. The usurper Erzeta was attacked by Guatemalan forces, leading to his downfall.[10]

The important point is that the Liberal Party cooperated with the so-called *catorce,* the fourteen families that supposedly owned and ruled the country. Sometimes this ruling oligarchy is called "the 40." The actual number of families that ran the country and divided the spoils seems to be approximately two hundred. Membership was elastic. Newer members in the nineteenth century included the coffee and merchant elite, the latter encompassing a fair number of Levantines. As long as the Liberal state enlarged the amount of land available to the planters—at the expense of peasants—everyone was happy, at least everyone who had a real vote.

It was a long, upgrade pull until we came to Santa Ana, El Salvador's second most populous city, with a population of about one hundred thousand. The agricultural fields on the outskirts were larger compared to those across the border in Guatemala, probably machine cultivated, and the soil darker and more fertile too, due to the volcanic origin of much of the countryside. Living under a volcano is a two-edged sword. The upside, so to speak, is the soil, among the richest in the world. The downside is obvious. The eruption of Ilopango in this area in the late Preclassic Maya era, almost two thousand years ago, killed everything in a radius of sixty miles and retarded Maya social development in the southern highlands for two hundred years.[11] Nowadays that good, rich soil is still a double-edged sword; the control over its use—for subsistence or export cash crops—was the major impetus for the El Salvadoran civil war.

Santa Ana was a not-quite-picturesque town of walled Spanish courtyards and green trees. All else was brown. Due to its location in the center of the coffee-growing region, it was at one time—one hundred years ago—more populous and prosperous than the capital, San Salvador. Now it was simply a dreary overgrown provincial town, whose principal interest lay in its claim to being a semiactive theater during the ongoing civil war. Those associations were not always—or do I mean ever?—pleasant. For instance, ten circus workers were summarily killed by the Maximiliano Hernández-Martínez Anti-Communist Brigade (read "death squad"), not for political crimes but out of ordinary vigilantism—the gandy dancers and roustabouts were suspected of dealing drugs. On the other side, the largest force the guerrillas ever mustered, more than one thousand men, attacked the National Telecommunication Administration in Santa Ana, putting it out of commission for a time. That happened almost seven years before in June 1985.

We blundered into the central market. It was grubby, but the stalls were loaded with interesting knickknacks. I was so ill I could not give these curiosities the inspection I desired. After receiving the standard, "Recto, recto (straight ahead)," to our pleas for directions, we ended hopelessly lost in a slum barrio. Then some youngsters in a nice-looking passenger sedan, students at a Catholic high school, led us through the maze of streets because they thought that it was too confusing to try to direct us orally.

Once on the highway outside of town, we noticed that the road was lined on both sides with what seemed to be continuous and contiguous houses pushed right up on the shoulder. The road between, though all but empty of motorized traffic, was alive with people and animals—cattle, horses, dogs, burros, chickens, kids. It appeared to be the world's longest and narrowest village. Construction was of sticks and mud. Beyond the houses coffee bushes were growing. It seemed very hot for coffee, which grows best in moderately high and cool (for the tropics) areas, but presently the road began to climb. Soon it was cooler, and both sides of the mountain were planted to the miracle bean.

Coffee, its scientific name of *Coffea arabica* notwithstanding, is thought to have originated in Ethiopia. The bean, which botanists insist on calling a seed, began its great migration in the fifteenth century, when plants were taken to Yemen and put under cultivation. With the dawn of the modern age and the attendant craving for novel consumables, the drink became faddish in the Middle East and later in European countries where it gained notoriety or disapproval as a religious, political, or medical beverage. Even as late as World War II, American troops sometimes employed it in an extremely strong brew, given as an enema, to treat battle shock.

Socially, coffeehouses transformed Europe, as they provided a sober commercial venue where men could gather. As every schoolboy knows, the term "cafe" is an outgrowth of this custom. Every other schoolboy knows that Lloyd's of London started off as one such place, where underwriters for any venture could be found. The War of 1812, which cut off American access to Asian tea, turned America's interest to coffee. By the Civil War, Union troops were doled out a ration of thirty-six pounds of beans per year. By the end of the nineteenth century, Americans were consuming about half of the world production. In Stephens's time, circa 1840, coffee was just beginning to become an important commercial crop in Central America.[12]

The coffee plant is an attractive, evergreen bush with shiny leaves that grows to fifteen feet. Rather astonishingly, it produces the second most valuable export commodity in the world (after petroleum and not counting illegal substances).[13] The fruit, known as the coffee cherry, turns a bright red when ripe. Large corporate enterprises in Central America remove the flesh by running the harvested cherries through a pulping machine. After a short fermentation period, during which a naturally occurring enzyme loosens the residual meat, the seeds are washed, cleaned, and kiln-dried. Owners of small coffee plots simply dry the fruit in the sun and remove the flesh later, a process that produces a superior product. Roasting is done at about 440 degrees. The bean expands while roasting and develops its characteristic aroma and taste.

From the point of view of Central American politics, the most cogent feature of the coffee plant is that it takes five years to come into production. That means a grower, whether he be a large *hacendado* or a peasant tending a plot, needs capital. When United Fruit disposed of its Guatemalan banana holdings, it shifted to buying fruit grown by small producers. Because the banana yields a crop in about a year, workers with a little land and initiative were able to cash in on that opportunity. For the little guy—especially in El Salvador— growing coffee was a much dicier proposition.

During the heyday of the Liberal state, from about 1875 to the 1920s, laws were passed that allowed the common ground between villages to be platted out and sold to private individuals. The hillsides were planted to coffee, the valleys and coastal plain to cotton. The peasants who formerly used these lands to grow their corn and beans or graze their herds were offered employment in the way of becoming a *colón*. The colón was given use of a piece of land sufficient to produce food for himself and his family, for which he paid by toiling in the planter's fields. Because this arrangement was not likely to be greeted with glee, a special police force was mandated to keep order in the countryside. (Indeed, of the country's ten thousand or so men under arms before the outbreak of civil war, all but two hundred or so were trained to deal with internal disturbances.) All went along smoothly until the end of World War I. Then the ingenious idea of enlarging the planter's acreage by eliminating the colón's gardens gained currency. Machinery or low-paid seasonal help took the colón's place in the fields.[14]

All the ingredients were in place: a dense population, semi-itinerant seasonal workers, and wages too low to sustain life. Ethnic tension existed as well; the Pipil Indians were stripped of their remaining communal lands. Then came the triggering mechanism: the Great Depression. It spelled the end of the Liberal State, although the last Liberal president, Arturo Araujo, tried to live up to the name of his party. He made a few slight reforms and promised free elections. Even the Communist Party was allowed to run a slate of candidates. But the army deposed him, and put his vice president, General Maximiliano Hernández-Martínez, in his place. Martínez, a rather strange man who went by his maternal last name among many other oddities, allowed the elections to proceed. (Like many totalitarian dictators, Duvalier in Haiti and Noreiga in Panama for example, he dabbled in the black arts; Martínez once hung colored lights around San Salvador to ward off a smallpox epidemic; the treatment, needless to say, did not work.) The Communists won many municipal posts in the area around Santa Ana. Martínez barred them from assuming office.

But worse was to come. The communists were well organized under the leadership of a young El Salvadoran by the name of Agustín Farabundo Martí. Martí was the preeminent Central American Marxist, having ties with the revolutionaries in Mexico and the Sandino rebellion in Nicaragua in the 1920s. The communists' peasant supporters plotted a rural insurrection. The army, alerted in advance, arrested Martí and the other ringleaders. The peasants rose up anyway. The army moved in. Martí and others were executed, as were up to thirty thousand supporters (the best estimate is fifteen to twenty thousand perished), most of them Indians. The event, called *la matanza* (the slaughter), ushered in fifty years of military control of the government, the hallmark of which was more land being taken from the populace and put at the disposal of the planter class.[15] The long narrow shacks pushed up against the road that Raphael and I noted are called fence houses. They became a conspicuous feature of the countryside after la matanza, when the peasants were forced into such digs for want of a better place to live.

We ascended to the top of the slope, the pickup running at 210 degrees, then barreled down the other side, and thanks to the Belizean mechanic who discarded the Ranger's thermostat, the temperature of the engine dropped to 120 degrees—same numbers, but rearranged. Stephens, though just recovering from the worst bout of fever he had yet to suffer, determined to climb Izalco Volcano, which was now visible to Raphael and me.

Our guide got lost, tied his horse, and left us to wait while he searched the way. We knew that we were near the volcano, for the explosions sounded like the deep mutterings of dreadful thunder. Shut up as we were in the woods, these reports were awful. Our horses snorted with terror, and the mountains quaked beneath our feet. Our guide returned, and in a few minutes we came out suddenly upon an open point, higher than the top of the volcano commanding a view of the interior of the crater, and so near it that we saw the huge stones as they separated in the air, and fell pattering around the sides of the volcano. In a few minutes our clothes were white with ashes, which fell around us with a noise like the sprinkling of rain.[16]

Raphael planned to save us a few *colones* by bunking with a priest friend in Sonsonate. Raphael's friend, Father Napoleón, we learned on finding his church, was away on a day trip to Acajutla. His parish church could have been designed by the architect that did the El Salvadoran border checkpoint. It was modernistic with ornamental concrete-block flourishes that went well with the city's eateries, Popeye's Chicken, Big Burger, and Deli Pizza, whose blandishments, given the state of my stomach, held little fascination for me. *It is hard to feel worse than I did when I mounted. I passed three hours of agony, scorched by the intense heat, and a little before dark arrived at Zonzonate* [Sonsonate], *fortunate, as Dr. Drivin afterward told me, in not having suffered a stroke of the sun.*[17]

Before entering the town and crossing the bridge over the Río Grande, I met a gentleman well mounted, having a scarlet Peruvian pellon over his saddle, with whose appearance I was struck, and we exchanged low bows. This gentleman, as I afterward learned, was the government I was looking for. He was Don Diego Vigil, the vice-president of the republic, and the only existing officer of the federal government. His business at Zonzonate showed the wretched state of the country. He had come expressly to treat with Rascon, the head of the band[its] which had prevented my coming from Guatemala by land. If there was any government, I had treed *it. Was it the real thing or not? In Guatemala they said it was not. Here they said it was. It was a knotty question. He was legally elected vice-president;* [Señor Vigil said] *the act of the four states in declaring themselves independent was unconstitutional and rebellious. I referred to the shattered condition of the government, its absolute impotence in other states, the nonexistence of senate and other coordinate branches, or even of a secretary of state, the officer to whom my credentials were addressed. He answered that he had in his suite an acting secretary of state, confirming what had been told me before, that the "government" would, at a moment's notice, make any officer I wanted.*[18] All this was too much for Stephens, the amateur diplomat. He refused to present his credentials and continued on his trek southward. Or, in other words, he decided the treaty was moribund.

Seldom had Raphael and I been as disappointed—to the point of despair—as we were with Acajutla, fifteen miles farther on. Stephens's description of a few miserable huts was infinitely preferable to the slum village we found, part port city, part proletarian resort. The black sand beach, though lovely, was littered with discarded trash and old tires, and the smoke of cook fires made the drive along the seafront oppressive. We stopped at the best-looking hotel-restaurant with a half-formed resolve of eating and perhaps spending the night. A closer view showed grounds that looked like Rome after the Visigoths took over. The swimming pool was cracked and filled with trash. Scratch spending the night. But we had only a snack-lunch in the truck. We claimed a seat in one of the dirty molded plastic chairs, ubiquitous third-world seating, at an attractive tile table under an untended pergola while I sought the comfort station. Next to the restroom, which reeked, a large smoked fish, half consumed, was laid out on a ledge on greasy brown paper as though put down and forgotten about.

We limited ourselves to a *refresco,* or soda, at that depressing hotel/restaurant and pushed on forty more miles to La Libertad, snaking along a ledge high above the Pacific, which foamed and crashed at our feet. The road led through five unguarded tunnels, the last of which terminated in the blazing orange-red glory of a grove of poinciana trees, often dubbed the world's most beautiful flowering tree. I was almost as delighted by the smoldering beauty of those trees as I was by not meeting a troupe of guerrillas or bandits in the dark of the tunnels. The countryside here was more lush, more humid, and cooler. The population was sparser and was occupied, it seemed, by pulling small-wheeled carts loaded with water jugs along the road.

With night approaching, on the outskirts of La Libertad we stopped at a roadhouse motel that could have been bodily lifted from the seedy motel strip of Anytown, U.S.A. It even had a row of mangy arbor-vitae-looking trees, and a half full swimming pool clouded gray-green from algae. The management charged us extra for air conditioning and forgot to mention that the electricity did not come on until later, the dim lights in the common area coming from a reserve battery system. We were thirty-two kilometers from the capital, San Salvador. Still feeling ill, I fell into bed in stifling heat.

Stephens had the great fortune—and honor—of being borne to Costa Rica by the brig *La Cosmopolita, the only vessel on the Pacific that bore the Central American flag. I had on board Gil Blas and Don Quixote in the original, and all day I sat under an awning, my attention divided between them and the great range of gigantic volcanoes which stud the coast. We passed in regular succession the volcanoes of San Salvador, San Vicente, San Miguel, Telega, Momotombo, each one a noble spectacle, and all together forming a chain with which no other in the world can be compared. Indeed, this coast has well been described as "bristling with volcanic cones."*[19]

The next morning we rolled along the Pacific coast, going through countryside with that deep deltaesque soil of the littoral, humid with big trees, poincianas flaming here and there, plus some other trees in bloom I did not recognize, notably some with white flowers in the hedgerows. That curious rain shadow effect that is seen around mountains, especially near the sea, was shown by quick changes of climate as we passed under the volcanoes that Stephens had enumerated. Once Raphael counted as many as six volcanic cones visible at the same time.

The arid regions were not picturesque. No big cactuses, just huge milkweeds with pretensions of being trees. Many ox carts were in evidence, and in one spot there were goat carts, the *cabritos* yoked by the horns. In other places, tractors rolled along the road and in the fields, and there were other indications of agribusiness operations. We went over four one-lane Bailey (temporary) bridges, the originals having been blown up by the guerrillas. Most of the streams under the bridges were dry. We were stopped for some minutes waiting for oncoming traffic on the bridge over the Lempa, the country's principal river, and the dividing line between the territory claimed by the Pipil Indians and the Lenca in days gone by.[20] Some girls with bottles of soda in plastic trays on their heads stuck their faces in the car. I asked one her name and how many anuses (anos) she had, instead of her age, or how many years (años) in Spanish. She upheld the modesty of El Salvadoran women by only smiling instead of giggling out loud as most Belizean woman would have done.

For almost forty years after *la matanza,* the army kept the country firmly in control. The escape valve for the ever burgeoning population was Honduras. El Salvadorans, who are known to be exceptionally industrious, went there to work. Many squatted on unused lands in that vastly larger and more underpopulated territory. In the late 1960s, for internal political reasons, Honduran strongman Oswaldo López Arellano started to expel the El Salvadorans. The situation reached fever pitch when El Salvadorans jeered the Honduran national soccer team during a game in El Salvador. The result: war, the infamous Soccer War of 1969. The Salvadoran military got the best of the Hondurans, but they also got the two hundred thousand settlers back. For ten years these repatriated squatters put a strain on the country's social fabric, which the military government tried to control by turning up the pressure on the underclasses. Finally, in 1979, the year the Sandinistas took control in neighboring Nicaragua, the fabric tore.[21]

Fearing a repeat of the Nicaraguan model where a supposed broad-based anti-Somoza movement was taken over by the communists, a group of Young Turk military officers overthrew the far-right government. It sought to bring in politicians from the center to help reform the country. With the government now officially out of its hands, the military rightists responded by unleashing their death squads, their most notable victim being Archbishop Oscar Arnulfo Romero, who was murdered while saying Mass in a hospital chapel. Some twenty to thirty thousand others, including a fair number of American nuns, clergy, union organizers, and the like, fell victim to right-wing oppression. The leftist political parties, including some from the center Christian Democrats, took to the hills, and others became urban guerrillas, kidnapping or assassinating key figures, including the occasional American Marine or foreign businessman. The dominant rebel faction was known as the Farabundo Martí National Liberation Front (FMLN).

By the early 1980s, the centrist coalition was led by José Napoleón Duarte, a charismatic politician who was equally courageous and wily. He had been among the hearty souls who founded the Christian Democrat Party in the early 1960s as a rejection of Castro and east-bloc communism, on the one hand, and right-wing militarism on the other. In the meantime, Duarte had been mayor of San Salvador and had had the 1972 presidential election stolen from him. As president he was confronted with a gigantic case of déjá vu. Emboldened by the victory in Nicaragua, Castro had called the leaders of the Salvadoran revolutionary factions (pro-Soviet, Maoist, Castroites) to Havana, where he forged a united front. However, Duarte's severest challenge came from the right—from destabilizing paramilitary activity and from the electorate.[22]

Even though the peasantry and the proletariat were sorely taxed by overpopulation and limited access to resources, their political consciousness had been shrewdly Balkanized. The peasants who depended on wage labor—either seasonal or full time—tended to support the landowners who employed them. Also, the military government had not been wholly without guile. It had developed a sort of paramilitary auxiliary in the countryside called *Orden* (Order). Government largesse to the poor went mostly to the Ordenistas. Orden was officially abandoned in the 1970s, but the military continued to work

with and favor these supporters. When Duarte instituted a modest land reform package, he turned to the military to implement it—because the military was the only institution in the government that had the muscle to buck
large estate owners. The military parceled out the acreage mostly to its former
allies in Orden.

Cuba was not the only nearby country dispensing counsel to the warring
factions. In 1979, a group of young businessmen and militarists were called to
Guatemala City. There Mario Sandoval, a Guatemalan with long experience
in Central American practical politics, addressed them. Sandoval, who was
recovering from a cancer operation, spoke like some underworld figure, his
voice an electronic rasp. He encouraged the El Salvadorans to form death
squads. To help train them in this grisly activity, he lent them French advisors
who had perfected their techniques in Algeria in the late 1950s. But perhaps
the most destabilizing advice tendered was to develop a political party. They
did. It was called ARENA (Alianza Repulicana Nacional).[23]

By the time of the first free election in recent El Salvadoran history, in 1983
(before that, Duarte had been provisional president appointed by the centrist
junta), ARENA garnered 25.8 percent of the popular vote, which along with
the 16.8 percent for the PCN, the official military party, surpassed Duarte and
the PDC's 35.5. Suddenly the specter of ARENA's Roberto D'Aubuisson
("Fighting Bob," as the young, distressingly attractive dispatcher of death
squads liked to style himself) as president became a very real prospect. That
extremely unsavory likelihood was averted by some ham-fisted tactics of the
Reagan administration, notably the threat to withhold aid. Because the Marxist guerrillas, the FMLN, had the El Salvadoran army on the ropes—never
minding the right-wing terror—a victory by D'Aubuisson would most likely
have paved the way for a Nicaragua-like collapse. A D'Aubuisson presidency
would have driven the centrists into the arms of the guerrillas.

As it happened, Duarte, with a great deal of American assistance, returned
to the presidency in the 1984 election. Despite liver cancer and the kidnapping
of his eldest daughter, Duarte fought desperately to hold the center for the
next five years. It was not an altogether successful fight. American threats to
cut off military aid helped curb death squad activity by the armed forces. On
the other hand, the United States insisted Duarte placate the elite landholder
class—at the expense of the peasants and workers, Duarte's natural constitu-
ency. In addition, his party suffered from corruption, which he was unable to
control. Nevertheless, for five years Duarte adroitly held a middle position

between the communists and the rightists. He was turned out of office by the voters in 1989 in favor of the ARENA Party's candidate, Alfredo Cristiani. He succumbed to cancer the next year.[24]

Cristiani was immediately confronted by a massive FMLN assault, which saw hundreds perish in the capital of San Salvador as entire neighborhoods became controlled by the Marxists for days. The ESAF (El Salvadoran Armed Forces) resorted to bombing neighborhoods in the city to dislodge the guerrillas. Casualty totals ran into the thousands, although neither side officially claimed more than five hundred lost. The civilian toll was at least two thousand. On the heels of the offensive, a death squad dispatched by the armed forces high command gunned down six Jesuits and two bystanders at the Central American University. The cowardice of this act, as much as the psychological defeat of the San Salvador assault and the electoral defeat of the Sandinistas a couple of months later (which made El Salvador much less important in the larger cold war scenario), set the stage for negotiations.

President Bush and the Soviet Union's Premier Gorbachev encouraged talks. Finally in November 1991, the year before Raphael and I rolled across El Salvador, the FMLN announced a unilateral halt to offensive operations. In December, just five months before, serious negotiations got under way in New York, the upshot of which would allow some FMLN members to be absorbed into a new national police force, the disbandment of the present police forces (including my special favorite, the Customs Police), the creation of a National Truth Commission, and a commitment by all sides to use the democratic process to effect political change.[25] Perhaps even more importantly, the military lost its constitutional mandate to maintain internal security and intelligence. Many of its component parts, such as the command of the military academy, came under civilian or joint civilian-military control.[26]

As we progressed, the country grew more uniformly arid. Cactuses appeared in fencerows, and often a pineapple-like bromeliad was used as a living fence between fields. We arrived in La Unión, the former auto-ferry port to Nicaragua, at about 12:30 P.M., having traversed almost the entire breadth of the country in a morning. Astonishingly, given the country was still technically in a state of civil war, our travel papers were checked here for the first time.

Stephens met Francisco Morazán near the El Salvadoran frontier. *General Morazan was about forty-five years old, 5 feet 10 inches high, thin, with a black mustache and week's beard, and wore a military frock coat, buttoned up to the throat, and sword. His hat was off, and the expression of his face mild and intel-*

*ligent. Though still young, for ten years he had been the first man in the country,
and eighth president of the Republic. He had risen and had sustained himself by
military skill and personal bravery, always led his forces himself, had been in innumerable battles, and often wounded, but never beaten. A year before, the people
of Guatemala, of both parties, had implored him to come to their relief, as the
only man who could save them from Carrera and destruction. He had marched
against Guatemala with fourteen hundred men, and forced his way into the
plaza. Forty of his oldest officers and his eldest son were shot down by his side.
Cutting his way through masses of human flesh, with about four hundred fifty
men, [he] made his escape. From the best information I could acquire and in fact
by every one else in his own state, I have conceived almost a feeling of admiration
for General Morazan and my interest in him was increased by his misfortunes.*
Stephens's interview with Morazán was brief, the general said he was sorry the
treaty could not be renewed (because the republic he represented was shattered). The general also asked after his family. *It spoke volumes that, at such a
moment, with the wreck of his followers before him, and the memory of his murdered companions fresh in his mind, in the overthrow of all his hopes and fortunes,
his heart turned to his domestic relations.*[27]

In many ways—certainly as being great, if flawed, political leaders—
presidents Duarte and Morazán bear some resemblance. Both were forlorn
and ultimately defeated figures, fighting long odds, who nevertheless kept on
fighting for what they and most fair-minded observers would agree was right
(if perhaps not always worth the price). Duarte's enemies circulated many
nasty things about him in both El Salvador and the United States. For instance, American leftists reviled him for being a Reagan stooge, claiming that
being a Notre Dame graduate was his sole claim to political favor (and supposedly the reason he was selected as the American puppet-president). These
critics, however, had not looked deeply into the man's career.

In 1972, Duarte had a presidential election stolen from him. The official
party, the PCN, stuffed the ballot box with one hundred thousand votes, the
number thought required to win. When it became apparent the party in
power had miscounted, it restuffed the boxes, and still came up a few thousand short, so the PCN partisans simply confiscated the necessary number of
ballots. Seeing where all this was heading, Duarte sought refuge in a Venezue-
lan diplomatic compound. Paying no attention to diplomatic immunity, the
police rousted him, handcuffed him, and beat him to a pulp without a word
being said. He then was set free. He fled into exile—but returned a few years
later to resume political office.[28] If one would like to find political models to

General Francisco Morazán, the failed George Washington of Central America. Stephens finally caught up with him in El Salvador. This monument stands in the town square of Copán Ruinas, Honduras.

look up to and admire, Central America, where a politician has to put his life as well as his convictions on the line, as both Morazán and Duarte did, is the place to look.

A half hour brought us to the Honduran frontier. If you imagine the Christmas rush at Kennedy and Miami airports rolled together, you would have a pretty good idea of what that border checkpoint was like. Vehicles were jammed together and people were running all over the place. No one seemed to know what was going on, with the exception of the horde of coyoteros, none older than high-school age, who clamored at us offering their services. One wanted twenty-five colones (four dollars), I offered him ten, which he took. We started with the police inspection. The coyotero said if we gave the cop twenty-five colones we could speed up the search. The four bucks was handed over, which the kid secreted in my passport. The cop snatched up the passport, whisked the banknotes into his pocket, and checked off the papers in the blink of an eye. Then the young fellow told me to give him 225 colones and he would take care of everything. I told him I would go with him. So we went through the red tape together. I paid one guy more than a one hundred colones, which seemed legit. The next guy wanted twenty-five colones. I gave him the twenty-five but demanded a receipt. He gave the twenty-five back. After about twenty minutes, we got to the Honduran side, where Raphael hired a guide by the name of José.

José demanded fifty dollars in *lempiras,* which Raphael forked over, then the kid told us to back up to a concrete dock and unload. By now I was beginning to get with the program. I asked José if we could perhaps show the customs officials a token of our appreciation and not bother with the inspection. I regret to report, as Stephens would have said, that the Hondurans were idealists and we were stuck with the procedure. Worse, I had an olive-drab duffel bag "confiscated" by a fatigue-clad captain with an acne-scarred face wearing Ray-Ban sunglasses. He strutted like a martinet as though trying to live up to some pulp-fiction cliché. My consolation came from watching the man next to us. He was traveling with his family in a Mitsubishi pickup with a trailer full of boxes. Like us, he was made to unload his wagon box and trailer and unseal all the boxes. I overheard his college-age children speaking English. Then I caught a glimpse of their license tag with the familiar orange peninsula, Palm Beach County. The father was a Nicaraguan who had lived in the States for the past thirteen years. He was more annoyed than I to be put through the routine bureaucratic harassment. One of the kids said it had cost $456 in "fees" to cross Mexico. I told them, facetiously, that I was going to sell my truck and fly home. Both father and son thought that was an excellent idea.

We arrived in Choluteca, Honduras, just as the market was breaking up. Stalls crowded cheek by jowl in the central park, which was ringed by tallish, modern buildings. The place, which was buzzing with activity, looked like a combined outdoor supermarket and church bazaar. The campesinos who had brought in enough money for the day were tearing stalls down, while others sat patiently by piles of mangoes or handicrafts or whatever. Bodies scurried around and buses took off pouring out huge clouds of blue exhaust. All this made Choluteca seem the very center of the world, in a place that had not even managed to attract my attention on the map before that day. Raphael, being more knowledgeable about things Central American, said he had long heard of Choluteca, but he had never known anyone who had actually been here.

We spent the night in the best hotel in the city, the Pierre, complete with air conditioning and cable TV, for fourteen dollars. We had to eat in the hotel coffee shop because when we ventured out at 9 P.M. there was not an eating establishment or anything else open in town. There was hardly even a streetlight to be seen. With the exception of the proprietor, who was an Englishman and thus not quite the real thing, not another gringo was in evidence. His son, a redhead named William, was eating supper in the lobby when we returned from our futile search for a restaurant. He was a young fellow of about twenty or perhaps less. For company he had insects of many different species—not cockroaches—about one for every floor tile. The young man looked like a gringo but spoke English as though Peter Lorre had been his TEFL (Teaching English as a Foreign Language) instructor. Speaking of Honduras's Bay Island, he said, "They are worthy islands. One day you must visit them."

A statue in the town square was of the local hero and failed politician, José Cecilio Del Valle. Born in 1777, died in 1834, Del Valle accomplished little in his life except to get thrown into jail by General Iturbide for more or less opposing the absorption of the Kingdom of Guatemala into Mexico after liberation from Spain. He also stood in elections twice against Morazán, winning the second contest, but dying before taking office. Del Valle, nicknamed "El Sabio" for his wisdom, was remembered in this corner of Honduras as a local hero. His family domicile still stood on the corner of the square. His statue and house, plus the local church of La Merced, which is claimed (perhaps erroneously) to date from the mid-1500s, all seemed to be the very model of Central America, so eagerly clinging to its past, ever so humble and noble.

After our quick tour around downtown Choluteca, we loaded up the Ranger, regained the highway, and shortly found ourselves on the Nicaraguan frontier. We hired Wilfor, a youngster of seventeen, to shepherd us through Honduran exit border customs. There were a bewildering number of stops, which I'm sorry I did not count. We got through fairly quickly, thanks to Wilfor's expertise, then it was down a long unpaved grade past shanty establishments to a Bailey bridge over a muddy, knee-deep river to Nicaragua. A checkpoint on the other side of the river was passed quickly enough, and I allowed myself to hope that the Nicaraguan authorities would quickly be put behind us.

A cinder-block building painted an official blue dashed that hope. As I parked under a tree a lean, muscular fellow in his late forties or early fifties ambled toward me from a van with Arizona plates. He started bitching about the border officials. I marked him down as a jerk. He had the sort of New York accent that did not help his credibility. Then I hired a coyotero and waded into the melee. My choice in Nicaraguan coyoteros was not a happy one. The young fellow would wander off and fool around. I supposed he was working some sort of elliptical maneuver, so I was reluctant to get him on track.

But after a while it was apparent I had a loser, because even when he stood on line he was letting people crowd in ahead, and the authorities were taking locals ahead of him. Finally we got through the first check, immigration, and went to the police check, which was more Kafkaesque than usual. My coyotero waited behind a closed door. Once he had the temerity to crack the door open, which with an astonished expression he snapped immediately shut. Then he walked away from the door, leaving me jealously guarding our position at the front of the line. Another coyotero came up and I hustled to prevent him from taking the lead spot. The second kid reached over me, opened the door and quickly shut it before I could see what was going on in the cubicle. Being a foreigner, I did not have the presumption to turn the doorknob myself.

While I waited behind the door, a jolly fellow in a baggy Hawaiian shirt and loose trousers, wearing a baseball cap with the insignia of the national police, wandered in. He had a Goofy-like face and he was shouting and joking with the regulars. In his pocket, as casually as he joked, the butt of a huge pistol bounced. He disappeared, laughing, behind "the door" and reappeared a few minutes later, still laughing. A short time later, an ordinary-looking local with plastic-rim glasses emerged, seeming quite satisfied with himself and his transaction, whatever it was. We were ushered into the small hot room—not even a fan by way of ventilation. The door was left open. The guy in T-shirt and trousers behind the desk puffed himself up with an important expression as he tried to look busy with other work for a time. After the requisite wait had been endured, he fiddled with our papers, and then at long last a checkmark was penciled on a scrap of paper. We were sent on our way to the next such booth, with never a clue being divulged as to the mysterious carrying-on behind the closed door.

Nicaragua, unlike Honduras, was on daylight savings time so lunch break arrived early. Although I had all the stamps except one, I was told I would have to wait until after lunch. By now I was as steamed as the guys from Arizona. The four of us converged under a tree. Frank and Ernie, ironworkers by trade, gave Raphael and me a beer each, and we entertained ourselves with one of the chief amusements of travelers in Central America, grumbling about the bureaucracy. The cake-taker was the Nicaraguan border officials' refusal to accept payment in their own currency. They demanded greenbacks.

The black market money-changers on the Nicaraguan side, the only kind to be had, would not take traveler's checks, so having plenty of time, I decided to walk back to Honduras to change some money. The guys at the bridge offered me a four-to-one rate and laughed at me when I told them I wanted five and a half. The no man's land around the bridge was dusty and hot and lined with big trucks. The poorest imaginable food stands catered to truckers. I stopped at a roadside kiosk where an old woman in an embroidered blouse, squatting in the dust, was frying chicken in a large woklike vessel over a charcoal fire. She wanted a dollar for a lunch that consisted of one piece of chicken, rice, beans, two tortillas, cabbage, and two slices of tomato, and which was among the best meals I had eaten since embarking on this journey. Unfortunately, by accident I had shuffled the five-lempiras note back in my pocket, like a con artist. She had to demand her money of me, which made me feel bad. It confirmed, you could read on her face, her opinion that gringos were not to be trusted.

At the Honduran border facility I was given an exchange rate of five-to-the-dollar, which I bragged about to the guys on the Nicaraguan side. We all had a good laugh about that. About 2 P.M. we were finally able to leave the frontier. The Nicaraguan countryside, in marked contrast to the Honduran, was low and dry, almost a desert, no-fooling tierra caliente. There were a lot of calabash trees, which in Belize grow in only the most unpromising locations. Little or no water ran in the rivers, which were a lot like the braided rivers of the western plains with two or more beds, with only one broad, shallow channel that runs water except in times of flood. In short, it seemed a flat, arid country where rain sometimes really pours down, but often does not come at all. The scruffiest, yet friendliest, of "officials" ran the inside-the-country checkpoint, ten or so miles inland. The man who stopped the car, wearing a dirty Mickey Mouse T-shirt, was eating a muskmelon, carving the peel off with a knife as needed. He had the daintiness to offer my papers to another "official," and the generosity to offer me a bite of his cantaloupe, which I hope I politely refused. After perusing our documents, his cohort bummed a cigarette from Raphael.

Off to the left some big mountains jutted up, and then after a while, the countryside suddenly became agricultural. There was a banana plantation, only a couple hundred acres of a spindly Cavendish strain. Other plots were being prepared for crops, probably cultivated by machines. Then the landscape became arid-looking again, but with signs of large-scale farming. The houses looked as destitute as any we had seen. The Sandinistas evidently had not been in power long enough to do the campesinos much good, if they ever really tried.

Before us at a great distance, rising above the level of the plain, we saw the spires of the Cathedral of Leon. This magnificent plain, in richness of soil not surpassed by any land in the world, lay as desolate as when the Spaniards first traversed it. The dry season was near its close. For four months there had been no rain, and the dust hung around us in thick clouds, hot and fine as the sands of Egypt. At nine o'clock we reached León. The suburbs were more miserable than anything I had yet seen. Passing up a long street, across which a sentinel was patrolling, I saw in front of the quartel a group of vagabond soldiers, a match for Carrera's, who cried out insolently, "Take off your hat."

[León] had an appearance of old and aristocratic respectability, which no other city in Central America possessed. The houses were large and many of the fronts were full of stucco ornaments. The plaza was spacious, and the squares of the churches and the churches themselves magnificent. But in walking through its streets I saw palaces in which nobles had lived dismantled and roofless, and occupied by half-starved wretches, pictures of misery and want, and on one side an immense field of ruins, covering half the city.[29]

North America was settled by self-imposed exiles with a jealous sense of the rights of man imparted by their English patrimony. This happened in the seventeenth century—the morning of the modern age: Shakespeare had defined the language we still speak and provided a role for social behavior; James I was king; and Newton was about to discover the laws of physics and calculus. Upon arriving on American shores, the first thing these willing refugees from the tyranny of old-world religion and poverty did was hold elections, each adult English male casting a ballot. Some 150 years later, when the colonies rebelled against the crown, a suitable framework for self-government, politically (democratic), socially (egalitarian but with a well-defined quasi-aristocratic leadership class), religiously (pluralistic but generally Protestant), had grown up along with the recently emerged states.

Spanish America, on the other hand, was settled a century earlier and imported the encomienda system, a social and political framework that harked back to a feudalism that was passé even in Spain at the time. The system ruled from the top down, the uppermost posts always going to Spanish-born *peninsulares*. Those in the lower echelons had little voice in matters governing their existence, let alone a vote. The closest thing to a political infrastructure was the forming of loose alliances in the early 1700s during the War of Spanish Succession, which became in time the so-called Liberal and Conservative parties. The various states of Central America, isolated from one another by ranges of rugged mountains, impenetrable forests, deserts or large bodies of water, developed identifiable social and linguistic peculiarities.

Nevertheless, the leadership class in these states frequently felt more affinity with those of similar economic and class interests elsewhere than patriotic allegiance to their own locales. Independence was not fought for or, perhaps, even greatly desired. After the jolt of Napoleon's conquest of Iberia, the Spanish crown had neither the moral nor the military authority to hold its New World possessions. When Mexico broke free of Spain, Central America—as noted earlier—came with it. In brief, Central America was miserably ready for independence and nowhere was that fact more evident—to Stephens— than Nicaragua in general and León in particular.

Almost immediately on the establishment of independence and the drawing of the great party lines between the [Conservatives] *and* [Liberals], *the State of Nicaragua became the theater of a furious struggle. In an unfortunate hour the people elected a Conservative governor and Liberal vice governor. A divided administration led to drawing of blood and the most sanguinary conflict known in civil wars. Inch by inch the ground was disputed, til the whole physical force and deadly animosity of the state were concentrated in the capital. The contending parties fought up to the very heart of the city. The streets were barricaded, and for three months not a person could pass the line without being shot at. Scenes of horror surpassing human belief are fresh in the memory of the inhabitants. The Liberals prevailed. The Conservative chief was killed, his forces massacred, and in the frenzy of the moment the part of the city occupied by the Conservatives was burned and razed to the ground. Besides the blood of murdered citizens, the tears and curses of widows and orphans, the victors had the rich enjoyment of a desolated country and a ruined capital.*[30]

At León, Stephens was thrown into a quandary. The rabble army he found in the streets *(at every corner was a group of scoundrels, who stared at me as if disposed to pick a quarrel)* was mustering to march in the same direction as he on the morrow. Already, he had heard reports of *pickets scouring the city for men and mules and had entered the yard of a padre near by and taken three of his animals. Fortunately for us,* [my servant Nicolas] *had learned that the troops were destined on another, but even more inglorious expedition. In order that Granada might be taken unawares, it was given out that the troops were destined for San Salvador.*[31]

Granada was the so-called Conservative capital, León the Liberal. As Stephens shows, the parties were willing to go to any lengths to achieve their ends. Fifteen years later, León played an even dirtier trick on Granada, one that both cities and the entire isthmus were soon to regret. In a word, León officials hired a mercenary army to fight their battles. León's *führer* was a minuscule—he weighed hardly one hundred pounds sopping wet and fighting mad—gray-eyed man of destiny, one William Walker. A veritable renaissance man from Tennessee, he studied medicine in Edinburgh, Heidelberg, and the Sorbonne before taking a degree at the University of Pennsylvania at the age of nineteen. He abandoned medicine for the law (he received his law degree at twenty-three). He practiced neither profession, as it happened, following the career of journalist to the gold fields of California, where, taking the lead of some French adventurers, he conceived a plot to sever the states of Sonora and Lower California from Mexico. His pretext was that he and his band of filibusters (a word that at the time was synonymous with "freebooter" or "pirate") could better protect the residents from Apache depredation than Santa Anna's government. Neither his soldiers of fortune nor the Mexican troops watching him seem to have so much as seen an Apache, let alone protected the locals from them during his reign. After the collapse of this scheme, Walker repaired to California, where a friend tried to convince him to raise a private army for the service of the Nicaraguan Liberals.

By then, Nicaragua was a vastly more important territory to the United States than Sonora. Thousands of Americans a month were crossing the Nicaraguan isthmus—drawn by the promise of easy pickings in California. It was openly bruited, that given its strategic location, Nicaragua would one day become a U.S. dependency. Nevertheless, Walker turned down his friend's proposal. His legal training, plus his recent brush with American neutrality laws, argued persuasively that such a proposition would only land him in a U.S. jail. He suggested that the Nicaraguan government tender a charter to permit him to bring several hundred armed settlers to its shores. In a few months, such a document was procured, and shortly thereafter Walker arrived in Nicaragua, organized his men into military companies, and became an immediate force in Nicaraguan politics.

He proved to be a fickle ally for his patrons as he played Conservative Granada off against Liberal León as it suited his interests. His power base was significant. Cornelius Vanderbilt, the Bill Gates of the time, had junketed off to Europe to receive his due as the world's richest man, leaving two of his cronies, Morgan and Garrison, in charge of the Accessory Transit Company, the corporation shuttling Forty-Niners across the isthmus. At regular intervals, Morgan and Garrison shipped Walker new stocks of filibusters, who were quickly used up by the Nicaraguan climate. (The country is lower and hotter than the other Central American republics.) At the same time, Morgan and Garrison, the corporation's trustees, were systematically manipulating the stock of the Transit Company to their advantage. Vanderbilt returned to the United States several million dollars poorer and vowed to ruin his former associates. "I will not sue you," he is reported to have said. "That will take too long." He offered to bankroll Walker, and the man who had shown a Talleyrandian ability to mix it up with Central American politicians made a fatal error. He stayed loyal to Morgan and Garrison, and so Vanderbilt added him to his list of those to be ruined.[32]

In the meantime, the unthinkable happened. The Liberals and Conservatives took time out from warring against each other to gang up against Walker. Forces of both political stripes from Guatemala, Honduras, and Costa Rica joined the Nicaraguans against the Yankee adventurers. The British, not at all pleased by the American strategic advantage that Walker presented, happily armed them. All in all, Walker lasted a bit more than two years in Central America, about the average for a local administration. His only really noteworthy accomplishment was the permanent cessation of traffic across Nicaragua, as the Nicaraguans had had enough of gringos in their country, whether passing through or no. The only clear winner in this tale was Cornelius Vanderbilt.

By the time of Walker's adventure, Stephens was in Panama working for the rival transportation magnate William Aspinwall's Panamanian transit company. Aspinwall was a man more to Stephens's liking. Not just a steamship tycoon—he operated a fleet of mail and passenger ships on the Pacific Coast—Aspinwall was an early (for an American) art collector and patron of New York's public library, which he helped forge into a first-rate research institution. Despite all this, his great rival got the better of him on the transit issue. Aspinwall agreed to pay Vanderbilt $56,000 *a month,* should he agree not to reopen his Nicaraguan route, which even Vanderbilt probably could not have done in 1856. Naturally Vanderbilt accepted, and the payments went on until the eve of the Civil War. The pint-sized, gray-eyed man of destiny, William Walker, was probably a winner, too, in the sense that he escaped (Nicaragua at least) with his neck, a better fate than many of the poor lads who gathered under his flag.

León is a city not without cultural pretension. Its cathedral is said to be the largest in the Americas, and indeed it made the basilica at Esquipulas look like a mountain chapel. In a crypt inside lie the remains of Rubén Darío, 1867–1916, the great poet of Nicaragua and one of the great literary figures of Spanish America. Rubén Darío became the cultural darling of the Sandinistas, who played up his anti-imperialist essays. Outside, there were indications everywhere of violence, presumably of the people's struggle against Somoza, as spontaneously organized gangs of youth helped the Sandinistas wrest control of the city during the last days of Somoza's rule in 1979. A huge mural showed peasants struggling to the top of the ladder, being held ineffectually back by snake figures, labeled "CIA."

On the outskirts of the city a young woman was trying to hitch a ride with a sexy come-on, a shoulder roll with some fancy eyebrow and thumb work. It was the first time I had seen anything like that since leaving Belize. There are certain disadvantages to traveling with a priest, and also some advantages, and sometimes it's hard to tell which is which. In any case, that damsel was left for someone else to rescue.

Stephens's encounter with a Nicaraguan maiden came at closer quarters. *I heard a lively voice at the door. A young lady entered, put out her hand, said that she had heard in church that I was at her house, and was so glad of it. No strangers ever came there. She was not regularly handsome, but her mouth and eyes were beautiful. Her manner was so different from the cold, awkward and bashful air of her countrywomen that if the table had not been between us I could have taken her in my arms and kissed her. Though living in that little town, she had a fancy for strangers. The simplest stories of other countries and other people were to her romance, and her eye kindled as she listened. Soon the transition from facts to feelings, and then that highest earthly pleasure, of being lifted above every-day thoughts by the enthusiasms of a high-minded girl. The mother pressed me to remain two or three days and rest.* [She] *said that her daughter would try to make it agreeable. Her daughter said nothing, but looked unutterable things.* Three hours later, at 3 A.M., the guide knocked at the door. The mules were saddled.

It was time to move on. *I had often clung to my pillow but never as I did to that pink one with its ruffled border. I told Nicolas that the guide must go home and wait another day. The guide refused. Very soon I heard a light footstep, and a soft voice expostulating with the guide. Indignant at his obstinacy, I ordered him away, but very soon I reflected that I could not procure another and might lose the great object I had in view in making this long journey. I walked out of doors and resolved it was folly to lose the chance for a belle. I hurried through my preparations and bade her, I may say, an affectionate farewell.*[33]

The road to Managua was potholed, and the bridges were under repair in at least a dozen places. The countryside consisted mostly of dry woods. The road climbed gradually and the temperature fell dramatically, even though still dry. In one valley the forest was completely deciduous, the leaves on the ground under the trees. In this dry wood, the yellow-flowered tabebuia trees were blooming. Tropical trees bloom year round—and deciduous tropical trees may lose their leaves at any month of the year. For instance, you may see three or four ceibas in varying stages, from completely bare to completely leafed out, all in the same field of view. The tabebuia in an area, to the contrary, tend to bloom simultaneously, giving the deciduous wood the illusion of a northern forest in spring, when the dogwood or redbud are in flower. The yellow blossoms on the ground were as bright and plentiful as those on the tree, giving a reflecting-pool effect. The valley was full of these trees, and in the deciduous wood they made for a nice view. It was cool here after the desert heat earlier in the day, thanks to a shower of rain that had fallen. The smell of rain on worked soil also produced another illusion of spring, aided by the sight of a hint of green here and there. Finally we crested a little range of hills and down in the valley lay Managua.

Nicaragua is the largest country by area in Central America, being just fractionally larger than Honduras and Guatemala, and being about the same size as Mississippi. Its population in 1992 was about four million; by comparison, Mississippi has three million.[34] It is said to have the lowest population density in all of Spanish Central America. In reality, Nicaragua is almost two countries. The Atlantic drainage has few roads leading to the Pacific slope and consequently has large areas of almost uninhabited pine and hardwood forest. The people living on the Caribbean or Mosquito Coast, as the area was traditionally known, are a creolized race of Indian, black, European, and exotic oriental blood, the so-called Miskito Indians. Up until 1894, the Mosquito Coast, which included much of the Honduran Gulf coastal plain, was administered by Britain, and English is still a leading language of the area.

The Caribbean coast and adjacent lands are sparsely populated. Therefore, most of the four million people live in about half the country, the central highlands and the Pacific lowlands. These areas are volcanic and thus very rich agricultural lands between the great lakes of Nicaragua (Lagos de Nicaragua and Managua) and the Pacific Ocean. In spite of its rich agricultural lands, Nicaragua is also among the poorest countries in the Western Hemisphere, with a 1992 per capita income of $425. It is estimated there were 1.5 telephones for every one hundred people.[35]

For a generation after William Walker was deposed, the Conservatives ruled Nicaragua in relative peace and stability. This kind of interlude was so unusual that it is simply referred to as The Thirty Years. The gay nineties ushered in a new age of controversy when Liberal José Santos Zelaya came to power by overturning the Liberal-Conservative coalition, which in turn had overthrown the elected Conservative president.

Zelaya was responsible for the development of a transportation infrastructure and a professional army, and he invited foreign concerns to develop banana and coffee crops for export. Nevertheless, he was widely reviled by internal opponents as well as by the United States and Britain. A 1903 Conservative rebellion led by Emiliano Chamorro failed. The coup attempt in 1909 secured the assistance of four hundred U.S. Marines. The pretext for sending the marines was the death by firing squad of two American mercenaries.[36]

The coalition of Liberals and Conservatives fighting Zelaya fell apart. More marines were requested. Some 2,700 were sent. Order was quickly restored, but it was determined that a standing force of one hundred marines was needed to keep the peace. That force remained in the country, on and off, for most of the next two decades. Four Conservative presidents (the party then in favor with Washington), two of them by the name of Chamorro, assumed office while the marines were there.

By the mid-1920s, American interventionist ardor had cooled. The time of Teddy Roosevelt, the Bull Moose who was always in favor of acting first and thinking later, and the academic Wilson, who was just as energetic on the world stage, had come and gone. Old-fashioned rock-ribbed Republicans, Harding and Coolidge, had reclaimed the White House. The old American bugaboo, isolationism, was back in fashion. Harding wanted the marines out of Nicaragua, and in 1925 Coolidge withdrew the last of the American force. But "guaranteeing a country's stability," as the euphemism went, was a tar baby. Without the Marine presence, the Conservatives and Liberals went back to making politics, Central America style. In short, the shooting started again. In the meantime, the Mexican revolution had taken a radical turn to the left. Would the Marxists exploit the violence in Nicaragua? Jettisoning isolationism, Coolidge sent back the marines. Finally, Henry Stimson, later secretary of state during the war years under FDR, was dispatched to oil the waters. Elections supervised by the United States would be held. Also, a non-partisan military force, one that would simply keep order, would be developed by the United States. General Moncada, the leader of the Liberal insurrection, laid down his arms—as did the government. Everyone was happy.

Well, not everyone. Augusto César Sandino, the illegitimate son of a Liberal planter—his mother was an Indian worker on the estate—was incensed by the breach of Nicaraguan sovereignty. Conor Cruise O'Brien has described Sandino as "a skinny, morose little man"—he was hardly larger than the banty-rooster Walker, his historical nemesis—"invariably wearing a 10-gallon hat and looking like a figure out of a 1920s movie."[37] Supposedly, he killed a man in 1920 when he was twenty-five. He fled to Mexico, where his egalitarian ideas were forged in the Mexican revolution. He worked for an American oil company at Tampico and developed his own rather mystical blend of Marxism, a sort of Freemasonry mixed with Communism. The Masonic group he belonged to was called the Bolshevik Grand Lodge. A powerful secondary influence was the so-called magnetic spiritualism of Argentine Joaquín Trincado.[38]

Back in Nicaragua, Sandino obtained employment as a paymaster at an American-owned mine and began organizing the workers and local peasants into a militia that he put at the service of the Liberal cause. When Moncada cut the deal with the Americans, Sandino took on the marines by himself. It was machetes against machine guns, biceps against biplanes. But Sandino's force acquitted itself so well that General Moncada, who was hoping to assume the presidency, sent Sandino's father to the rebel. The elder is said to have told his son, "In this world saviors end up on crosses, and the people are never grateful."[39]

Yet, the father came to support his illegitimate son as he laid siege to Marine strongholds such as Ocotal, where Captain G. D. Hatfield demanded his surrender. Sandino came with his little band—and eight hundred unarmed peasants. They stormed the garrison, which, with machine guns blazing, held on for half a day until five warplanes arrived. The aircraft bombed and strafed the attackers. The Marine detachment was saved and the American public was alternately thrilled and horrified by the use of flying machines on peasant rabble. Senator Borah, the Idaho isolationist and one of the brightest minds in the Senate, called for immediate withdrawal. Washington sent more marines. The Sandinistas fled to the mountains of northeast Nicaragua.

Walter Lippmann, the renowned columnist, called for the withdrawal of troops. The Panamerican Conference taking place in Havana was thrown into turmoil. Anti-American regimes, namely Mexico, denounced U.S. policies. Moderate states were almost as vocal. Moscow assigned Farabundo Martí as the Comintern control for Sandino. Sandino accepted the war matériel but refused the party line. Martí, disappointed by Sandino's lack of political consciousness, slipped across the border to El Salvador and organized the rebellion that led to la matanza, the massacre of up to thirty thousand constituents in his home country, as previously discussed.

Ultimately, Sandino agreed to disarm all but one hundred of his followers and to work within the framework of the Liberal Party. President Sacasa invited him to dinner. On the way home he was abducted and killed by armed men. The man believed by many to have been behind the plot claimed to have been at a poetry reading; this man was the head of the putatively nonpolitical police force that the marines had trained, as a means of quelling the Liberal-Conservative clashes. A graduate of a Philadelphia business college, fluent speaker of English, and fervent admirer of all things American, as well as a member in good standing of the Liberal Party, the man seemed a natural for the top job with the National Guard. His name was Anastasio "Tacho" Somoza García. In 1934, with the National Guard behind him, he bullied Sacasa, who was his uncle, from the presidency and later had himself elected by the curious vote tally of 107,201 to 108. Thus began the dynasty that occupied the president's mansion for the next forty-five years.

Once in Managua, we headed for the cathedral, which is always at the nerve center of a Latin American city—or so we reasoned. As we approached the city center, traffic thinned noticeably. High weeds were growing in unusual places. The buildings had a rundown aspect that was remarkable even for Central America. The cathedral, a huge colonial edifice, had a peculiar look about it, too, one that took us a moment to identify. Its windows were broken out. The building was derelict, obviously abandoned as a deathtrap after the massive earthquake that shook Managua in 1972. Although all of Central America is a land of ruins, rarely are the abandonments so recent. In any case, that massive building standing vacant in the downtown area was a strange and ghostly sight. Catty-corner stood the National Palace, a government building that Éden Pastora, the later Contra commander in his first incarnation as an anti-Somoza rebel, captured—along with the national legislature and many bureaucrats—in a daring raid back in 1978. It was one of the blows that shook the Somoza dynasty and showed just how vulnerable the old dictator was.

We took a wrong turn not far from the cathedral and ended up on the bank of the famous lake from which the city takes its name, one of the few places where freshwater sharks exist, or at least did exist before the lake became one of the more polluted bodies of freshwater on the planet. The shoreline, future prime real estate, was being utilized as a garbage dump. People were living among refuse in houses made of cardboard with tin roofs. We waved meekly, fearing these down-and-outers as the somewhat better-off always do. For their part, they smiled and waved back friendlylike, looking neither threatening nor the least bit aware of the strangeness of living in a cardboard house in a garbage pile. As it happened, though surrounded by a city, not a hotel, posada, boarding house, or anything resembling a lodging for travelers was to be seen, making us almost envy those landfill squatters.

For the moment Raphael and I would have been pleased to settle for decent directions to a hotel. Back on a principal street, Raphael asked a young man on the sidewalk for his recommendation. Experience had taught us not to ask directions from just anyone. Campesino women were never consulted—because they never drove and their knowledge of local geography was limited, which, however, does not mean they were not happy to give you advice that would probably be incorrect. Older men were questionable for the same reason. Now we learned about asking younger men. This fellow recommended without a moment's hesitation the Hotel Recreo. "All the foreigners stay there," he said.

Managua was hot, and finding one's way was confusing. Also, the place was depressing, in a large part owing to the failed revolution. Instead of buses, one-ton Soviet trucks functioned as jitneys, the cargo bed so loaded down with passengers that the front wheels came off the ground at dips. Still many of the young women dressed very attractively, perhaps even a bit racily. We kept getting lost but finally ended up at two suspicious-looking establishments, which backed one onto the other. While we sized up the first place, a young couple arrived without luggage. A couple of bills were passed to the landlady and a key handed over. No one seemed to think there was anything unusual about dispensing with the usual paperwork. We were shown a small room with one double bed, the mattress of which was exposed to view. It was covered with a thick linoleum-like cover. We told the woman thanks but no thanks and tried the neighboring place. The clientele there, it turned out, was of the same quick-time, hot-pillow variety. We were exhausted, so, seeing no better alternative, we took two rooms.

Stephens suffered a similar fate. *At length we heard the distant sound of the vesper bell and very soon were greeted by the barking of dogs in the suburbs of Nicaragua. Fires were burning in the streets, which served as the kitchens for the miserable inhabitants, and at which they were cooking their suppers. We passed around a miserable plaza and stopped at the house of the Licenciado Pineda. A large door was wide open. The licenciado was swinging in one hammock, his wife and a mulatto woman in another. I dismounted and entered his house and told him I had a letter to him from Don Manuel de Aguila. He asked me what I wished and when I told him a night's lodging, said he could accommodate me, but had no room for the mules. In a word his reception was very cool. I was indignant and went to the door but without it was dark as Erebus.* Stephens not only stayed, he added *that the ice once broken, they did all they could for my comfort. A traveler never forgets the kindness shown him in a strange land and I never felt so sensible of it as in Central America. In other countries, with money, a man can command comforts. Here, whatever his means may be, he is entirely dependent upon individual hospitality.*[40]

The miserable state of hostelry in central Managua in our time could be laid squarely on the head of the Somoza family. And in fact, twentieth-century Nicaraguan history, for better and worse, was shaped by the dynasty's founder, Anastasio "Tacho" Somoza. He was an incredibly cagey politician and businessman. By the end of World War II, he had amassed a fortune of more than $60 million. He had taken control of many of the country's leading industries: rum distilleries, textile factories, the airlines, the merchant marine, and even the only dairy capable of pasteurizing milk. Not without abundant charm, he schmoozed American politicians and local leaders alike, even allowing token political opposition. Nevertheless, in 1956, after twenty years of rule, a young poet and self-anointed assassin put a bullet in him during a party in León.

For the next ten years, the country limped along with son Luis running the show. Luis was bright, ruthless, oppressive, without heart, or at least without a good heart. He died of a coronary. That brought Anastasio Somoza Junior or "Tachito" to the fore, who was "elected" to the presidency in 1967. The lesser son with the lesser talent, still Tachito was a crafty-enough politician to keep his various constituencies—National Guard, business leaders, American politicians and diplomats (these were the Nixon years)—more or less happy with his regime. In the meantime he amassed a personal fortune of somewhere between $500 million and $1 billion. It is estimated he owned half the country.

Not satisfied with that, after the devastating Managua earthquake of 1972, Tachito and his cronies began pilfering the aid flowing into the country, hence the derelict look of the capital's downtown district. The legitimate political opposition was led by the old-time Conservative family, the Chamorros, who owned the leading newspaper, *La Prensa*. (Yes, as reported earlier, the Somozas were of the Liberal persuasion and even ran on the Liberal ticket.) The illegitimate opposition went under the heading of the Sandinista National Liberation Front (FSLN). Inspired by Castro's success, Tomás Borge and others founded the FSLN in 1961. But it was not until after the 1972 earthquake, to be precise, that the FSLN scored its first real triumph, the kidnapping and subsequent $1 million ransoming of a former government official. Fourteen Sandinista prisoners were released and flown to Cuba. The cycle of state terrorism, repression, and media censorship yielded an ever-growing popular opposition.

Groups of leading citizens, such as Los Doce, a group of twelve academics and business people, formed councils to encourage the end of Somozaism. The FSLN split into three camps. The hard-line Marxists were led by Moscow-trained Jaime Wheelock. He headed the Proletarian faction. Borge's Maoist group believed a long, peasant-driven insurrection was the proper strategy for assuming control. The Third Way faction of Daniel and Humberto Ortega advocated cooperation with non-FSLN anti-Somocistas.

The beginning of the end was heralded when Pedro Joaquín Chamorro, the publisher of *La Prensa*, was gunned down in 1978 by unidentified assailants (who may or may not have been Somoza's men). Spontaneous street demonstrations closed Managua down. A universally observed ten-day strike was called. The FSLN launched assaults around the country. The National Guard fended them off, but the international reputation of the regime became even more tarnished by the needless civilian deaths. The United States cut off military aid. A few months later, Éden Pastora took over the National Palace. It took another year before the regime collapsed in July 1979, when Tachito fled to Miami. Hope and joy reigned in the countryside, and also in Caracas, San José, Havana, and even Washington, D.C., the capitals of countries that actively supported the rebellion (or in the case of Jimmy Carter's White House, declined to assist the tottering regime). The tyrant was gone.[41]

A pluralist junta of five persons was formed to rule the country. Two of the five were non-Marxist, non-Sandinista. An agreement signed by interested parties in the last days of Somoza guaranteed political plurality in the new regime. And at first it appeared those guarantees would be kept. Somoza's agricultural property was seized and turned into state farms. The banks were nationalized. The new government reversed the age-old policy of government repression of civil rights. Although it is estimated fifty thousand were killed during Somoza's overthrow, human rights agencies reported few instances of retribution toward incarcerated National Guardsmen. A mixed economy and democratic elections were promised.

Within a year, right-wing naysayers in Washington were proclaiming a dangerous tilt to the left. Havana had become the new regional power hub. Sandinista leaders flew there regularly to meet with Castro and other leaders.[42] Hundreds, then thousands, of medical, educational, and military "volunteers" from Cuba arrived to assist in the development of the new state. First one, then the other of the non-Marxist junta members resigned. The promised elections kept being put off. The armed forces, which were supposed to be nonpolitical (as the National Guard was in the 1920s), came under the complete control of the Sandinistas.

Were the Jesse Helmses in the north correct in their judgment that Nicaragua was becoming a totalitarian state? Harry Vanden and Gary Prevost claim that the Sandinista regime, at this period, was actually one of the more democratic third-world governments on the face of the globe.[43] True, plans for conducting representative elections kept being postponed, but Vanden and Prevost argue that the Sandinistas were experimenting with participatory democracy in a way that few modern countries have. The participation came from the establishment of neighborhood organizations, women's groups, a National Union of Farmers and Ranchers, and liberation theology–oriented popular church groups. These social units, composed in many instances of nearly illiterate peasants who had never before been integrated politically, had frequent and direct interaction with the members of the ruling bureaucracy. The bureaucrats told the groups the Sandinista's vision of the future, and the constituents had the chance to give their input at mass meetings. According to them, it was about as close to the Jeffersonian ideal as any country has ever gotten.

Not all Nicaraguans agreed with this assessment. State control of such minuscule areas as farmers' markets drew criticism. Private property was seized, including some small holdings. Ultimately, more than ten thousand Cubans were circulating inside the country—about double the number of U.S. Marines, at the peak of action against Sandino. The presence of so many foreigners was resented. Violeta Chamorro—newspaper publisher, former junta member, and widow of the slain political leader—pointed out that Nicaragua was willingly buying into a political system that was not entirely free of problems. For instance, she noted that Cuba, the country from which this political philosophy had been imported, had citizens fleeing in the hundreds of thousands during the Mariel boatlift, which was occurring at about the same time (1981). The Sandinistas began building the largest army in the region, of almost one hundred thousand men. Dozens, then hundreds, of tanks were ordered from Eastern Bloc countries. The Sandinistas seemed to be the pipeline for arms shipments to the insurrectionist forces in El Salvador. Rebel Salvadorian leaders were not shy about popping into Managua for rest and recreation.[44]

The Miskitos, of Nicaragua's non-Spanish-speaking and semiautonomous Carribean coast, became annoyed by Sandinista intrusions. Many defected to Honduras with Brooklyn Rivera at their head. Éden Pastora removed himself to Costa Rica and began armed resistance against the regime. In Honduras former Nicaraguan National Guardsmen bankrolled by Argentine rightists took up arms. Shortly, the Reagan administration cut off the hundreds of millions of dollars in aid promised by the Carter administration, slapped a total economic embargo on the country, and began backing the *Contras,* or counterrevolutionaries, the disparate guerilla movement based in Honduras and Costa Rica.

From the early 1980s until the fall of the Sandinistas in 1990, the battle was as much economic as military. The Contras were unable to unseat the regime, which was well fortified with copious assistance from Havana and Moscow. Meanwhile, the Sandinistas were unable to dislodge the Contras, who were given sanctuary by neighboring governments hostile to Sandinista policy. The Contras waged war primarily against economic targets. In Washington, liberal and leftist politicians were appalled by the suffering the war was engendering and fought to cut off Contra aid. In 1984, the regime scheduled elections to shore up its claim of being the only legitimate voice of the people. Daniel Ortega and his administration won two-thirds of the vote. Seventy-five percent of the registered voters went to the polls.

Still the war raged on. The Sandinistas came to believe the key to winning the conflict was to control the hearts and minds of the former middle class. And so they began subsidizing them—at the expense of the peasant class, which the regime assumed was in its pocket. Demands made by the International Monetary Fund were met, and the peasants were hardest hit. Finally, the continued prospect of civil war loomed if the Sandinista regime was permitted to remain. The final straw was the $7 million the Sandinistas spent on the 1990 election. Election favors, knapsacks, tortilla warmers, and so on, gaily festooned with Sandinista colors and mottoes, were distributed to an electorate who had nothing to put in the knapsacks and precious few tortillas to warm and who were worried about their sons being killed after conscription into the massive Sandinista army. The unemployment rate hovered at about a third of the work force, and, after more than a decade of the Sandinistas, the working poor still could not expect to see more than $20 to $40 a month. Come the election in late February 1990, the Sandinistas were shocked when they only garnered 40.8 percent of the vote, while the united opposition party received 54.7 percent.

Although out of office by the time Raphael and I rolled through the country, the Sandinistas were by no means an impotent political force. The greatly diminished army and police forces were still controlled by them. By June 1992 some of their number had joined renegade Contras to raid and pillage the still ravaged northern frontier country. The new president, Violeta Chamorro, had her hands full. She was the standard bearer of a fine old Conservative Party name that dated back to Independence from Spain. Her Conservative family had, as we've seen, bucked the Liberal Somoza regime from its inception.

Raphael and I had differing views on what to eat for dinner that evening. He had a hankering for spaghetti and wanted to go find a good Italian restaurant. I claimed I wanted to walk to a local eatery, of which there were a fair number of modest outdoor ones in the neighborhood, all completely jammed with people, as we had noted while driving to the hotel. Raphael insisted we take a taxi. As it happened, his was a good suggestion; we saw where the real post-earthquake heart of Managua was, on a suburban boulevard. Somoza and his cronies had diverted some of the earthquake relief funds to develop subdivisions. Naturally the shopping and services followed. The fancier restaurants, out on the beltway, were just as full up as those closer in to downtown. I wonder if a single person ate at home in that city. The driver, on learning we were Americans, volunteered that there had been Russians here before. Raphael asked if they were nice guys. The man said he did not associate with them. He said times were better now, not good but better. He said Nicaraguans were used to putting up with what they were handed by the authorities.

I woke up at about 2 A.M. drenched in sweat even though I had left the ceiling fan on. I placed a towel under me and went back to sleep. At 6:30 A.M.

I woke again in sweat. Otherwise the (literally as well as figuratively) hot-sheet joint was quite pleasant. There had been no noise overnight, no drunks, no loud music or TV. The guests had evidently been too busy getting it on to bother with any of those other staples of Central American lodgings. We slipped the night auditor, Dooglas, who planned to immigrate to Los Angeles, five colones to add to his grubstake, and headed out.

While we gassed up, the attendants practically washed the truck. At first I was embarrassed, but when I figured up the price of half a tank, $30, I was bothered much less. The countryside near Managua was dry. The houses of the local folk were scruffy. Most of the land was occupied by agribusiness concerns, haciendas, or collectives. Shortly we were in Granada, the old Conservative capital. Granada looked old and interesting with the wind-whipped Lago de Nicaragua, a veritable inland sea, behind it. *Built by those hardy adventurers who conquered America, even yet it is a monument to their fame. The houses are of stone, large and spacious, with balconies to the windows of turned wood, and projecting roofs, with pendent ornaments of wood curiously carved.*[45]

South of Granada, the countryside surrounding the Pan American Highway, wide and fast, was almost depopulated. I maintained 60 mph. A few people stood on the side of the road waiting for buses. It was good-looking countryside given over mainly to grazing. At 9 A.M. we turned off the Pan American Highway where the Río San Juan emptied out of Lake Nicaragua, almost on the Costa Rican border. At first the road was surprisingly level, but after a time it fell off sharply.

We reached the River St. John, the mouth of which was the terminating point of the great canal to connect the Atlantic and Pacific Oceans. Our encampment was about in the center of the harbor, which was the finest I saw on the Pacific. It is not large, but beautifully protected, being almost in the form of the letter U. It seemed preposterous to consider it the focus of a great commercial enterprise; to imagine that a city was to rise up out of the forest, the desolate harbor to be filled with ships and become a great portal for the thoroughfare of nations.[46]

And why was that? Because Stephens had retraced the survey made by a Mr. Bailey, a half-pay British naval officer residing in Granada, Nicaragua, who had laid out a proposed canal for the Central American government. *By a vigorous use of the machete I was enabled to follow the line of Mr. Bailey up the ravine to the [first] station. Up to this place manifestly there could be no difficulty in cutting a canal. Beyond, the line of survey follows the small stream of El Cacao for another league, when it crosses the mountain. My guide pulled off his shirt and commenced with his machete. The side of the mountain was very steep and besides large trees, was full of brambles, thorn-bushes, and ticks.*[47] In its sixteen-mile course from Lake Nicaragua to the Pacific, the proposed canal route rose from 130 feet at the lake to more than six hundred feet over the mountain and then back down to sea level. However, it did not take the always-sanguine Stephens long to change his mind about the viability of this route. *A canal large enough for the passage of boats could be made at a trifling expense.* Getting around that mountain could easily be accomplished by means of a tunnel—*a tunnel of the length required is not considered a great work in the United States.*[48] *Looking back, I saw the two great mountain ranges, standing like giant portals and could but think what a magnificent spectacle it would be to see a ship, with all its spars and rigging, cross the plain, pass through the great door, and move on to the Pacific.*[49]

The village of San Juan on the Pacific Ocean, seventeen road miles from the lake, which Stephens found a howling wilderness, was the most pleasant place we saw in Nicaragua, with perhaps the exception of Granada. Ships were anchored in the harbor with mountains all around, and the wide volcanic sand beach was festooned with attractive-looking, if modest, restaurants and bars. Stephens allotted three days' rations for the trip along the proposed canal route and was reduced to supping on wild game and chocolate. Raphael and I spent most of the twenty minutes it took us to regain the Pan American Highway roaring at the absurdity of attempting to build a canal there with early-nineteenth-century technology.

The Río San Juan del Sur and its sister river, the San Juan del Norte (the latter curiously being entirely south of the former), along with Lake Nicaragua, which both rivers flow out of, narrowly missed becoming the canal route. The first serious discussion of an isthmian canal occurred in 1811 when the great German scientist and explorer, Alexander von Humboldt, determined Nicaragua would be the best possible site. As we have seen, serious thought was still given to this choice during Stephens's time. President Grant dispatched a commission to the area (as well as to Panama and Mexico) to study the proposed route. Even after the French failed in their effort to build a canal across Panama, it was generally held that the American canal crossing middle America would go through Nicaragua.

The person most responsible for this perception was Senator John Tyler Morgan from Alabama. During his years in the Senate Morgan was known as a prickly character. His early experiences in the Civil War probably did not help engender a kindly personality. He led a charge at that most grisly of battles, Chicamauga, and later became a general in the Confederate army. He was elected to the Senate in 1876 and carefully accumulated and guarded the privilege that comes with seniority. Anything having to do with the interoceanic canal he considered his business, and hardly anyone in the Senate dared cross him. Although just about all Americans desired a canal, few had a vested interest in where the canal sliced across the isthmus—except those with commercial interests in the Deep South.

A Nicaraguan canal would have been seven to eight hundred miles closer to New Orleans, Mobile, and Galveston than one through Panama, ensuring those cities of becoming important rail and shipping centers. Teddy Roosevelt, who early on had been one of Senator Morgan's greatest admirers, put the worm in the apple. In part, the French turned Roosevelt's head, selling (some would say unloading) their Panama concession to (on) him. In any case, Roosevelt championed the Panamanian cause, going at it with characteristic Bull Moose enthusiasm.[50] The upshot was that the canal was put through Panama, which profited from the transit and collateral business. Nicaragua returned to lethargy.

The Costa Rican border lay fifteen miles to the south. A local coyotero guided us through the Nicaraguan checkpoint in a jiffy, but Costa Rica was the usual nightmare—no order, all confusion—having to vie with a dozen other people to catch the eye of the officials. All told it took an hour and a half, but we were back on the road by noon. We had visions of spending the night in San José, long known as one of the most pleasant and gringo-friendly towns in Central America.

6 / Costa Rica and Passage through Honduras

As we continued ascending, every moment the view became more grand and beautiful, [Stephens wrote of Costa Rica]. *Suddenly, from a height of six thousand feet, I looked down upon the Gulf of Nicoya. Here on the very highest points were the huts of miners. The sun touched the sea, lighted up the surface of the water, and softened the rugged mountains. It was the most beautiful scene I ever saw.*[1]

Stephens's appreciation of Costa Rica has since been shared by many visitors from North America. About the same size as West Virginia, Costa Rica is the smallest of the original confederation of Central American countries by population and next smallest in size to El Salvador. It is also by far the most peaceful (but hardly pacific) of those states.[2] Like West Virginia, Costa Rica is high and mountainous but also has generous portions of lowland. Approximately half of its 1990 population of slightly more than three million lived in the temperate Central Valley, which included the major urban centers, Alajuela, Cartago, Heredia, and San José, the capital where we were bound that day. As everyone seems to know, Costa Rica—in stark contrast to its neighbors—has been a functioning democracy for more than a generation, since 1949 to be exact. However, none of that background information should mask the fact that it is still a third-world country with a per capita income of about $1800 (only $600 more than Guatemala) per year and a functional literacy rate of about 70 percent (by the least flattering estimate).[3]

The houses near the frontier were far from lavish, hardly better than on the Nicaraguan side. Cattle and horses grazed on the shoulders and ranged freely

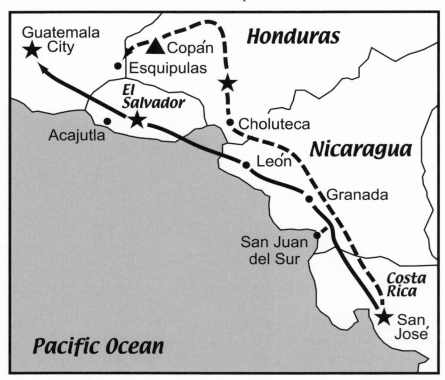

Costa Rica and the passage through Honduras
Stephens returned from Costa Rica to Guatemala City by land. The route he followed was approximately the same as the one the author drove from Esquipulas to Costa Rica.

On the return trip, the author visited Copán ruins in the southwestern corner of that country. Copán was visited by Stephens on his way from Belize to Guatemala City.

along the road. Farther south, a look of prosperity came over the country. The homes began to resemble North American ones, small frame or stucco houses, nicely kept, generally with an automobile under a carport. Every few miles a roadhouse promised relief for the weary traveler and, as we progressed, we went up higher and the country became cooler and moister. I got a fleeting glimpse of what I hope was a lovely cotinga. It flitted across the highway accompanied by a brown bird, probably its drab-colored mate. Also, I observed a magpie jay, a bird that would be revered worldwide for its astonishing beauty if it were not, as its name implies, of the lowly magpie and jay clan, and indeed it looks like a magpie crossed with a blue jay.

In one way Costa Rica did not vary from anyplace else in Central America

—in the way the streets were marked. Even though every river had a name-plate, the exits on the *autopista* (or freeway) leading into San José were unsigned. *I did not know where I should sleep that night. In the large towns of Central America I was always at a loss where to stop. Hezoos had told me there was an old chapiton in whose house I could have a room to myself and pay for it. Unfortunately, time had made its changes, and the old Spaniard had been gone so long that the occupants of his house did not know what had become of him. The cura was at his hacienda, and his house was shut up. In the midst of this street consultation, I longed for a hotel at a hundred dollars a day.*[4] Like Stephens, we spent interminable minutes looking for the way to downtown; once we found it we were jammed in traffic. Finally we found a hotel and turned in immediately.

After a good night's sleep in a very soft bed, I set out on foot for a tour of the city. Walking was so pleasant I just kept on going. In a surprisingly short time I reached the outskirts of town. I took a left onto a country lane, and suddenly the vista was not that different from the one Stephen's had described.

On top of the ravine we came upon a large table of land covered with the rich coffee plantations of San José. It was laid out into squares of two hundred feet, enclosed by living fences of trees bearing flowers, with roads sixty feet wide and except the small horsepath, the roads had a sod of unbroken green. The deep green of the coffee plantations, the sward of the roads and the vistas through the trees at all the crossroads were lovely; at a distance on each side were mountains, and in front, rising above all, was the great Volcano of Cartago. The vista was soft, and it addressed itself to other senses than sight, for it was not, like the rest of Central America, retrograding and going to ruin, but smiling as the reward of industry.[5]

The valley in front of me was completely boxed in with coffee bushes; a little stream purled through the bottom. The vegetation regime was tropical montane, meaning anything could grow here. Fuchsias and crepe myrtles and hibiscus and alamanda grew side by side. The road going up was incredibly steep, yet two joggers sprinted up it. The scene would not only have met with Stephens's approval, but with another Democrat and sharer of the title of Father of American Archaeology, Thomas Jefferson, who as every schoolchild knows believed small farmers were the backbone of civilization. The coffee plots seemed a bit larger than the two-hundred-foot squares Stephens described, but the living fences made of yucca trees were still there.

How was Costa Rica able to develop an economy based to a great extent on the small farm, while the rest of Central America was torn between serfs and plantation holders? The answer has much to do with Costa Rica's having the great luck of lacking significant precious metals.[6] Columbus whiled away two weeks of his last voyage in the area now known as Port Limon, where he formed the opinion, based on the gold trinkets of the Carib Indians, that much of that precious metal was to be found inland. He was so impressed that he gave the country the ironic name of Costa Rica or Rich Coast. He left his brother Bartolomé to search for the yellow stuff. But the Carib attacks and harassment were too much even for Spanish greed, and the mission ended in failure.

By the late sixteenth century, the early conquistadors had given up on finding riches in the area. And the Indians—who had colonized the land both from South America and northern Mesoamerica—were extremely fierce, discouraging settlement. In the seventeenth and eighteenth centuries a few hardy settlers, Spanish peasant farmers mainly, immigrated into the area, which was so backward that it was ruled by the Kingdom of Guatemala as a territory of Nicaragua. By then, the only human resource, Indian labor, had vanished. Epidemics of European disease had done what the redoubtable conquistadors could not. Today, the population of Costa Rica is only 7 percent mestizo. This meant Tico (the national nickname) farmers had to till their own plots or hire people much like themselves. Therefore, the racial tension seen in other Central American countries is not as noticeable here (overlooking the problems of the Caribbean coast where there is a substantial English-speaking black minority).

Independence from Spain brought the people of various Costa Rican towns with populations numbering in the low thousands to blows. The leaders of Cartago and Heredia wanted to join the new Mexican empire. San José's city fathers did not. One bloody battle settled the issue in San José's favor. In the meantime, that is in the early 1820s, Iturbide was deposed in Mexico. Costa Rica, whipped by Liberal Party fervor, chose to throw in its lot with the United Provinces of Central America. It was not long before the country regretted this choice, as it was drawn into the armed machinations of the warring factions of the new republic. Salvation came in the way of a Liberal strongman, Braulio Carrillo Colina.

Carrillo, whom we will meet shortly through Stephens's eyes, established San José, once and for all, as the country's capital. He also destroyed his enemies, fellow coffee barons generally, by confiscating their estates. Sad as the losses were for the former coffee barons, Carrillo established a practice that had much to do with Costa Rica's present democratic character. He divided the estates and parceled them out to landless peasants.[7] He also promoted a sort of homestead mentality by allowing the cultivation and ownership of public lands by small farmers. Other nineteenth-century caudillos followed his example, distributing plots to landless citizens who showed they could work them. Education among the masses was encouraged. The 1871 constitution called for a popular selection of an electoral college, resulting in administrations more or less democratically chosen—at least some of the time. In the meantime, migration continued from Italy, Germany, and other European countries. In short, institutions that could support democratic government gradually developed.

Early the next morning, accompanied by my countryman Mr. Lawrence, and mounted on a noble mule, I set off for Cartago. We left the city by a long, well-paved street, and a little beyond the suburbs passed a neat coffee plantation. On both sides were mountains, and in front was the great Volcano of Cartago. The fields were cultivated with corn, plantains, and potatoes.

Coming from San José, Cartago's appearance was that of an ancient city. The churches were large and imposing, the houses had yardwalls as high as themselves, and its quiet was extraordinary. Immediately we set out to ascend the volcano. Passing down the principal street, we crossed in front of the Cathedral and began to ascend. Very soon we reached a height which commanded a view of a river, a village and an extensive valley not visible from the plain below. The sides of the volcano are particularly favorable for cattle, and while the plains below were appropriated, all the way up were potreros or pasture grounds.[8]

Those were Stephens's observations. Here are my notes: "Off to Cartago after got truck's oil changed. Truck ran like a top up to top of Mt. Irazú, 11,128 by my calculations, i.e., conversion from meters to feet. The volcano was 30 kilometers outside of Cartago and on the slopes of the mountain were nicely tended dairy farms and higher up, potato patches. Soil volcanic of course and very rich. Beautiful country. The volcano had several craters, one of which we parked in. Walked across a stretch of black volcanic gravel. Temperature a pleasant 70 degrees, little wind. The view unfortunately was only of clouds even though it was perfectly clear on top of the mountain. One small crater had a pool of green water in it. The vegetation was unusual stuff, a small red firecracker-plant like thing and a spectacular skunk cabbage sort with large rice plant like leaves and an interesting bloom."

The crater was about two miles in circumference, rent and broken by time or some great convulsion, the fragments stood high, bare, and grand as mountains, and within were three or four smaller craters. We ascended on the south side by a ridge running east and west till we reached a high point, at which there was an immense gap in the crater impossible to cross. The lofty point on which we stood was perfectly clear, the atmosphere was of transparent purity, and looking beyond the region of desolation, below us, at a distance of perhaps two thousand feet, the whole country was covered with clouds. By degrees the more distant clouds lifted, and over the immense bed we saw at the same moment the Atlantic and Pacific Oceans. This was the grand spectacle we had hoped, but scarcely expected to behold. The points at which they were visible were the Gulf of Nicoya and the harbor of San Juan, not directly opposite. In a right line over the tops of the mountains neither was more than twenty miles distant, and from the great height at which we stood they seemed almost at our feet. This was one of the occasions in which I regretted the loss of my barometer, as the height of the mountain has never been measured, but is believed to be about eleven thousand feet. We returned to our horses and descended. In an hour we reached the hut at which we had slept, and at two o'clock Cartago.[9]

"Got off mountain about 2 and R wanted to pass Father Bernardo's gift off to his mother; I wanted to go to the orchid garden first." As it turned out, we had already passed by the garden and were near Bernardo's mother. So we went through the incredibly medieval process of finding a street address in Cartago. Seventy-two *varas* (the vara is about two and a half feet) south of the Farmacia something or another. Fortunately, the neighbors, although not familiar with the lady, understood the directions and told us to go about three and a half blocks and surprisingly we were brought to within a few feet of the woman's door.

Cartago is the ancient capital of the country and has associations as historic as its colonial cobblestones and architecture. Its founder in 1564 was Juan Vásquez de Coronado, whose namesake, Francisco Vázquez de Coronado was seeking at roughly the same time—give or take a quarter century—the Seven Cities of Cibola in what is now the southwestern United States. Coronado tried a different tack. He made peace with the Indians and started exploring for the gold everyone assumed the country had an abundance of. When his personal fortune was exhausted, he shipped aboard a galleon to Spain. Although successful in his quest for more capital, he was lost at sea on the return voyage. A second great name associated with Cartago was Henry Morgan, the pirate. In 1666 he assembled a company of seven hundred freebooters and marched on the capital. An outnumbered and outgunned militia was able to save the day with the intercession of the Virgin of Ujarrás, under whose banner they fought, or at least so the story is told today.[10]

After a refreshing lunch, Stephens, accompanied by an American resident, stretched his legs. He too wanted to visit a garden, a garden of stone. *We were intercepted by a procession coming down a cross street. It was headed by boys playing on violins and then came a small barrow tastefully decorated and strewed with flowers. It was a bier carrying the body of a child to the cemetery. We followed, and passing it at the gate, entered through a chapel, at the door of which sat three or four men selling lottery tickets.*[11] One of the ticket sellers volunteered to show Stephens the grave of an American who had died the year before, a man with whose family Stephens was acquainted. Since the American was not Catholic, or Christian in the parlance of the country, the vicar refused to bury him in consecrated ground. The Englishman in whose house he had died rode to San José and begged the government in the interests of good relations with the United States to intercede. He returned with two companies of soldiers who escorted the body to the cemetery. The next day the fanatical vicar held a procession to formally reconsecrate the sacred ground.

While standing among the tombstones Stephens *saw pass the man who had accompanied the bier, with the child in his arms. He was its father, and with a smile on his face, was carrying it to its grave. He was followed by two boys playing on violins, and others were laughing around. The child was dressed in white, with a wreath of roses around its head. As it lay in its father's arms it did not seem dead but sleeping. The grave was not quite ready and the boys sat on the heap of dirt thrown out and played the violin till it was finished. The father then laid the child carefully in its final resting place, with its head to the rising sun, folded its little hands across its breast and closed its fingers around a wooden crucifix. It seemed, as they thought it was, happy at escaping the troubles of an uncertain world. There were no tears shed. On the contrary, all were cheerful and though it appeared heartless, it was because they were firm in the conviction that, taken away so young, it was transferred immediately to a better world. The father sprinkled a handful of dirt over its face, the grave digger took his shovel, in a few moments the little grave was filled up and preceded by the boy playing on his violin, we all went away together.*[12] Stephens's fascination with death was that of one who— like my brother who showed a similar interest—was destined for an early grave. He could hardly pass a cemetery without entering, and, to him, funerals were social occasions meant to be crashed, which he did with glorious abandon.

I lost the entire morning and the best part of the afternoon of the following day dealing with bureaucracy, and all for naught. A consular clerk in the Guatemalan Embassy explained patiently—as to a child— that for "Americans only" a thirty-day visa was good for ninety days. I thanked her for that information but said that I was afraid I would meet up with *migración* officials who were not as knowledgeable as she (such as the folks in the Guatemalan Consulate in Belize who insisted I apply for a visa at a regular embassy). After a fair bit of going round and round, and shaking her head at the impropriety of it all, she made an asterisk and stamped over the original "30" days with a "90."

Stephens's brush with Costa Rican officialdom was at a somewhat higher level. *My first visit of ceremony was to Señor Carillo, the Gefe del Estado. The State of Costa Rica enjoyed at that time a degree of prosperity unequaled by any in the disjointed confederacy. He was about fifty, short and stout, plain, but careful in his dress, and with an appearance of dogged resolution in his face. His house was republican enough, and had nothing to distinguish it from that of any other citizen. In one part his wife had a little store, and in the other was his office for government business. It was not larger than the counting-room of a third-class merchant. He had three clerks, who at the moment of my entering were engaged writing, while he, with his coat off, was looking over papers. He had heard of my coming and welcomed me to Costa Rica. In fact, usurper and despot as he is, Carillo works hard for the good of the state, and for twelve hundred dollars a year (with perquisites, and leave to be his own paymaster.) In the meantime all who do not interfere with him are protected. A few who cannot submit to despotism talk of leaving the country, but the great mass are contented and the state prospers. As for myself, I admire him. In that country the alternative is a strong government or none at all. Throughout his state I felt a sense of security, which I did not enjoy in any other.*[13]

Stable as Carrillo's regime may have seemed to Stephens, trouble was brewing. The country's relative isolation could not shelter it forever from the calamities of the now disunited provinces of Central America. With his army shattered, Morazán had no choice but to fall back on the only possible Liberal sanctuary left to him, Costa Rica. Carrillo, although a Liberal like Morazán, was no fool. He dispatched a deputy, General Vicente Villaseñor, to arrest the fallen national leader. Charismatic character that Morazán was, he charmed Villaseñor into becoming his lieutenant. Together, they marched on San José and deposed Carrillo, who had illegally maintained power after losing the election four years before and had recently named himself president for life. Morazán, unfortunately schooled in the politics of upper Central America, immediately raised taxes and set about conscripting the country's youth into his army. Not liking this turn, the populace rose up. Morazán and his erstwhile assistant, Villaseñor, were put against a wall and shot. So the tyrant was disposed of, but the price was an inglorious end for Central America's greatest patriot, Francisco Morazán.[14] These events occurred in 1841, the year after Stephens's visit.

It did not take us long to get bored with San José. It was too well ordered and clean to suit our tastes, not enough harassing police searches and no machine guns or shotguns stuck in our faces to provide that existential edge that the traveler to Central America comes to expect. We rose about 5:45 the next day with the intention of heading back north. The next couple of days we planned to spend in Costa Rican nature preserves. Then we would transit Nicaragua and Honduras, completing the trip, as noted earlier, at Copán, the great Maya site Stephens not only visited but bought for $50. Finally, we would return to Raphael's old home base in Esquipulas, Guatemala.

In order to get on our way, we merely had to wait for Vanessa, the chambermaid, to bring us our laundry, which we had entrusted to her two days previously, and which she had assured us would be done well before this morning. Our assumption was that Vanessa took our clothes home with her, a not uncommon practice. Seven came and went. No Vanessa. I asked the cook where Vanessa was and she said something about *ropas*. I said, "sí," and, after awhile, she arrived with keys and opened the chambermaid's closet and showed me our clothes soaking in tubs. We squeezed the water out of our duds, stuffed them in plastic bags and headed for the truck.

When we got to the autopista tollbooth, I asked for directions and received the usual "Recto, recto" but for once those were the correct instructions. We planned to spend just one night at the Monteverde cloud forest reserve, and I wanted to have plenty of daylight for a good look around. As the four-lane autopista devolved into a two-lane highway, the jeep ahead of me, in a friendly gesture, pulled its right wheels onto the shoulder to let me go around. I passed, but there was a yellow stripe on my side of the road and hidden on the other side of the bridge that occasioned the yellow line lurked a cop, a real bull of a cop, with a Smokey Bear hat and a Jack Webb drill instructor face, and a lump of coal for a heart. He motioned me to the shoulder and told me he was going to take my license plate and that I would have to go back to San José and face a judge the next day. I said those magic words that work just as well in San José as in Chicago, "Isn't there another way to handle this, officer?" His price was three thousand colones (twenty-four bucks). To keep up appearances, he took down my auto information on a very unofficial looking form, a medical notepad. I was offered no receipt, nor did I care to ask for one.

Five miles down the pike, I got nailed again, this time by radar for going eighty-seven kilometers in an eighty-kilometer zone. Raphael told the cop that the force had just hit us up for three thousand colones a couple of miles back. I was not sure whether spilling the beans regarding our history as speed violators was a good strategy. But the cop, who was young and sensitive looking and wore a Star of David around his neck, wrote me up a real ticket and charged a mere one thousand colones or eight dollars, giving a discount, he explained, because of the earlier ticket. I asked the cop, who was very earnest and seemed a decent sort, despite being a bit quick on the trigger of that radar gun, for directions to Monteverde. (Alas, I learned too late one wants to be especially careful when driving in the late morning when traffic cops need to raise lunch money.)

The guidebook said the Monteverde cloud forest preserve was the brainchild of American Quakers who were drawn to Costa Rica in 1951 by the pacific nature of the country, specifically the disbandment of the armed forces and the restoration of democratic institutions. Indeed, one hears much about how Costa Rica embraced democracy in those days. Seldom does the intensity of the labor pains of this birthing come across in the telling. It all started when the legitimate and socially conservative president, Calderón, declared war on Japan hours after the attack on Pearl Harbor—ahead even of the declaration of war by the U.S. Congress. Stalin had previously instructed all Comintern (Communist International) cells to assist regimes that were united in the fight against fascism. Now that President Calderón was lined up with the Americans against the Axis powers (and even though Costa Rica had exactly zero war-making capability), the head of the local Communists, Manuel Mora Valverde, came immediately to heel. During the 1944 election this strange alliance of social conservatives and Communists held. Calderón's hand-picked successor was elected president. By 1948 the electorate was ready for a change. Ex-President Calderón stood for office again, and lost by at least ten thousand of the one hundred thousand votes cast. Nevertheless, he protested, and the election ended up in the legislative assembly, still controlled by his supporters, who selected him as president. The opposition, led by José Figueres Ferrer, had expected a maneuver of this sort. Lying in wait on an estate south of Cartago was Figueres's own private army. The nation's armed forces only amounted to a few hundred poorly trained men. The real power resided in the three-thousand-man Communist militia kept on a short leash by Calderon's ally Mora. After a stormy period of civil war, Figueres's forces, backed by popular support, came out on top. He personally supervised the much-boasted-of dismantling of the Costa Rican army and the Communist militia, while keeping his National Liberation Army intact. The duly elected president, Ulate, a conservative, was after a time installed in office, but Figueres, a moderate leftist, ran for president on the next go-round and was elected.[15]

Often overlooked in Central American politics is the courage and nobility of character that the best politicians display. Figueres, affectionately called Don Pepe, is universally and deservedly revered in Central America (despite a few peccadilloes of his own, such as his sponsorship of the renegade Nixon backer Robert Vesco's Costa Rican exile, and his meddling in the affairs of neighboring countries whose politics he abhorred). Even the Sandinistas could not have a full-dress event without him in attendance.[16]

The road to Monteverde was an object lesson in rain forest clearing. The steep gravel roadway started its ascent at very close to sea level, and the weather was hot and, although there were trees, dry. We had not climbed very high when we saw that the mountainside began to look shaved clean and the pastures overgrazed and almost arid. Things improved a bit higher still. It looked like Switzerland, with cattle grazing on green slopes, and all around the vistas were spectacular, although lacking what we had come to see, forest. Then, finally, at the top of the mountain a bit of cloud forest had been spared.

I made for the nature trails through the cloud forest. This was one of the few sanctuaries of the quetzal bird, the bird of Maya royalty, one of nature's rarest and most spectacular feathered creatures. I had never glimpsed one. Nor did I have any luck this time, which even serious quetzal questers need. The most interesting bird, of the many I saw, was a yellow-bellied songbird with a slate back and brilliant red crown. Peterson's Guide told me it was a collared redstart. The forest was something of a disappointment, as I expected a cloud forest to harbor all sorts of exotic botanical forms, but I got standard issue lowland tropical stuff, the same luxuriance that grew in Belize and even Florida. Bonsai-like gumbo-limbo trees, no more than four feet high, grew in the elfin forest dwarfed by mountain storms on the ridge line. I did come up on, in a vale, a huge oak tree growing among the tropical vegetation and, as in Florida, it was hung with all sorts of bromeliads. The most conspicuous flower was a member of the coffee family called hot lips because the flower resembled two extremely sensuous lips, meant no doubt to draw humming-birds and other pollinators.

Despite our best efforts for an early departure, we arrived at Parque Nacional Santa Rosa just off Ruta Uno on the northern frontier at about 1 P.M. the following day. The gatekeeper said my truck could not make it all the way to the campsite on the ocean, twenty kilometers distant, so we pitched camp at the first campground, seven kilometers from the highway. Raphael wanted to make a forced march through Nicaragua the following day, ending in Honduras. The campsite closer to the Pan American Highway, from that point of view, was a good choice.

We camped under a huge *amate,* or strangler fig, tree. The ground underneath the tree was muddy, it having rained in earnest here in the days since we had passed by earlier. The countryside was semi-desert scrub, and I did not really expect it to rain again, but I went to considerable care finding the highest spot on which to pitch the tent all the same. It was after 2 P.M. by the time I got the tent up and had lunched on some bread and fruit. I threw a half-gallon container of water in my backpack and headed down the road toward the sea. After a few kilometers I came to a nature trail that simply crawled with interesting species. I saw two trogons with iridescent green backs and brilliant orange-red bellies. Had I seen them the day before, I would have thought they were quetzals, being first cousins to that most famous bird of Central America and lacking only the immense tail. The trail was also good for a racquet-tailed motmot, a flock of two dozen parrots, some white-winged doves, and a troop of white-faced monkeys, the latter interesting as they, when threatened, are reported as dangerous to humans.

The road to the ocean headed sharply down, dropping several hundred feet, and finally when I was about ready to turn around I saw the sea in the distance. That spurred me on and shortly I came to a fork in the road and a sign that said only three kilometers to the beach campsite. I also saw two whitetail deer, identical to those roaming the eastern United States, strolling casually across the road. They hiked up their tails before bounding off into the scrub.

After a half-mile or so the trees got taller. Some huge strangler figs grew there with lots of bromeliads and epiphytic cactus, with cereus cactus and a spiny bromeliad growing in the understory. The smell of composting tropical leaf litter hung in the close, humid atmosphere. The earth was cratered by innumerable holes, each with its own red-legged fiddler crab. All those crabs with their brilliantly red legs clattered like so many chopsticks as I passed.

I could hear the surf, not more than a quarter of a mile away, crashing on the other side of a low range of hills to which the road ran parallel. Daylight was pushing on but I was loath to turn around now. Another mile—that three kilometer sign obviously was wrong—brought me to a tidal swamp with mangroves on the lower side of the road and buttonwood trees on the slightly higher upland one. Finally the road turned across the swamp. It was muddy and hard-going on foot, and then right before the littoral a tidal creek flowed. It was perhaps thirty feet wide and fifteen inches deep. Thoughtfully placed stones allowed me to cross without getting my feet wet. Then it was through a grove of trees into a very pleasant campsite with drinkable water (unheard of in the Third World), thanks to a primitive chlorinating mechanism affixed to a fifty-five-gallon drum of water. The black-sand beach was quite narrow. Goat-foot morning glories pushed toward the surging surfline. In the distance several ranges of mountains plunged right down to the water, each successive range being a bit dimmer in the mist and fog. There was a rock island one hundred yards out in the water and another a quarter mile off. The sun, looking like a giant vanilla wafer in the ocean mist, was pushing toward the sea. All in all it may be the prettiest beach I have ever visited and well worth the hike.

Night caught me on the road about halfway back to camp. Heat lightning —in the way of dim flickering sheets—illuminated the road well enough for me to be able to forge ahead at full speed. The lightning seemed to go away. Yea, I cheered. Then it came forking back, sending its bolts into the hills around. After a few nasty gusts, rain began to pelt down. The roadbed was unimproved clay and I slipped and slid, and critters—tree frogs and whatnot—were cheeping in the dark all about. A foul odor, sort of like a skunky peppergrass, seemed to be released by the deluge. The rain had completely stopped by the time I arrived at camp, where Raphael had considerately bought me a plate of dinner from the park restaurant. I set my passport and immigration papers on the front seat of the truck to dry then showered in an outdoor stall. I gobbled down the plate of oh-so-delicious food while Raphael told me about the park exhibits honoring the Costa Rican patriots who foiled General William Walker's plans to extend the two-year reich of the Mosquito Republic.

Urged on by Cornelius Vanderbilt, Costa Rican president Mora Porras declared war on Walker's regime in February 1855. He mustered a force of nine thousand men. Walker sent an expedition of several hundred of his filibusters toward the border. The armies clashed at Rivas, south of Granada, Nicaragua. The battle was saved when a Costa Rican drummer boy, Juan Santamaría, set the town ablaze and routed the gringos. Young Juan lost his life but remains one of the country's greatest heroes. A second battle of Rivas, in April of the following year, spelled the end for Walker's Mosquito adventure. The pint-size general was evacuated by an American gunboat. Walker's defeat was something of a great divide in Costa Rican history. Prior to the days of engagement with Walker, the first loyalty of many Costa Ricans lay with the city in which they were born, rather than the country at large. Afterward, they became Costa Ricans. Unhappily, the war with Walker did not much help President Mora Porras, who lost almost half the army to battle losses, disease, and incompetence. He was overthrown by a military junta a few months after Walker was deposed. A year later he was arrested and shot for attempting a counter coup.[17]

Mid-afternoon the next day—on our forced march through Nicaragua—we rolled unimpeded through Estelí. A British backpacker had assured me the Sandinistas would detain us for some time with a roadblock. Raphael and I were pleased to find he was mistaken. Once we arrived at the Honduran border it was the familiar border-crossing blues all over again, with Nicaraguan officials taking their time to pass us through. The dawdling was just the usual bureaucratic insouciance. We hustled over to the Honduran side, which closed, so we had been informed by an enterprising kid, at 5 P.M. sharp.

The Honduran military, which seemed to be wholly in charge of border crossings, greeted us with more than the studied indifference of Central American officialdom. Our passports were held by an ugly character while three soldiers went through the truck, banging on the fenders and bed and so on for false walls. That inspection was the worst of the entire trip. We arrived in Choluteca, Honduras, running on fumes and greeted William, the hotel proprietor's son, like an old friend, to his mild consternation. Both Raphael and I were a bit hurt that he did not seem to harbor any great feeling for us. To us he was a legendary figure, the person to whom Peter Lorre taught English. "They are worthy islands." It would be a long time before we forgot him or that.

At 112,088 square kilometers, Honduras is about the same size as Pennsylvania. Like the Keystone State, the Central American country is longest on the east-west axis, with a Caribbean, or northern, shoreline of 735 kilometers. Guatemala borders the country on the west, Nicaragua the east, and El Salvador the south. Less than 20 percent is lowland, the Atlantic flatlands being the most valuable agricultural acreage as they account for almost all of the production of bananas, still, after a century, the country's most lucrative export. Honduras's Pacific region, where Choluteca is located, extends along the coast like a pedestal. The Pacific lowlands stretch for about 150 kilometers along the water in a band averaging twenty-five kilometers wide.

Back in the saddle the following day, the highway headed away from the

Pacific coastal plain and into the highlands. Although not as elevated as the mountains in Guatemala or Costa Rica, the central plateau is uniformly high and the climate tierra templada, or relatively moderate, for the four-fifths of the country where most of the population of about five million lives, divided evenly between rural and urban. The capital, Tegucigalpa, has a population of somewhere between half a million and one million. The commercial capital, San Pedro Sula, located in the banana lands of the Caribbean littoral, has a somewhat smaller population but is growing rapidly. Honduras was regarded as the poorest and most backward of the Central American states until the civil war wrecked Nicaragua. The per capita income in 1992 was a mere $548, half that of neighboring Guatemala and less than a third of Costa Rica. Only 0.7 telephones existed for each one hundred persons.[18]

Despite these dismal-sounding figures, Honduras was by no means the worst off of the countries Raphael and I passed through. As so often occurs, its misfortune was also its fortune. The country's upland soils are not volcanic, so fertility is low. Therefore, no coffee-baron class developed. Most of the coffee, the country's second export, is produced by small farmers. Politically, Honduras has been called the "essential banana republic." During its sixty-one years of independence in the nineteenth century, Honduras boasted sixty-four presidents plus a number of juntas.[19] In the early part of the twentieth century its politics were dominated by three (then two) American banana companies, each sometimes supporting its own candidates for office. Political instability and mismanagement figured largely in the outbreak of the debilitating Soccer War of 1969. Strongman Oswaldo López Arellano needed an issue with which to take the heat off his own administrative shortcomings. Also, Honduras's border with its politically volatile neighbors—Guatemala, El Salvador, Nicaragua—resulted in its becoming a sanctuary and staging ground. In the early 1950s, the CIA and Guatemalan would-be dictator Carlos Castillo Armas assembled their anti-Arbenz force here. Honduras also lacks anything resembling an independent police force or judiciary system.

Nonetheless, Honduras escaped the troubles of the 1980s much better than any of its neighbors. Because there was no intense class or ethnic hatred, there was less class and ethnic conflict, and when the specter of fascism of the grander scale of other Central American countries of the time tried to take root, institutional forces foiled it. For instance, Argentine-trained chief of the army General Alvarez Martínez encouraged the "disappearance" of political enemies; however, Alvarez overstepped himself by trying to replace the council of senior officers with his own handpicked group of eight. He was forcibly put on a plane to Miami with a permanent wave goodbye to this would-be usurper.[20] Not taking the hint, he was later assassinated when he returned to Honduras on a nefarious errand.

During the Sandinista times, up to twenty thousand Nicaraguan Contras were operating out of bases in Honduras. Honduras's own military force was less than two-thirds that size, a situation that could have caused big trouble. Nevertheless, the Contras disbanded and returned to Nicaragua after the Sandinista electoral defeat without undue social disruption in Honduras. The hundreds of millions of dollars of U.S. aid that flowed into the country in the 1980s, though mostly military, helped support the economy in a time of collapsing coffee prices.

The highlight of our forced march across Honduras came in the pine-clad mountains on the outskirts of Tegucigalpa, where I overran a red light, snudging maybe ten feet over the line. A mean-looking cop, a regular pit bull, burst out of a hut, jabbed a finger at me, and pointed inside. Raphael muttered, "Uh oh, this is going to cost you." Then out loud he said, "He's a *profesor de universidad en los Estados Unidas.*"

Central America is a great place to trade on titles. Normally Raphael referred to me as Don Esteban. Once, when I asked him not to do that, he said, "In Guatemala you can be called a *don* (*de* [of] *origen noble*) if you own three cows." Inside the filthy shack, the cop looked at my passport and then asked me whether I really was a professor in the States. I said yes. He handed the passport back to me and bade me a pleasant *adiós.* Or at least that was my interpretation of events. Raphael told me later that his utterance was simply as one good old Central American boy to another implying that, "Because he is a professor you've got to expect him to be a bit dopey and confused."

For two hours we barreled through prosperous-looking fields in the mountains on the way to the banana town of San Pedro Sula. The traditional occupation of the land-owning elite here is stock raising. Every male head in rural Honduras sports a ten-gallon straw stockman's hat, unlike elsewhere in Central America where the ubiquitous baseball cap has made serious and rather unattractive inroads. In the early afternoon we lunched at a local tourist resort. A waterfall coming down the hill had a concrete pool at its base. Two families were swimming and eating at the comedor attached to it. The cooking was done over an open fire in full view of the patrons.

On the San Pedro Sula highway, we encountered a few tidy-looking prefab buildings, each generally surrounded by chain-link fences, with small professional-looking signs bearing anonymous industrial names. Sometimes there would be a few oriental characters written under the name. These were

Man making adobe bricks by the side of the road in Honduras.

the so-called maquiladoras, or factories, generally of Korean, Taiwanese, or sometimes American ownership. The going rate for the workers was about $4 a day, and not surprisingly, North American labor unions denounce them as exploitive sweatshops. Many locals look down on them as well because "now we cannot get any maids," as I was told by a man who identified himself as a tourist guide.

We arrived at La Entrada de Copán at about 5 P.M. only to learn we still had sixty-five kilometers to go to get to the ruins. To two weary travelers with a bad case of cab fever, who had come all the way from Costa Rica, it did not seem that even Stephens had to endure more to reach Copán. In no mood to enjoy the scenery, we lead-footed it along the Río Copán, a pretty little stream bounded on both sides by low mountains. In the river bottom, campesinos were setting out tobacco plants, which in time would become the cigars for which the area is locally renowned. In less than an hour, which nevertheless seemed like an afternoon, we arrived at the pleasant village of Copán Ruinas.

7 / Copán

To reach Copán, which as you recall Stephens headed for immediately on arriving in Central America, he underwent several of the minor tribulations of Job. He had to best the Mico Mountains, spend a night in jail, suffer the inhospitality of a surly don whose *house had two sides, an inside and an out; the don* [his far from obliging host] *and his family occupied the former, and* [Stephens and Catherwood] *the latter.*[1] The don also tried to thwart Stephens's access to the ruins. At long last, Stephens procured a guide, José.

Fording the Río Copán, Stephens rode along the bank on a path that José opened with his machete, *until we came to the foot of the wall. The wall was of cut stone, well laid, and in a good state of preservation. We ascended by large stone steps, in some places perfect, and in others thrown down by trees which had grown up between the crevices, and reached a terrace, the form of which it was impossible to make out, from the density of the forest in which it was enveloped. Our guide cleared a way, and we came upon a square stone column about fourteen feet high and three feet on each side, sculptured in very bold relief, and on all four of the sides, from the base to the top.*

The front was the figure of a man curiously and richly dressed, and the face, evidently a portrait, solemn, stern, and well fitted to excite terror. The sides were covered with hieroglyphics. This our guide called an "Idol." Before it, at a distance of three feet, was a large block of stone, also sculptured with figures and emblematical devices, which he called an altar. We followed our guide to fourteen monuments of the same character and appearance, some with more elegant designs, and some in workmanship equal to the finest monuments of the Egyptians, one

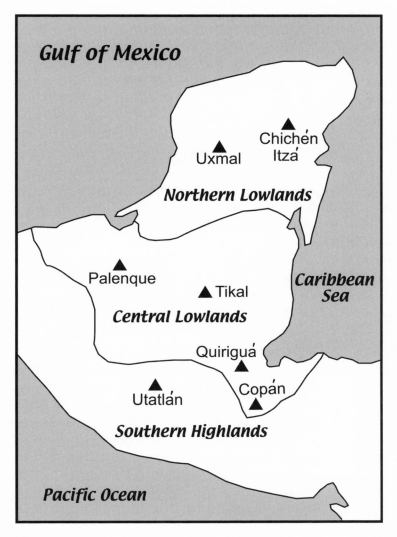

Maya area

The area inhabited by the Maya takes in the Yucatán peninsula and most of the territory directly south of it including a sliver of western Honduras and approximately a third of modern day El Salvador. To the west the land inhabited by the Maya stretches to the Isthmus of Tehuantipec in Mexico. Altogether the Maya area comprises about 125,000 square miles. The region is broken into three parts. The Southern Highlands is the location where Maya culture first flourished. The Maya reached their greatest development in the Central Lowlands during the Late Classic period. Copán is placed here because of its situation in a mountain valley and because of its cultural affinity. Maya culture continued to flourish in the northern lowlands (as well as in the southern highlands) in the Postclassic period after the great central centers such as Copán had fallen to ruin.

displaced from its pedestal by enormous roots, another locked in the close embrace of branches of trees and almost lifted out of the earth, another hurled to the ground and bound down by huge vines and creepers and one standing, with its altar before it, in a grove of trees which grew around it, seemingly to shade and shroud it as a sacred thing.

In the solemn stillness of the woods, it seemed a divinity mourning over a fallen people. We asked the Indians who made them, and their dull answer was "Quien sabe?" "who knows?" Architecture, sculpture and painting, all the arts which embellish life, had flourished in this overgrown forest. Orators, warriors and statesmen, beauty, ambition and glory had lived and passed away, and none knew that such things had been or could tell of their past existence. Books are silent on this theme. The place where we sat, was it a citadel from which an unknown people had sounded the trumpet of war? Or a temple for the worship of the God of peace? Or did the inhabitants worship the idols made with their own hands and offer sacrifices on the stones before them. All was mystery, dark, impenetrable mystery, and every circumstance increased it. The city was desolate. The only sounds that disturbed the quiet of this buried city were the noise of monkeys moving among the tops of the trees, with a noise like a current of wind, passed on into the depths of the forest. With the strange monuments around us, they seemed like wandering spirits of the departed race guarding the ruins of their former habitations.[2]

Stephens and Catherwood were by no means the first Europeans to view a Maya ruin. The first Westerner to leave a firsthand account of Copán was Diego García de Palacio, who sent a detailed report to King Philip II in 1576. Stephens traveled with a copy of Francisco Antonio Fuentes y Guzmán's history of Guatemala, published in 1689, which included a section on Copán. It is assumed, because of his account's inaccuracy, that Fuentes did not visit the ruins. The Mexican cities of Palenque and Uxmal, in particular, had been paid a fair amount of attention by the Spanish colonial authorities and other travelers. Colonel Juan Galindo of the Liberal army had visited Copán in 1834 and Palenque some time before that. The publication of an article by him in London and New York newspapers focused Stephens's attention on Copán.

Galindo was an interesting fellow, one Stephens much wanted to meet. Despite his rather misleading name, he was Irish by birth.[3] His great-grandfather had emigrated to the Emerald Isle from Spain. Both his father and mother were actors who toured Great Britain. He immigrated to Central America, changed his name from John to Juan, and offered his services to the Liberal government. His talents were put to good use as governor of the Petén, during which tenure he scurried off to survey Palenque in adjacent Chiapas, Mexico.

Later he was sent to Washington to talk to Secretary of State John Forsyth about the possibility of an American-controlled rail and canal route across the isthmus. Then he went on to London to try to talk Lord Palmerston, the prime minister, into recognizing his grant in what is now Belize. In exchange for Galindo spilling everything he had learned about American plans in Central America, Palmerston agreed to let the Irish-cum-Central American have his way in Belize—but later rescinded the deal, much to Galindo's annoyance.[4] In short, Galindo was the sort of Renaissance character frequently found in the nineteenth-century Americas. He exhibited a burning curiosity, lively intelligence, and, most of all, an eye to the main chance.

Galindo was the first modern commentator on Copán. He was fortunate in having a clean slate with which to work, rather than one sullied with many false and misleading assumptions. Early Mayanists, before Stephens and Galindo and for one hundred years afterward, were remarkable for their crackpot ideas and behavior. The self-appointed noble Count Waldeck produced plate after plate of "illustrations" of the Yucatán site of Uxmal, which bore only the remotest resemblance to what future archaeologists were to discover. (He placed an exquisitely drawn male figure clothed only in grass mantle and helmet at the entrance to the Temple of the Dwarf at Uxmal; no one has since seen this sculpture.[5]) Brasseur de Bourbourg, cleric, scholar, and accomplished linguist, insisted on shuffling Atlantean theories in with his archaeology; he also marked down Scandinavia as the original homeland of the Maya. Augustus Le Plongeon was fortunate in having a sensible wife who toned down his hypothesizing. One of his milder speculations was that the Maya colonized the Nile valley and from there sent out missions to the north and west to bring about Western civilization. Even respectable twentieth-century professional archaeologists, such as J. Eric Thompson and Sylvanus Morley, were not above promulgating hokum about their pet subject, the Maya. Thompson and Morley insisted, in the face of substantial evidence to the contrary, that the Maya lived in a peaceful theocratic state ruled by priest-kings and devoted chiefly to intellectual and artistic pursuits.

Ultimately Stephens was to rough out a picture of Maya life that in its broad outlines resembles the conventional archaeological wisdom at the turn of the twenty-first century.[6] In this regard he was fortunate to have been exposed to Galindo's work, which also displayed a level-headed, commonsense approach to dealing with the ruins. For instance, when describing the Temple of the Cross at Palenque, Galindo merely noted the resemblance to the Christian symbol without making an inference about direct Christian influence.

He also intuited that the hieroglyphics were a form of writing. Galindo made a connection, despite the large number of differences, between Copán and Palenque, arguing that they were of the same cultural origin, if perhaps not of the same culture. He noted that the tools of daily life found in the ruins (*metates* [grinding stones] and rollers used for processing corn) were similar to those used by local natives in his day. Finally, Galindo claimed that the builders of the ruined cities he visited were the ancestors of the present Indians of Central America and that the vernacular of contemporary natives was likely related to the language of the builders of the cities. Eventually, Stephens was to agree with all these claims and to make them himself in a much more forceful manner.

Stephens noted *a remarkable altar, which perhaps presents as curious a subject of speculation as any monument in Copán. The altars, like the idols, are all a single block of stone. This stands on four globules cut out of the same stone. The sculpture is bas-relief, and it is the only specimen of that kind of sculpture found at Copán, all the rest being in bold alto-relievo. It is six feet square and four feet high, and the top is divided into thirty-six tablets of hieroglyphics, which beyond doubt record some event in the history of the mysterious people who once inhabited the city. The lines are still distinctly visible. The next two engravings exhibit the four sides of this altar. Each side represents four individuals. On the west side are the two principal personages, chiefs or warriors, with their faces opposite each other, and apparently engaged in argument or negotiation. The other fourteen are divided into two equal parties, and seem to be following their leaders. Each of the two principal figures is seated cross-legged, in the Oriental fashion, on a hieroglyphic which probably designates his name and office, or character, and on three sides of which the serpent forms part. Between the two principal personages is a remarkable cartouche, containing two hieroglyphics well preserved, which reminded us strongly of the Egyptian method of giving the names of the kings or heroes in whose honor the monuments were erected. The headdresses are remarkable for their curious and complicated form. The figures have all breastplates, and one of the two principal characters holds in his hand an instrument which may perhaps be a scepter.*[7]

Subsequent Mayanists have been as puzzled and intrigued by this object, now known as Altar Q, as Stephens was. The sculpture is one of the best known of all Maya works of art. Somehow it seemed to offer a clue to what the mysterious Maya were all about. Who were the sixteen figures depicted on its sides? Here's the answer given by Sir J. Eric Thompson, who in 1954, the publication date of this passage, was unquestionably the world's most

West side of Altar Q, Copán. Yax K'uk Mo', second from left, is handing the scepter—as Stephens suggested—to Yax Pac, the sixteenth in line of succession. For many years this famous Maya monument was believed to depict a gathering of astronomers.

highly regarded Mayanist: "About A.D. 700, Copán appears to have produced the most up-to-date computation of the length of the tropical year, and recorded it on a number of monuments. The sides of one altar commemorating this achievement are carved with the figures of sixteen persons who face inward toward the date in question. [John E.] Teeple, who first advanced the explanation that this was a computation of the length of the solar year, speaks felicitously of this 'group photograph of the Copán Academy of Sciences taken just after their sessions.'"[8] Indeed, Mayanists in days gone by frequently referred to the figures depicted on Altar Q as "the 16 astronomers."

A half-century after Thompson, the questions Stephens posed about the larger culture he rediscovered are now finally being answered in something approaching complete detail, thanks to more level-headed archaeological analysis and the unraveling of the Maya hieroglyphic code. Current scholarship, while less fanciful and even less interesting than Thompson and Teeple, strikes a tone much closer to Stephens. Here's the caption under a photograph of Altar Q in Harvard archaeologist William Fash's *Scribes, Warriors and Kings:* "Altar Q, west side. The left-central figure represents the revered founder of the Copán dynasty (Yax K'uk' Mo'), passing a scepter of office to the right-center figure (Yax Pac), the 16th ruler in that dynasty. Yax K'uk' Mo's name appears in his headdress, while all the other figures are identified by the hieroglyphs they sit upon. The date of Yax Pac's accession to power (2 July 763) is shown between the two central figures. On the far left sits the 2nd ruler; on the far right sits the 15th ruler, Smoke Shell."[9]

As Stephens speculated, all are seated on hieroglyphic representations of their names, the object held by one of the two principals is a scepter, and the gentlemen in questions are kings, or "chiefs," as Stephens styles them. Stephens missed the element of dynastic succession as did scholars for many years. Tumbling intuitively to the idea of a dynasty that lasted for 394 years, as the rulers on Altar Q represent, was too much to expect of him. After all, Stephens hailed from a country whose current government dated back only sixty-three years to the Declaration of Independence, and whose Pilgrim forefathers had arrived a mere 150 years before that. The Maya fascination with time and the civilization's long extension are two of the culture's distinguishing idiosyncrasies. The first Maya, or proto-Maya, settled in the Copán area approximately 1,800 years prior to the erection of Altar Q.

The scholar who solved the puzzle of Altar Q was, surprisingly, a German, Berthold Riese of the University of Hamburg. The Germans were generally the bad guys in the unraveling of the Maya code. As the famous Mayanist (and arch Stephens fan; he calls him "the great Stephens") Michael Coe has pointed out, it took less than two decades from the discovery of the Rosetta stone to the deciphering of the Egyptian hieroglyphics by the young Frenchman Jean François Champollion, which in the nineteenth century was considered a vast triumph of the human mind.[10] More than a century passed from the uncovering of the Maya equivalent of the Rosetta stone to the time Maya glyphs came to be understood in a more or less systematic way. The German school was indeed an impediment in the final decipherment, but many more cultural and political hurdles tripped the various scholars who tried their hand at what would become an intellectual milepost of the twentieth century, in its way as challenging as landing on the moon. Those hurdles included racism, the cold war, and plain old intellectual boneheadedness.

In the seventeenth century a Jesuit by the name of Athanasius Kircher, following Coe, declared that the Egyptian hieroglyphics represented ideas that could be transmitted without recourse to any spoken language. Kircher's point of view prevailed even after the Rosetta stone was uncovered. What contributed most to Champollion's breakthrough was his study of the contemporary Coptic language. Coptic was believed to be a descendent of the language of the pharaohs. Working backward from Coptic, Champollion was able to develop phonetic components of the hieroglyphs.

Using Champollion's example, then, a code-breaker would need to learn what language was likely to have been spoken at the major Maya sites. The next step would be to ransack local libraries and international archives for written examples of the language. Stephens searched for dictionaries and other documentary sources of Maya writing on his second trip to the land of the Maya in 1841. Although his efforts were not fruitless, no Rosetta stone was uncovered.

The discovery of the Mayan equivalent of the stone was saved for Charles E. Brasseur de Bourbourg about twenty years later. Although Brasseur de Bourbourg entertained foolish notions as to the provenance of the Maya (thinking they were Atlanteans), his linguistic and scholarly credentials were considerable. In fact, his reputation was such that the Spanish allowed him to look through their Archives of the Americas in Seville, which generally was jealously guarded against foreign snooping. Filed away in a forgotten box on a nameless shelf was a manuscript copy of Bishop Diego de Landa's *Relación de las cosas de Yucatán*.[11]

If the business of history is irony, which it sometimes seems, Landa surely qualifies as a prime exemplar. He was the man, more than anyone else, who destroyed historical knowledge of the Maya, just as he was the man most responsible for passing on to posterity what is known of Maya life at the time of contact. While a lowly friar he set upon an auto-da-fé (Inquisition) to rout the devil worship of the Maya. Anything having to do with their religion was destroyed. In short, the Maya bodies were tortured for the sake of their souls. In Landa's defense, it should be noted that the statues of Maya gods he destroyed were clotted with blood from human sacrifices, and the books burnt all seemed to speak to the mysterious rites of this human-immolating religion. In short, to Landa and to the far-from-fastidious Spanish conquistadors, the entire culture seemed to be organized around the idolatry of evil.

Unfortunately for Landa, but fortunately for Maya studies, he had enemies who reported his activities to the royal authorities. Most likely the informers were the conquistadors who felt he was interfering with the serfs they claimed as prizes of the Conquest. Because only a bishop could institute an inquisition, Landa was called back to Spain. In part to atone for his destruction of the Yucatec culture (which the king, only in nominal control of what went on in the Americas, did not sanction), he penned his famous *Relation*. His intimate knowledge of the Maya may have included an understanding of their language and writing; in any case, he set down hieroglyphic representations of the Spanish alphabet, given to him by informants, without quite explaining his methodology. A century after Brasseur de Bourbourg's discovery of Landa's Maya "alphabet," it would come to be considered the key to breaking the code.

Brasseur de Bourbourg had the linguistic ability to crack the Maya enigma. Among his various talents was a speaking knowledge of some highland Mayan languages. But he lacked two things to accomplish the job. The first was faithful reproductions of Maya writing. As good as Catherwood's illustrations were, they were not good enough. The second was emancipation from the racist belief that the present inhabitants of the country were not descended from the people whose culture he admired and studied. Of these two deficiencies, the latter was by far the more efficient barrier.

The next phase of the story was a face-off between a bucolic American ethnologist and a formidable champion of the German academy. The American Cyrus Thomas was by birth a citizen of Tennessee, the state Davy Crockett represented in the U.S. House of Representatives in the mid-1820s. His opposite number in Bismark's Imperial Germany, the world's bastion of learning and culture, was Eduard Seler. He was called the Nestor of Mesoamerica for the good reason that he had an encyclopedic command of all phases of Americanist studies. Seler spoke Mayan languages, knew Maya cultural history and archaeology, and had access to every known codex, or book (at the time three Postclassic Maya books were known to have survived Landa's auto-da-fé). According to Coe, "his devotion to detail and his suspicion of intuitive thought effectively blocked any such breakthrough."[12] His erudition crushed the frontiersman Thomas, who, like Champollion, believed that contemporary Mayan languages could guide a phonetic translation of the hieroglyphs. In fact, Thomas managed correctly to translate a number of words, and helped show the way to future Maya code-breakers.

The strange story of the deciphering of Maya hieroglyphic writing, up to this point, would probably chart not that differently from any other great intellectual endeavor: a few steps up, a step to the side, two steps down, a big stride forward, and so on. The next phase, when the professional archaeologists take over in the twentieth century, is where the story becomes truly weird. Sylvanus Morley, 1883–1948, who has been described as a "small, nearsighted, dynamic bundle of energy," had the great good fortune of enrolling at Harvard University when it was taking the lead in Maya studies. After receiving an M.A. in 1908, he became the beneficiary of the munificence of the Carnegie Institution, which supported his plan for a massive expedition to Mesoamerica. From all this came Morley's belief, still quite widespread among tourist guides, voice-over narrators of TV specials, and those of the general populace vaguely interested in Maya studies, that Maya history splits into two phases. The Old Empire consisted of a more or less unified league of Classic Maya cities in the central lowlands, stretching from Copán in the southeast to Palenque, and, above all, to mighty Tikal in the heartland center. War and violence were next to unknown to these people, ruled as they were by benevolent priest-kings devoted to artistic matters and scientific and astronomical speculation. Around the ninth century the Old Empire collapsed. The Maya moved north into the Yucatán peninsula founding such cities as Uxmal and Chichén Itzá. There they were invaded by a war-mongering race from points north and west that adulterated their culture. Nowadays, most authorities consider Morley's chronology to be pure fantasy.

First Morley's acolyte, then his equal, and ultimately his widely acknowledged intellectual superior was the British-Argentine J. Eric Thompson. Thompson's genius, according to Michael Coe, and perhaps his greatest lasting contribution to Maya studies stemmed from his work unraveling the multitudinous calendrical sequences, such as his decipherment of the 819-day cycle of the Maya, a still not completely understood observance of a "year" as the product of 7, the earth number; 9, the heaven number; and 13, for the underworld. Thompson assiduously defended his belief that the Maya inscriptions were devoted almost entirely to mathematical-astronomical (or perhaps astrological) calculations with a fair bit of mythology mixed in. The stone monuments, he contended, "bear witness to the incredible preoccupation with the mysteries of time which so profoundly affected Maya culture. Priest-astronomers recorded on these stone shafts their progress in astronomy and mathematics; the best artists were employed in carving on them representations of their gods; and for them were reserved the most important positions before pyramid or palace."[13]

He also held the notion, better expressed by his contemporary Paul Schellhas, that the principle of Maya hieroglyphic writing was logographic, or word-based, as opposed to phonetic. In short, the Maya glyphs were "by no means real writing" because they did not replicate language. Put another way, Thompson, Schellhas, and others held that so-called Maya writing was a sophisticated means of taking notes, with each logograph representing a full-blown word or idea rather than phonetic components that could be assembled into words and strung together by rules of grammar. In short, it was not a genuine representation of a spoken language.

Then, in 1952, came an academic, Y. V. Knorosov, who turned epigraphic studies on its ear. This scholar began by studying contemporary Mayan languages. He showed that Landa's Maya glyphs did indeed express a phonetic representation of a spoken language. Previous scholars had mistakenly assumed that each glyph stood for a simple letter. Instead, the glyphs indicated syllables. Among other things, he learned that the usual word order in contemporary Mayan languages is verb first, then object and lastly subject. Next, he applied this syntactic structure to the glyphs. Finally, he pored over the Maya codices, which are liberally illustrated, for clues to the subject matter of nearby sentences. He used the pioneering work of Cyrus Thomas to guide him. The method, elegant in its simplicity, flew in the face of the conventional wisdom of the giants in the field. Morley had been dead a few years, but Thompson was very much alive and quite willing to take on any challenger. And Thompson very much wanted to take on this challenger because Yuri Valentinovich Knorosov was not only Russian but a Soviet. (Interestingly, Coe claims Knorosov, who participated in the invasion of Berlin during World War II, was able to retrieve only one book from the burning National Library, an edition of one of the three then known Maya codices, which he used to develop his code-breaking system. This story seems too good to be true, and indeed a leading German Mayanist claims it is apocryphal.) Knorosov's landmark paper was published in a Soviet journal with a foreword that taunted the decadent science of the West for failing to make the discovery. In short, the key to breaking the Maya code may have been found, but most Western scholars showed little interest in recognizing Knorosov or his system.

The next milepost in returning to Stephens's vision of what the inscriptions and monuments of Copán represented was attained a few years later by a White Russian émigré, Tatiana Proskouriakoff. Raised in Philadelphia and a graduate of Pennsylvania State University, Proskouriakoff's first job as a Mayanist came as a staff artist in the central lowlands. Like the charismatic Harvard biologist Alexander Agassiz, who forced his students to draw the creatures they studied, Proskouriakoff applied formal structural analysis to the four hundred monuments she sketched. By classifying various structural elements on the monuments, she charted "a peculiar pattern of dates." That pattern could mean only one thing, she decided, and ultimately her archaeological colleagues agreed. The dated monuments referred to Maya history. The figures in the stone were of political personages, those with the clout to get others to erect monuments to them. The figures were not of gods or priests, as Morley and Thompson had believed.

Most of all, Proskouriakoff's discovery directed epigraphers (those who study ancient inscriptions) to the proper subject matter of the glyphs, historical text. As Coe puts it, "I was truly thunderstruck. In one brilliant stroke, this extraordinary woman opened up a world of dynastic rivalry, royal marriages, taking of captives, and all the other elite doings which have held the attention of kingdoms around the world since the remotest antiquity."[14] Maya archaeologists, after 120 years, finally got back to Stephens's position in the passage about Copán's Altar Q. (As we shall see, Stephens later elaborated on these sentiments after he observed more sites and his thinking matured.) Finally, after decades of ethereal beliefs about the Maya being ruled by scholar-priests and being unlike any other known culture, as the twentieth century came to a close, scholars began to regard the Maya as a historical people analogous to other historical peoples in roughly similar circumstances in other places around the globe.

The dam did not truly break until 1973, when a semiformal conference was held at Palenque, Mexico. Participants included professors, graduate students, locals, foreigners, tourists wandering in off the street (such as the fellow dubbed Daddy Warbucks because of his resemblance to the cartoon-strip character, who was known to no one but was warmly welcomed according to the always entertaining Michael Coe, then chairman of anthropology at Yale).

The distinguished Ivy League–educated linguist Floyd Lounsbury was in attendance as was the at-the-time much less distinguished University of South Alabama art teacher Linda Schele. The North American champion of the Soviet Knorosov's method, David Kelley, could not make it because he was on sabbatical in England. He sent an undergraduate in his place, the Australian Peter Mathews, who was studying at the University of Calgary. Mathews's mentor had put him to the task of transcribing and ordering every published glyph from Palenque. One afternoon these three, Schele, Mathews, and Lounsbury, with their various talents, sat down at the kitchen table of the conference organizer—and the result was magic. Lounsbury had a formula for quickly determining dates. Mathews knew practically by heart every glyph at the site. Schele was a longtime Palenquephile. By evening, they had worked out the dynastic succession for seven of the city's rulers from Palenque's flowering at about A.D. 600 to its demise in the ninth century. Using Knorosov's method and guided by Proskouriakoff's findings, finally the Maya hiero-glyphic code could be said to have been deciphered—even though thirty years later some Maya hieroglyphic writing is still not completely understood.

For the moment, let us return to Stephens in 1839, whom we left making his shrewd commonsense surmises about the puzzling New World ruins sur-rounding him. At this time, Stephens had not a clue as to whether Copán stood in cultural isolation or was just one in a network of many ruined cities. For more than one hundred years, archaeologists have known the answer to that question. Maya territory takes in the Yucatán peninsula including the Mexican states of Campeche, Yucatán, and Quintana Roo, the country of Belize, and the Guatemalan department of Petén. Much of the Mexican states of Tabasco and Chiapas were peopled by Maya. In addition, the extreme west-ern part of Honduras (where at the moment we find ourselves and Stephens at Copán), parts of western El Salvador, and all of the Guatemalan highlands were, and, for the most part, still are occupied by Maya, the most conspicuous exceptions being along the Pacific coastal plain where Uto-Aztecan speak-ers settled from the north.[15]

Altogether, the Maya area is about the size of the state of New Mexico or approximately 125,000 square miles. The topography of this land is extremely diverse, ranging from peaks so high that frost can occur any night of the year to lowland tropical rain forests with annual precipitation of up to ten feet. Also, as we have seen, there are deserts as well as scrub jungle and temperate highlands. The Maya, as Stephens gradually came to decide, settled all these biospheres and adapted their culture to them. Literally hundreds of ancient ruined Maya towns and cities have been located. More are being discovered or rediscovered. Only a very few match the artistic apogee Copán repre-sents, but almost every one—as Stephens learned in a subsequent trip to the Yucatán—has one and sometimes many more interesting aesthetic arrange-ments.

The geographical and topographical spread of the Maya area pales in com-parison to its temporal sweep. The river valleys of this area came to be peopled by folks who may have been early Maya speakers somewhere around 1000 B.C. By 400 to 250 B.C., Maya centers had started to develop monumental archi-tecture and sculpture and could already be considered sophisticated cultures (such as Nakbe in Petén, Guatemala). The most advanced centers, early on, were located in the Guatemalan highlands. They had cultural interactions with neighboring Mesoamerican cultures to the west and north. By the late Preclassic period, about the time of the birth of Christ, the people of some highland sites were erecting stone monuments bearing calendar dates and early hieroglyphic writing. In the central zone huge pyramids were being erected, as at El Mirador on the Guatemalan-Mexican border; the site's El Tigre pyramid is the largest of all Maya buildings. The Protoclassic period, which began in about A.D. 100, spelled the end of high civilization in the Guatemalan highlands. As pointed out on our tour of western El Salvador, the eruption of Ilopango Volcano wiped out everything within sixty miles and diminished for centuries the people-carrying capacity of the physical environment in the contiguous highlands.

The central lowlands, in which Copán is placed because, among other reasons, of its situation in a mountain valley, became the focal point of Maya culture. About A.D. 600, competition between the sites provided the impetus for the true flowering of the culture when rulers began to try to outdo one another in the erection of monuments. Unfortunately, competition in this period also became increasingly more self-destructive. Warfare increased. Conflict among centers continued to intensify until the lights, one by one, winked out on all the great cities of the central area by about A.D. 900. For a while the center remained fairly well peopled, if less so than at the height of the culture. Then even the remnant populations seemed to have disappeared from the heart of the central area, the Petén. The central area's loss appears to have been the gain of the southern Guatemala highlands and the northern lowlands, where Maya culture continued to flourish.

Maya culture, inspired by massive Mexican cultural influence that may have included conquest, then flourished throughout the Yucatán peninsula. Chichén Itzá, the vast site that many a day-tripping Cancún vacationer takes in, became the dominant city from about A.D. 1000 until its collapse in A.D. 1200 or so. After that a league of cities led by Mayapán became the chief political organization of the Maya. This league was in retrograde when the Spanish arrived and conquered the peninsula. A recrudescence began in the Guatemalan highlands about A.D. 1000 as peoples began occupying and fortifying hilltop sites there. By about A.D. 1200 a warrior elite from the Gulf Coast conquered these highland polities and forged the mighty Quiché empire that the Spaniards would confront in the sixteenth century and that Stephens will describe for us.

Today, almost five hundred years later, much of this territory is still occupied by Maya, many of whom are living much like their nonelite forebears in the formative period, more than two thousand years ago. Their houses are constructed in round or square designs similar to ones used 2,500 years ago, and the thatch is of the same type. They worship the same gods (mixed some-what with Catholicism now), farm the same crops, and eat the same diet con-sisting of about 80 percent corn, 11 percent vegetables (beans, squash, chile peppers) and 9 percent flesh (whatever can be shot [deer, gibnut, guan], caught [iguana, fish], or grown, [chickens, pigs, sheep, beef—very little of the latter]).

Maya intellectual accomplishments, perhaps not surprisingly, had to do with the keeping of time and the mathematics necessary to do so. Whether this preoccupation was accidental or stemmed from the great staying power of their culture is difficult to ascertain. They shared the 52-year calendar round with other Mesoamerican cultures. This calendar consists of two inter-meshing calendars, one composed of 20 weeks of 13 days (making a 260-day "year"), and another of eighteen 20-day months plus an extra 5-day period (making a 365-day "vague" year; i.e., not leap-corrected for the additional quarter-day of the actual orbit of the sun). Each day in each "year" had its own name. Therefore, a particular short-year/vague-year conjunction could come only once in 18,980 days, or 52 years. The Maya also observed the Long Count year, which consisted of 360 days. These years were organized into larger periods of twenty 360-day years, known as *katuns*. As we have seen from Thompson's decipherment of the $7 \times 9 \times 13$ "year," the Maya had other increments of time as well. As Thompson pointed out, these various years can be likened to a car with several odometers calibrated to miles, kilometers, furlongs, chains, Spanish leagues, Roman stadia, Russian versts and so on. Why anyone would need a car with so many odometers is a question that is still under review.[16]

Thanks to the work of pioneer epigraphers, and with a smattering of Maya historical and intellectual background, some of the questions Stephens posed in the ruins at Copán can now be answered. For instance, most of the visages in the stone columns Stephens contemplated were that of Waxaklahun-Ubah-K'awil, more commonly known among archaeologists as 18 Rabbit. (The de-piction of 18 Rabbit on Altar Q clearly shows him sitting on a glyph bearing the three dots [units] and three lines [representing fives] indicating the 18 part of his name. Maya numbers were first deciphered by another brilliant but eccentric early Mayanist, the French-American Constantine Rafinesque, who died in 1840, the year Stephens returned from his first trip to Mesoamerica. Rafinesque made his discovery by poring over the rather poor illustrations by Waldeck and other early visitors to the ruins.) The "rabbit" part of his com-mon name seems to come from his namesake glyph's fancied resemblance to that animal. He is sometimes called 18 Jog, which is evidently a more accurate portrayal of his name glyph.[17] Schele and Mathews claim he was named after the great War Serpent of the Maya.[18]

The career of 18 Rabbit, interestingly enough, bears some resemblance to that of Juan Galindo, Stephens's archaeological predecessor at Copán. Both were ruthlessly ambitious and were willing to use the canvas at hand to best advantage. 18 Rabbit commissioned seven of the stelae (tall stone monuments) that so impressed Stephens, and he was responsible for making over the city architecturally, including the development of the ball court and the starting of the hieroglyphic staircase, for which Copán is now famous.

18 Rabbit ascended the throne on 19 July A.D. 695, taking over from his father who had ruled for sixty-seven years. His father had expanded the economic and political base of the kingdom. Quiriguá, which Catherwood visited and we discussed earlier, had come under Copán's suzerainty during that period, if not before. Cities located as far away as southern Belize had also become subject to Copán's political influence. In other words, 18 Rabbit had the good fortune of being left with the economic and political resources to fulfill his artistic vision.

Before 18 Rabbit, Copán was just another Maya city. It boasted a few massive stone platforms, which today are known as "buildings," that were used for ceremonial and aesthetic purposes. It was 18 Rabbit, or someone in his entourage, who conceived of richly embellishing the stelae in the manner that would, a millennium later, make Copán familiar to art aficionados the world over.

At the distance of one hundred and twenty feet north is the monument marked O, which unhappily is fallen and broken. In workmanship [it is] *equal to the best remains of Egyptian art. The fallen part was completely bound to the earth by vines and creepers, and before it could be drawn it was necessary to unlace them, and tear the fibers out of the crevices. The paint is very perfect and has preserved the stone, which makes it more to be regretted that it is broken. The altar is buried, with the top barely visible, which, by excavating, we made out to represent the back of a tortoise.*[19]

The monument Stephens designated "O" is now known as Stela C. It was erected to commemorate the end of the first katun (20-year cycle) after 18 Rabbit took power. Fortunately for us, the pioneer epigraphers Schele and Mathews undertook a study of this stone monument.[20] Generally, this stela does two things. First, it commemorates 18 Rabbit as ruler at this important juncture in Maya time. Second, it shows his "divine right" to reign by tying

Catherwood's illustration of Stela C as he and Stephens found it.

him to his ancestors and Maya mythology. It also gives us a taste of the incredible sophistication of Maya culture and art.

This stela has a larger-than-life image of 18 Rabbit carved on both broad sides of the monument. Inscribed text occupies the narrow north and south sides. The writing on the south links the erection of Stela C to an event 4,617 years in the past, this event evidently being the hypothetical setting of a stone base for the stela. (The great pity of the deciphering of the Maya hieroglyphs is that almost all extant inscriptions are on public monuments, whose relation to the true history of the Maya probably bears about the same relationship as a representation of the Civil War gleaned from courthouse statuary in the Deep South.) Not to be outdone, glyphs on the north side of Stela C describe events that occurred two million years before the creation of the world. Epigraphers are not sure what is being claimed to have happened on those early dates, but they are certain that the reappearance of Venus on the day the stela was commemorated is significant. In terms of heavenly bodies, Venus was second only to the sun in importance to the Maya. The planet boded war and misfortune; an effective king naturally had to have this heavenly body under his control.

On the broad east side of the stela, 18 Rabbit wears an elaborate headdress showing three heads and a serpent bar frames his face. The double-headed serpent bar represents a scepter, which, naturally, indicates royalty. Each of the serpent's mouths has heads emerging. These heads represent ancestral beings and each has a stacked headdress upon which other ancestral beings are depicted. Of the three heads on 18 Rabbit's pate, the last has been identified by Schele and Mathews as the Jester God, again, a sign of royalty. For whatever reason, the Jester God (named for a resemblance to a court jester in the days before a Maya name was known) usually has fish fins on his face. An unknown ancestor sits behind 18 Rabbit holding a serpent bar from which yet more figures emerge. Shooting out of the mouths of the serpent bars are flint blades, which indicate war and sacrifice; during the dedication ceremony 18 Rabbit perforated his private parts with stingray spines and offered the gods the resulting blood. Ropes entwine 18 Rabbit's headdress. They are knotted three times and encircle a bat's head. The ropes, according to Linda Schele and Peter Mathews, symbolize the umbilical cord, both human (stating his legitimate right to rule) and cosmic (showing 18 Rabbit is connected to celestial sources of light and power).

The bottom half of 18 Rabbit's body represents the crocodile-tree motif, an elaborate and somewhat fluid zoomorphic (crocodile head, deer ears, and hooves) representation of the Milky Way. Tree imagery appears in two forms. 18 Rabbit's loin apron shows one version. The crocodile head, which also overlays the apron, shows another. The World Tree is another symbol of the Milky Way, and the king was the royal personification of it, thereby demonstrating 18 Rabbit's legitimacy once again. We are not finished yet. Two mountain monsters hang upside down in the World Tree. The mountain monsters plus other symbols are probably meant to link 18 Rabbit to the Maya's great mythical Hero Twins, who were responsible for the making of man (out of maize) and the dawn of the modern era, the so-called Fourth Creation. The below-the-waist imagery, in toto, represents the Milky Way on 5 December A.D. 711, when Venus made its first reappearance as the evening star. And all this is the Cliff Notes version of the side of Stela C shown in Catherwood's illustration. Even if a naive viewer, such as Stephens, did not comprehend the meaning of the work, the richness and artistic accomplishment were readily apparent.

An explorer stumbling on another Maya city, taken in isolation, could have considered it merely a curious anomaly. Copán, with its rich sculpture, represented a world-class artistic site. Oddly enough, Copán was (and is) tucked into the southeastern corner of the Maya area. Indeed, its name in Mayan is *Xukpi,* or corner. The next valley over is inhabited by non-Mayas, so Stephens's luck at finding it was pretty good. The fortune of the writer of the article that led Stephens to Copán was not so good. Galindo's luck ran out while Stephens was making his way back from Costa Rica. After a defeat in battle, he was captured by partisans in a Honduran village and summarily shot. 18 Rabbit's run of luck broke one year after he erected his last stone monument. He was captured by the ruler of Quiriguá, and, after a suitable amount of torture, which both kings recognized as necessary lubrication for their blood-craving deities, was executed in A.D. 738.

Copán had less than a century of civilized life left. Its last dated monument clocked in at A.D. 822. Only two of that stone altar's four faces were finished, leading archaeologists to speculate that the seventeenth known ruler of Copán, U Cit Tok, was the last.[21] Stephens spent the best part of three weeks at Copán, carefully surveying and inventorying the site, devoting approximately 6.5 percent of the text of *Incidents of Travel in Central America* to these investigations. Ultimately, the pressure of diplomatic business forced him to move on, but Catherwood stayed to finish his impressive drawings of the ruins. *Catherwood made the outline of all his drawings with the camera lucida and divided his paper into sections to preserve the utmost accuracy of proportion.*[22] The work Stephens and Catherwood did at Copán made them fa-

Catherwood's illustration of Stela D with altar.

Photograph of Stela D with altar. Note the superior clarity of detail in Catherwood's sketch (p. 163). Photo darkened to highlight detail.

mous at the time and given the long view, immortal. Even today, nearly every book on the Maya includes some of Catherwood's prints. Probably more than any other interpreter of Maya art, Catherwood was able to portray accurately the richness and detail of Maya statuary without getting lost in it. The explication of Stela C above indicates the ease with which one can completely founder in Maya art. As for Stephens, as long as antiquities are studied the Father of American Archaeology will be remembered. One day, even a literary culture as hard-nosed, ungrateful, narrow, and canon-oriented as our own may bestir itself to recognize him for the remarkable quality of his prose.

Raphael and I spent the day visiting the ruins, the restoration of which the government of Honduras had taken over from Pennsylvania State University. We spent a second evening in Copán Ruinas, which remains in my mind a pleasant little village despite the experience I had there during a later trip. Four men—three Chorti Maya and a ladino—were shot dead in a neighboring restaurant while I was putting away an enormous quantity of the country's beef. What had sounded to me like firecrackers was understood immediately by the restaurant staff, naturally more attuned to Central American conditions. Some claimed the Chorti had it in for the ladino because of the latter's misapplications of poor-box collections and also the death of a youngster some time before. Others claimed the Chorti, whose forebears included 18 Rabbit and the builders of Copán, were gunned down in the bathroom by the hired gunman of a landowner who staked claim to their tribal lands.

Our return to Esquipulas the following day was marred by nothing more startling than being shaken down for two dollars by a Guatemalan cop at an improvised roadblock. The fellow was so diffident and needful—he patted me on the back in gratitude after I forked over the lucre—that I almost passed him a couple of bucks more, but in the interests of future travelers I resisted the impulse. Although Raphael and I had been away from Esquipulas less than two weeks, we'd traveled through four countries. El Salvador was still nominally at war, and Nicaragua's society was shattered by civil war, while the other two, Honduras and Costa Rica, showed in various degrees the ordeals that all of Central America had to put up with as the cold war played out its final battles. All this made the welcome of the American priests at Raphael's old monastery seem almost like coming home.

8 / The Guatemalan Big Apple and Utatlán

My airplane acquaintance of some weeks before, the Caterpillar executive, said I would be impressed by the economic development in Guatemala, and I was able to see what he meant a couple of days later on the Atlantic Highway heading for Guatemala City. A half-mile of vegetable peddlers and food stalls lined the highway around a modern-looking Texaco station. On my first trip in that area back in the late 1970s, I remembered stopping at a modest gas station and looking down over the semi-arid plain in wonder at the perfect stillness of the place—not a diesel chuffing, an engine throbbing, or an electrical motor humming to disturb your inner peace. This scene was absolute freedom from the tyranny of the mechanized age.

Now the villages were, unfortunately, emptying into strip slums along the major highways. Here the Atlantic Highway was potholed and by no means the impressive throughway I had encountered back toward the Caribbean, nor did it seem from the armies of roadside peddlers asking rock-bottom prices that this supposed economic development had done much for the rank and file.

We passed the flat agricultural district around a town with the banefully ironic name of Progreso, and then started the climb up into the pine- and oak-clad foothills. There we found another graphic indication of my airplane friend's concept of economic progress. Trucks—miles of them—had pulled onto the shoulder near a cement plant, waiting to pick up a load. Raphael wondered, "How can it be that a country with high inflation and supposedly

Esquipulas to Guatemala City and Utatlán
This map shows the approximate route the author took from Esquipulas to the capital and then to the old capital of Antigua. From Antiqua he took a side trip to Utatlán.

on the verge of economic collapse seems to be booming?" That was indeed a good question, and one neither of us could readily answer.

Stephens, on the other hand, concentrated on the beauty of the scene. *Almost immediately we commenced ascending a rugged mountain, very steep, and commanding at every step a wild and magnificent view. We descended to the village and crossed the bridge, which was laid on a stone arch, thrown across a ravine with a cataract foaming through it. At this point we were completely encircled by mountains, wild to sublimity, and reminding me of some of the finest parts of Switzerland. On the other side of the bridge we commenced ascending another mountain. The road was winding, and when very high up, the view of the village and bridge at the immense distance below was surpassingly fine. Descending a short distance, we passed a village of huts, situated on the ridge of the mountain, commanding on both sides a view of an extensive valley four or five thousand feet below us. Continuing on this magnificent ridge, we descended upon a table of rich land, and saw a gate opening into grounds which reminded me of park scenery in England, undulating, and ornamented with trees. Along the table was a line of huts, and if adorned instead of being deformed by the hand of man, this would be a region of poetic beauty.*[1]

We entered the outer gate, still a mile and a half from Guatemala [City]. Inside were miserable huts, with large fires before them, surrounded by groups of drunken Indians and vagabond soldiers, firing their muskets at random in the air. We picked up a ragged Indian, who undertook to conduct us, and under his guidance, entered the city at the foot of a long, straight street. My country-bred mule seemed astonished at the sight of so many houses, and would not cross the gutters, which were wide, and in the middle of the street. She broke her bridle and I was obliged to dismount and lead her. Augustin's poor beast was really past carrying him, and he followed on foot, whipping mine, the guide lending a hand before and behind. Perhaps no diplomatist ever made a more unpretending entry into a capitol.[2]

With its population pushing two million, Guatemala City was no longer a pocket city, and the shantytown Stephens described on its outskirts had grown with it. The hovels were not as miserable as the cardboard shacks in the dump in Managua, but the slum barrio was much more extensive. Because the climate at five thousand feet elevation is more vigorous, the denizens constructed their hovels out of the most ingenious materials—flattened cans, patchwork quilts of castoff plywood, complete samplers of mixed media. The purpose for our visit to the capital was to visit a friend of Raphael who decidedly lived on the other side of the tracks. It would not be too much to say that her neighborhood did not resemble the first world so much as a fancier knockoff of it.

Jean Wunderlich, a native Guatemalan despite the German surname, was a tall, elegant, graceful woman who spoke idiomatic American English. "Golly," she said once, and another time she pronounced her son-in-law a "bum" (jokingly). Many of her industrialist husband's plentiful funds were diverted to the basilica at Esquipulas. Her relationship had long since ceased to be that of a simple benefactress. She was now a special friend, she and the distaff members of her family even being allowed to stay at the monastery (something the crusty Father Charles harrumphed would never have happened in his day).

She said she remembered me from years before. Then she impressed me mightily by referring to two of the world's most prominent Mayanists, J. Eric Thompson and Michael Coe, as Eric and Michael (or perhaps Mike). Now, like all of us, she had grown older and she seemed somewhat faded and more subdued than the woman I remembered—no chatty references to Eric or Mike this time. She seemed preoccupied and her thoughts were of domestic things, although even there she showed a largeness of heart. "The prices are just going through the roof. I used to say that no one ever died of hunger in Guatemala, malnutrition yes, but not hunger. Now I can no longer say that. A pound of black beans sometimes costs as much as three quetzales." Then, out of the blue, she said, "I won't be driven out. I won't."

Raphael made an oblique reference to "the misfortunes" that had befallen her family. After a time, her misfortunes boiled to the surface. First, her son's apartment had been burglarized. Second, a bookkeeper had absconded with a month's cash receipts. All this was pretty small beer compared to number three. Her husband's company's warehouse—he imported and assembled Asian electronics—had been looted. The entire Christmas inventory of electronic products had been wiped out. Obviously an inside job, she pronounced. Yes, and somewhat more, given the logistical nightmare that hauling off all those radar ranges, TV sets, VCRs, and whatnot must have required, not to mention disposing of the plunder without police interference in a relatively small country. Finally, someone had been calling during the last week threatening her with death. "I will not be driven out. I won't." Raphael took all this with equanimity as though such things happened all the time in Guatemala.

To lighten this gloomy spell, she asked about our travel plans. I said that we had decided to visit Utatlán, a fairly out-of-the-way Maya ruin. Utatlán was an important site to Stephens because it seemed to link contemporary Indians with the ancients since the site was still occupied during the Spanish Conquest. Mrs. Wunderlich assured me I was in good hands traveling with Raphael in the guerrilla-prone western highlands. He was closely acquainted with the bishop of Quiché province, Julio Cabrera, and the military commander there as well. When we left, after twenty-five or thirty minutes (not even a footnote to a real Central American chat), neither Raphael nor Mrs. Wunderlich seemed to feel that this parting was anything but routine. I asked

Raphael if those death threats were serious, as though any death threat is not. He said he did not know.

Situated in the "Tierras templadas," or temperate regions, the climate of Guatemala [City] is that of perpetual spring, and the general aspect reminded me of the best class of Italian cities. It is laid out in blocks of from three to four hundred feet square, the streets parallel and crossing each other at right angles. The foundation of the city was laid in 1776, a year memorable in our own annals, and when our ancestors thought but little of the troubles of their neighbors. At that time the old capital, twenty-five miles distant, shattered and destroyed by earthquakes was abandoned by its inhabitants, and the present was built in a style commensurate with the dignity of a captain-generalship of Spain. I have seldom been more favorably impressed with the first appearance of any city, and the only thing that pained me in a two hours' stroll through the streets was the sight of Carrera's ragged and insolent-looking soldiers.[3]

Today, Antigua, the old town that was abandoned by the Spanish 220 years before, bears a better resemblance to Stephens's description than the modern city, which is crowded, noisy, smoggy, and which was made over in the early twentieth century in the likeness of Louis Napoleon's Paris. It was to Antigua, one of the world's minor bohemian meccas, like Sante Fe or Taos in the 1930s, that Raphael and I repaired that night. I had some errands to run. Raphael suggested we meet at the San Carlos Cafe, a greasy spoon on the main plaza that seemed to be everyone's favorite meeting place in Antigua.

The San Carlos was crowded. I found Raphael sitting at a table with three strangers, all Americans. He and two of them were slugging down Gallo beers. The fourth was a clean-cut fellow in a crisp madras sport shirt who was rather conspicuously sipping coffee. Somehow Raphael had stumbled on a nest of religious types. That was not unusual but the religious folks at the table were all Protestants, and that was unusual. The older beer-drinking couple, Paul and Laura, was in their late forties or early fifties. Paul was an Episcopalian pastor from suburban New Jersey on a missionary sabbatical in Guatemala. He was outspoken and agreeably bluff, and Laura seemed, even at first glance, extraordinarily sensitive and handsome in a rather roughhewn way. Her eyes were remarkably sympathetic. Because the restaurant's few tables had been taken when Rob the coffee drinker walked in, they offered to let him sit with them.

Perhaps it was after they discovered that Rob was a Bible-thumping Assembly of God fundamentalist from Lubbock that they decided they needed to dilute the table talk, and they added a Catholic padre to their ecclesiastical

Maria, Maya woman in the Guatemalan highlands. Photograph by Sally Duncan.

assembly. In any case, by the time I arrived it was obvious there was a bit of tension, if nothing more than a good faith effort not to step on anyone's toes.

Because religion was out, we fell to talking about the political situation in Guatemala. Rob said he had heard that President Serrano, a fundamentalist, was a good chief executive. I threw in that my airplane friend, Juan Salazar, backed Serrano because he thought he was good for business. (He also thought Pinochet had been good for business in Chile.) This had Rob beaming. Then somehow the conversation drifted into the much less safe discussion of political violence. Someone, perhaps Raphael, told about the ten to twenty bodies discovered daily in ditches ten years or so ago. Rob said he had heard that much of that violence was the local people's way of dealing with lawbreakers. Because the government thought its job was to take in taxes, not to give out services, naturally the same was true of the police. They felt no obligation to arrest lawbreakers.

Of the five sitting around the table, only one believed Rob's explanation in any significant way, and that was Rob himself. But, in the ecumenical spirit, Paul said that he had once been in a village while two men were being buried. He asked if the dead were disappeared ones. No, they were *ladrones*—thieves. The local constabulary would not deal with the problem so the populace had. The gents were shot dead.

Rob liked this explanation. It appealed to his right-wing views—fundamentalist missionaries got on better with the government than the representatives of the old church because of their authoritarian political convictions. Rob praised Ríos Montt, the evangelical president of the early 1980s, for restoring some sense of order to society. This made for a bit of shiftiness at the table, especially from Paul and Raphael. Raphael, I remembered from letters he sent me, initially had been pleased by Ríos Montt's takeover, mainly because he had strong religious views. But Ríos Montt had been a gigantic disappointment. Death-squad activity topped out during his regime, and Paul told Rob as much, saying that, "They claim Ríos Montt drained the sea to get at the fish." Rob took this as well as he could, but seeing an open table, he decided he needed to go claim it for his family, which he was expecting momentarily. After Rob left Paul said a bit wistfully, "I hope I wasn't too hard on him."

Raphael said, "He needed to hear what you said."

"I just hope he did hear it," Paul said. Then he told us how he got out of the business of being a parson in New Jersey and into Central America— through his association with the Sandinistas. He had been invited to attend the victory celebration for Daniel Ortega's reelection at the Nicaraguan Embassy in Washington in February 1990. The state banquet had been a potluck supper. Paul had brought a bucket of Kentucky Fried Chicken. Ortega lost, and the victory celebration had turned into something quite different. Paul said that some people cried, others laughed, and still others gave the Sandinista version of the rebel yell.

Laura cautioned us about keeping our voices down. The people sitting around us were families and did not look potentially very dangerous, but we were in public and she and Paul were in a very dangerous occupation—in Guatemala. She told us of a Chicana nun in Antigua who had been kidnapped from her convent and taken on a public bus to Guatemala City, then put in a police car and blindfolded and taken away and tortured by having cigarettes stuck in her back. She was saved some time later by a man who burst in and hollered at the torturers, "Are you crazy? This woman is an American!" She was released. She had engaged in very little political activity, but she had been warned several times that her presence was not welcomed in the country.[4] Another American nun disappeared and was presumably killed, and no one understood what she had done to incite her assassins. Laura said that she had been told that back in the bad times it happened often that people disappeared for no apparent reason—just the kind of discussion you want to fall into when the next day you are heading for the hottest spot in the country, Santa Cruz del Quiché and the nearby ruins of Utatlán.

The next morning I drove the Ranger out of Antigua and climbed past coffee fincas and a *lavandería,* a large concrete basin where women communally hand-washed their clothes. Raphael asked if I remembered this road and I told him I did not believe I had ever passed down it before. He assured me I had. The vegetation was too jungly-scrubby, I said. I remembered high open fields with blooming elderberry plants and Spanish moss hanging in the trees. Hardly had I said that when the road ascended, and we spotted an elderberry in bloom, and shortly after that an oak tree festooned with moss. We continued to climb and shortly we were back in the sort of countryside I recalled as characteristic of central-west Guatemala. Very high, say, six thousand or more feet, and open, surrounded by lofty mountains.

We stopped at an overview with a little market area for a view of Lake Atitlán, part of the Cakchíquel Maya empire in the days of the Conquest. The vendors were pushy, and Raphael made a terrible mistake in passing out chewing gum to the kids just as we were getting back in the truck. We were suddenly surrounded, and hands shot into every aperture—reminiscent of Nixon in Caracas or Sebastian's untimely end in *Suddenly Last Summer,* although instead of crying "pan" the kids were screaming, "Chicle! Chicle!" What a worthless thing to be pulled apart by a mob for.

The spur road from the Pan American Highway to Santa Cruz is dissected by *barrancas,* or gorges, through which the road drops a thousand or more feet before switching back and going up the far wall. The U.S. State Department had issued a travel advisory for auto travelers in the area, warning of roadblocks and robbery, apparently by leftist guerrillas. I could hardly think of a better place to put a roadblock than on one of those *ganchos,* or hairpin turns, that autos have to negotiate as they work their way up and down the canyon walls. If you could take your choice of guerrilla roadblock or one of those parrot-colored Guatemalan market buses streaming more exhaust than a fully loaded 707 and going about as fast and swinging wide around a turn, the guerrillas would probably be the better alternative. Driving from Esquipulas to here we had encountered two terrible smashups, the buses completely gutted, the paint smoking.

A large military reservation guarded the southern flank of Santa Cruz del Quiché. Young men in fatigues with submachine guns slouched inside wooden pillboxes looking equal parts wary and bored. The town—actually a huge village—gobbled us up like a Venus flytrap. Narrow streets ran on and on with no directional signs. Finally in desperation we asked two women— seeing no more eligible persons—and they sent us out of town toward the ruins down the worst road we had traveled in Guatemala.

In Stephens's day a bit more caution was advised. *Early in the morning, with a Mestizo armed with a long basket-hilted sword, who advised us to carry our weapons, as the people were not to be trusted, we set out for the ruins. At about a mile from the village we came to a range of elevations, extending to a great distance, and connected by a ditch which had evidently formed the line of fortifications for the ruined city. They consisted of the remains of stone buildings, probably towers, the stones well cut and laid together, and the mass of rubbish around abounded with flint arrow-heads. Within this line was an elevation, which grew more imposing as we approached, square with terraces, and having in the center a tower, in all one hundred and twenty feet high. We ascended by steps to three ranges of terraces, and on the top entered an area enclosed by stone walls, and covered with hard cement, in many places still perfect. Thence we ascended by stone steps to the top of the tower, the whole of which was formerly covered with stucco, and stood as a fortress at the entrance of the great city of Utatlán, the capital of the kingdom of the Quiché Indians.*[5]

Stephens was impressed by the heroic resistance the Maya mounted against the Spanish invaders. *In a short time intelligence was received that Alvarado had marched to besiege Xelahuh, the second largest city of Quiche. At that time it had within its walls eighty thousand men. Such was the fame of the Spaniards that Tecum Uman, the Quiche ruler, determined to go to its assistance. He left the capital, at the threshold of which we stood, borne in his litter on the shoulders of the principal men of his kingdom, and preceded by the music of flutes, cornets, and drums, and seventy thousand men, commanded by his general Ahzob, his lieutenant Ahzumanche, the grand shield-bearer Ahpocob, other officers of dignity with still harder names, and numerous attendants bearing parasols and fans of feathers for the comfort of the royal person. Tecum Uman marshaled under his banner on the plain of Tzaccapa two hundred and thirty thousand warriors, and fortified his camp with a wall of loose stones, enclosing within its circuit several mountains. After a series of desperate and bloody battles, the Spaniards* [and their Mexican Indian allies] *routed this immense army and entered the city of Xelahuh. The fugitives rallied outside, and made a last effort to surround and crush the Spaniards. Tecum Umam commanded in person, singled out Alvarado, attacked him three times hand to hand, and wounded his horse. But the last time Alvarado pierced him with a lance and killed him on the spot. The fury of the Indians increased to madness. In immense masses they rushed upon the Spaniards, and seizing the tails of the horses, endeavored by main force to bring horse and rider to the ground. But at a critical moment, the Spaniards attacked in close column, broke the solid masses of the Quiches, routed the whole army, and slaying an immense number became completely masters of the field.*

At a council of war called at Utatlan by Tecum Umam's successor, it was determined to send an embassy to Alvarado, with a valuable present of gold, suing for pardon, promising submission, and inviting the Spaniards to the capital. Alvarado entered this city with his army. Observing the strength of the place, that it was well walled and surrounded by a deep ravine, having but two approaches to it, the one by an ascent of twenty-five steps, and the other by a causeway, and both extremely narrow, that the streets were but of trifling breadth and the houses very lofty, that there were neither women nor children to be seen, and that the Indians seemed agitated, the soldiers began to suspect some deceit. The troops were collected, and without any appearance of alarm, marched in good order to the plain. The king, with pretended courtesy, accompanied them, and Alvarado, taking advantage of the opportunity, made him prisoner, and after trial and proof of treachery, hung him on the spot. A new ebullition of animosity and rage broke forth. A general attack was made upon the Spaniards, but Spanish bravery and discipline increased with danger, and after a dreadful havoc by the artillery and horses, the Indians abandoned a field covered with their dead and Utatlan with the whole kingdom of Quiche fell into the hands of Alvarado.

Utatlán was the most disappointing ruin we visited. It was completely unrestored, being just mounds on the lip of a barranca (large ravine) for protection from attack. The mysteries of those hummocks were as tightly kept as those of Florida shell mounds, which they greatly resembled. Indeed, the ruin showed substantially better in Stephens's day. He wrote, [the palace] *is of hard cement, which, though year after year washed by the floods of the rainy season, is hard and durable as stone. The inner walls were covered with plaster of a finer description. The whole interior had been ornamented with paintings. It gave a strange sensation to walk the floor of that roofless palace, and think of that king who left it at the head of seventy thousand men to repel the invaders of his empire. Corn was now growing among the ruins. The ground was used by an Indian family which claimed to be descended from the royal house.*

The most important part remaining is called El Sacrificatorio or the place of sacrifice. It is a quadrangular stone structure, sixty-six feet on each side at the base, and rising in a pyramidal form to the height, in its present condition, of thirty-three feet. On three sides there is a range of steps, each step seventeen inches high, which makes the range so steep that in descending some caution is necessary. The top once supported an altar for those sacrifices of human victims which struck even the Spaniards with horror.

Stephens then gives a textbook account of how the Quiché performed human sacrifice. *The barbarous ministers carried up the victim entirely naked and extended him upon the altar. Four priests held the legs and arms, and another kept his head firm with a wooden instrument made in the form of a coiled serpent. The head priest, with a knife made of flint, cut an aperture in the breast and tore out the heart, which yet palpitating, he offered to the sun, and then threw it at the feet of the idol. If the victim was a prisoner of war, as soon as he was sacrificed, the priests cut off the head to preserve the skull and threw the body down the steps, when it was taken up by the officer or soldier to whom the prisoner had belonged, and carried to his house to be dressed and served up as an entertainment for his friends.*

Notwithstanding the temple overshadowing him where grisly deeds had been routinely played out, Stephens wrote *as we stood on the ruined fortress, the great plain, consecrated by the last struggle of a brave people, lay before us grand and beautiful, its bloodstains all washed out. We considered this place important from the fact that its history is known and its date fixed. It was in its greatest splendor when Alvarado conquered it. The point to which we directed our attention was to discover some resemblance to the ruins of Copan and Quirigua. We did not find statues or carved figures or hieroglyphics, nor could we learn that any had ever been found there.* From this Stephens concluded provisionally that *we believed that Copan and Quirigua were cities of another race and of a much older date.* Later, however, Stephens would come to the view that these ruins were part of the same culture. The most difficult element to deal with when assessing the Maya is their temporal extension in history. The central government of Copán collapsed in A.D. 832. Alvarado, with his Cakchíquel Maya and Mexican Indian allies, attacked Utatlán in 1524 almost seven hundred years later, time enough for several empires to rise and fall. Indeed, as noted earlier, the ruling elite in the Quiché highlands probably came from the Gulf Coast around A.D. 1200 to conquer the local Maya.[6]

While contemplating the faded splendor of the ruins, Stephens saw *a stranger come stumbling along under a red silk umbrella. We recognized him as the cura and descended to meet him. He laughed to see us grope our way down. By degrees his laugh became infectious and when we met we all laughed together. Our friend's dress was as unclerical as his manner, a broad brimmed black glazed hat, an old black coat reaching to his heels, glossy from long use, and pantaloons to match, a striped roundabout, a waistcoat, flannel shirt, and under it a cotton one, perhaps washed when he last shaved, some weeks before.*

He laughed at our coming to see the ruins, and said that he laughed prodigiously himself when he first saw them. He was from Old Spain, had seen the battle of Trafalgar, looking on from the heights on shore, and laughed whenever he thought of it. The French fleet was blown sky high, and the Spanish went with it. Lord Nelson was killed—all for glory. He could not help laughing. He had left Spain to get rid of wars and revolutions. Here we all laughed, sailed with twenty Dominican friars, was fired upon and chased in Jamaica by a French cruiser. Here we laughed again, got an English convoy to Omoa, where he arrived at the breaking out of a revolution, had been all his life in the midst of revolutions, and it was now better than ever. Here we all laughed incontinently. His own laugh was so rich and expressive that it was perfectly irresistible. In fact, we were not disposed to resist, and in half an hour we were as intimate as if acquainted for years. The world was our butt, and we laughed at it outrageously.[7]

The afternoon was wearing on, but Raphael insisted we pay our respects to the bishop. The cathedral, like everything else in the country, was under renovation. Hammers pounded, skill saws buzzed, and huge quantities of wood were stacked in covered passageways. While Raphael went in search of the bishop, I sat in the car and noted that the bishop's place, though modest even by middle-class Guatemalan standards, was glaringly opulent, given the rude neighboring dwellings. Even from the outside I was certain his place did not much resemble Stephens's curate, who claimed that *he always locked his room to prevent the women throwing things into confusion. When we entered it was of a class that beggars description. The room contained a table, chairs, and two settees, but there was not a vacant place even on the table to sit down or lay a hat upon. Every spot was encumbered with articles, of which four bottles, a cruet of mustard and another of oil, bones, cups, plates, minerals and large stones, shells, pieces of pottery, skulls, bones, cheese, books and manuscripts formed a part.*[8]

While I was cogitating on the presumed difference between the old curate and the contemporary bishop, a young man in his thirties with expressive, olive-colored eyes appeared and insisted I come inside. He led me through a courtyard, a very pleasant though modest place with potted ferns and blooming orchids neatly displayed on stools. The floor was painted and clean, in marked contrast to the dingy houses of the overgrown village. As I had expected, it bore no trace of the untidiness of the curate's sanctuary of sanctuaries, with the exception of a pile of unanswered mail. He told us he had just gotten back from a synod of bishops in Rome and was shell-shocked from jet lag. He pointed to his mail and laughed. Indeed he laughed as frequently and as heartily as Stephens's *cura*. The coincidence was remarkable, or perhaps the only way to survive the clerical life in Quiché province was by greeting each absurdity with a horse laugh.

The bishop told us about the huge range of his diocese. On two sides it abutted Mexico. Many of his congregation were in exile in Belize or in the Mexican states of Chiapas and Campeche. Again a laugh. Then he told us about the activities of the army in the area. He said his department and the neighboring department of San Marcos were in an open state of war (as opposed to most of the rest of the country, excepting the Petén, which was considered more or less pacified). I asked about the guerrillas and he said at first they had been just a few Communists. But the army would go in and commit atrocities and get the people all stirred up against the government, and so support for the insurgents had broadened. I asked the cause of the trouble, and he said greed. Outsiders wanted the Indians' land for farming and mineral rights. What about the reestablishment of democracy? Would it make any difference? No, he did not think a civilian government could get the military under control.

After all of this, I was champing at the bit to stop and see Raphael's friend, Colonel Otzoy, the military commander. Raphael said that he had learned from the bishop that Otzoy had been promoted to general and transferred. Parenthetically, he added that the colonel's promotion was the exception that made the rule insofar as getting ahead in the Guatemalan Army. Otzoy was a full-blooded Indian and a good man. Not many of either were found in the higher echelons of that institution. On the way out of town, I noticed a poster on a building proclaiming a local mayor's fidelity to Ríos Montt, the last military dictator, who was declared ineligible to run for president again for having assumed the presidency illegally. It seemed strange that local candidates would try to tie themselves to the coattails of Ríos Montt, the man who "drained the sea to get at the fish." My "Republican" friend on the plane, although not for Ríos Montt, saw him as a starting point of stability, but that was understandable. He was from the city. The folks out here were mostly Indians. They were part of the drained sea. Yet, there was the sign, for whatever it might mean.

9 / Under and on Top of the Volcano

During Stephens's sojourn in Antigua he climbed Agua Volcano, the spectacular, cloud-snaggled, 12,356-foot-high cone that not only dominated the old city but had destroyed its first incarnation back in 1541. Then the crater wall collapsed and a water and mud tsunami slammed into the early capital. Going Stephens one better, I ascended the *volcán* not just once, but twice. For many of the weeks I summered in Antigua in 1992 that deed was put off because of the nasty reputation the mountain had for harboring bandits and guerrillas. I did not want to try it alone, and no one would go with me. Finally toward the end of my stay I rose early and made my way to the foot of the volcano.

The jump-off spot for the ascent is a village called Santa María. At an elevation of seven thousand feet, it was two thousand feet above Antigua. Stephens arrived there the day before he made the hike. *We did not get off till seven o'clock the next morning. The day was very unpromising, and the whole mountain was covered with clouds. The side of the volcano was cultivated. In half an hour the road became so steep and slippery that we dismounted and commenced the ascent on foot. The Indians went on before, carrying water and provisions, and each of us was equipped with a strong staff. At a quarter before eight we entered the middle region, which is covered with a broad belt of thick forest. The path was steep and muddy, and every three or four minutes we were obliged to stop and rest. At a quarter before nine we reached a clearing, in which stood a large wooden cross. This was the first resting place, and we sat down at the foot of the cross and lunched. A drizzling rain had commenced but in the hope of a change at half past*

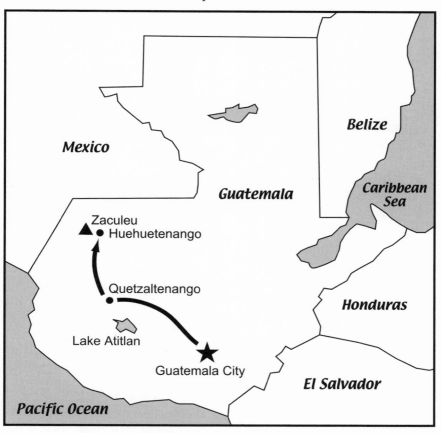

Guatemala City to Huehuetenango
The solid line shows Stephens's route from Guatemala City to Huehuetenango. The author's route is not shown because of its similarity.

nine we resumed our ascent. The path became steeper and muddier, the trees so thickly crowded together that the sun never found its way through them, and their branches and trunks covered with green excrescences. The path was made and kept open by Indians, who go up in the winter time to procure snow and ice for Guatemala City.

The labor of toiling up this muddy acclivity was excessive and very soon my young companion became fatigued and was unable to continue without help. The Indians were provided with ropes, one of which was tied around his waist and two Indians went before with the rope over the shoulders. At half past ten we were above the region of forest and came out upon the open side of the volcano. There were still scattering trees, long grass and a great variety of curious plants and flowers, furnishing materials for the botanist.

My companion, tired with the toil of ascending, even with the aid of the rope, at length mounted an Indian's shoulders. I was obliged to stop every two or three minutes, and my rests were about equal to the actual time of walking. The great difficulty was on account of the wet and mud, which in ascending, made us lose part of every step. It was so slippery that even with the staff and the assistance of branches of trees and bushes, it was difficult to keep from falling. About half an hour before reaching the top, and perhaps a thousand or fifteen hundred feet from it, the trees became scarce and seemed blasted by lightning or withered by cold. The clouds gathered thicker than before and I lost all hope of a clear day. At half an hour before twelve we reached the top and descended into the crater. A whirlwind of cloud and vapor was sweeping around it. We were in a perspiration. Our clothes were saturated with rain and mud. In a few minutes the cold penetrated our very bones. We could see nothing, and the shivering Indians begged me to return. While I was blowing my fingers, the vapors cleared away a little and gave me a view of the interior of the crater. It was a large oval basin, the area level and covered with grass. The sides were sloping about one hundred or one hundred and fifty feet high, and all around were masses of rock piled up in magnificent confusion, and rising to inaccessible peaks.[1]

It became quickly apparent that the dangers of this hike had been highly exaggerated. For many hundreds or even thousands of feet up the sides of the volcano, corn and potato patches and orchards of peaches, apples, and plums were visible. There were many people abroad. I might get robbed, but I could not imagine any serious crimes occurring with so many potential witnesses around.

I made the mistake of asking a local for directions. He indicated a path through the fields. This path was probably the spitting image of Stephens's Mico Mountains trail, a rut dug into the mountain, below the level of the surrounding fields. Almost the entire male line of a campesino family was ascending the mountain on the back of the family horse, the smallest hanging on to the pommel, the next smaller behind the saddle, Papa reaching back and encircling the little shaver with his arms on steeper grades. The eldest, about ten or twelve years old, walked ahead. Real family togetherness. They even had a portable radio blaring away, the Guatemalan version of salsa music. I passed a campesino digging a boulder out of the trail. Later on I saw that men were splitting boulders into granite tablets somewhat smaller than headstones.

The splitting was done by chisel and hammer. Other campesinos were picking corn into huge net bags slung over the backs of pack stock. Women were gathering flowers, a wild amaranthlike thing and the center stalk of a huge bromeliad, similar to the giant tillandsia of Florida only this one was much more showy, being of reddish color. It is called *pie de gallo,* meaning foot of the rooster, the spikes looking very much like a fighting cock's spurs.

When the path crossed the jeep trail, I took the road. The jeep road ran up to about ten thousand feet. About a thousand feet below its termination a Toyota pickup, with a ladino in the cab and two Indians in the wagon bed, passed me. Five hundred feet up, I found that the vehicle had slid off into the rut on the side of the trail. The Indians were tugging on ropes while the driver futilely tried to hie the truck farther up the mountain. I grabbed a rope and pretended to help in this effort, but after five minutes of no progress, I bid those folks adieu. The vegetation in this band was temperate zone stuff. Juniper trees grew here, as did trees that looked like basswood and oak. When I later showed some locals an oak leaf, they said "encina" (live oak). The basswood was unknown—they said it had no name. As for birds, I saw a couple of species of hummers; one buzzed me like a mockingbird giving a cat a pass, and the flowers seemed alive from the purring of the bees. Parrots screamed in the trees. Sunflowers grew on both sides of the trail. The rank herbal smell combined with that of the other wild plants made it smell like Kansas. There were grand views of the valley below every time the trail snaked back to a lookout point.

I hoped to make the top before the afternoon clouds obscured the view, but by 9:23 A.M. when I was at about eleven thousand feet, I could not see fifty feet in any direction. It had gotten pretty nippy and I lost the trail, which above the jeep road was simply a beaten path. Because the direction I needed to go was up, that's the way I headed, climbing up little washes by tree roots and whatever else was there to hang onto. A few gnarled pine trees grew up there, as did a low-growing plant that looked something like a strawberry. When I started pulling myself up the washes and mashing my nose into the dirt, I found that the plant smelled like a strawberry too. It started to rain, and I could barely see so I gave up and was heading back when I encountered the driver of the jeep that I had tried to help pull out of a ditch. He greeted me like an old friend and led me all the way to the top. We went right between the legs of the microwave-repeating tower that it was his job to service. He motioned me to follow him into the shed that housed the microwave equipment, old Motorola stuff with analog gauges. Anywhere else there would have been a hurricane fence around the installation with barbed wire on top, but here in a country in the midst of civil war—on a mountain supposedly infested with guerrillas—a major element in the communications system was completely unprotected. The rain—or rather, heavy drizzle—had not abated. I had on four layers of clothes and I was still cold. My hands were smarting.

The transmitter fellow told me to wait a few minutes, and shortly the two Indians started back down. They were not in very good shape, being smokers and having huffed and puffed behind the transmitter man and me on the way up. But very quickly they put me in the shade because they ran the steep parts of the trail. One had a machete stashed in his belt, without a sheath. The other's knife was in a net bag, tumpline around forehead, the tip of the blade pointing right at the base of his skull. I followed their lead and ran down the slippery, rocky trail, slipping and staggering with them. I arrived back in Antigua by 2:30. I repaired to the San Carlos restaurant for a bite of lunch. I brought my copy of Stephens along and was amused to learn he had gone down Agua pretty much the same way I had, only he had done it barefooted, since the heavy leather boots he normally wore were not suitable for running down mountains. The man sitting at the next table, a slight, sensitive, nervous, light-complexioned Latin American, surprised me by asking about Stephens in quite good English. We exchanged bona fides and I learned the man was a "Bolivian-American." He taught economics at Francisco Marroquín University, or he did until just recently, when he had resigned with the intention of returning to his home in Bolivia. He explained that he had come to Guatemala several years ago for a temporary appointment and before he knew it his life had gotten away from him. His wife and son traveled on a Bolivian passport, his daughter on a Guatemalan one, and he on an American. His father was American, he explained.

He asked me about Stephens's motivation for writing. Pure science? Not entirely, I told him. He wanted to make money and indeed had his own pavilion in New York, showing Catherwood's pictures and a few trinkets, until it burned. He said people still did not make money writing books. He himself had written two and had gotten nothing from either. The first was called *Latin American Inflation.* The North American edition had been published by Praeger.

Here was a man who could explain some of the things that had puzzled me. Why did a country that many claimed to be on the verge of economic collapse seem to be booming? That was easy. In periods of inflation investors put their money into material goods; therefore, building was a natural result.

Would inflation be the downfall of Guatemala? No. Seventy percent inflation was nothing. Guatemalans were spoiled by Latin American standards. Some countries had suffered that much in a month. All the building, in fact, was preparing an infrastructure for later growth. Guatemala would be the Chile of the 1990s, the leading Latin American economy.

Moving onto politics, I told him about seeing posters for strongman Ríos Montt. He dismissed Ríos Montt as a man whose time had come and gone. However, he pointed out that 60 percent of the vote in the last primary election had gone to rightist candidates, showing the strength of the right in Guatemala. In fairness he said he had to admit he too was a rightist, but he was certain that democracy and stability would take root in Guatemala. The army? He thought it wanted to stay out of politics and that it would, if given the toys it wanted to play with. Were there still piles of dead bodies discovered here and there? Not like ten years ago, but yes, dead people still showed up. Who killed them? He could not say. It was by no means apparent to him that the killings were the work of the army or the so-called death squads. It may well be the leftist guerrillas. Much was made of violence in Guatemala but he had never witnessed a single violent act. Nor had he ever been pulled over for a security check. I told him I had seen plenty of security checks.

The second time I climbed Agua Volcano was four and a half years later, in December 1996, when I returned to complete Stephens's journey. Peace talks that had been secretly going on even while I was climbing Agua the first time had finally succeeded. An agreement bringing peace to Guatemala would be signed in just a matter of days, on Christmas. My itinerary this time around had first taken me to the Petén, and, amazingly, the army units there did seem confined to their barracks. The bus I was on rolled through the former checkpoints without even slowing, and the watchtowers went unmanned.

The morning after I climbed, or rather hiked, the volcano the second time, I was typing up my notes in the courtyard of the *posada* when Roxana, the innkeeper, asked how the ascent went. I told her there was lots of frost on the mountain, and what was really strange was that the broadleaf vegetation all around seemed completely unharmed.

The conversation veered to Roxana and, after a while, to politics. Most Guatemalans refused to discuss politics. People who let their opinions be known too often ended up as a corpse in a ditch. Roxana, who was in her early thirties, had studied—she told me—hotel and restaurant management at Ohio University, living with an American family and learning, she said, how Americans lived and what they wanted, which was, namely, cleanliness. After she graduated, she spent a year in Miami and then went to New York, where she met a Greek shipping magnate, whom she married. Her Aristotle Onassis carried her off to Greece, but the relationship did not prosper.

Back home in Antigua, Roxana put all that hotel training and experience to work by overseeing the conversion of her family's courtyard-style home, where she had been born, into the Posada Doña María. The original walls were gutted and modern hotel rooms, each with its own bath, were constructed, leaving a very small courtyard. How was business I asked? Good enough, she said. The tourists were coming back. I told her the first time I had visited the town, in the late 1970s, many more tourists were around than when I had returned in 1990. And that there had been many more in 1990 than in 1992, and that now there seemed to be fewer still.

The worst times had been in the 1980s, she said, but it took the tourists a while to catch on and even longer to come back. Once when walking to school, back in the 80s, she had seen four bodies laid out in the street, victims of the army's campaign of intimidation. Other than that, Roxana's complaints were pretty typical of a businessperson anywhere, the high cost of utilities, taxes, and wages (the minimum wage, frequently not observed, $3 a day). I pointed out that money paid out for those things was made back during the course of business. Everything, she agreed grudgingly, except the taxes. The government just took the money and you got nothing for it, the people at the top simply helping themselves to what was in the cookie jar.

Roxana was not afraid of speaking her mind to me, and she also spoke it to the authorities. A neighborhood building belonging to the municipal government was being used as a clubhouse by a rowdy element. Roxana and a woman friend asked the municipal government to revoke the lease. A group of soldiers stopped by and told her bluntly to knock off efforts at civic improvement. Roxana said her friend was scared, fearing that nothing had changed, that it was just like the old days, when what the soldiers said went. Still, she and the friend pressed on, and finally they were assured the clubhouse would be closed.

After lunch I walked across town to see an old friend, to the neighborhood I had stayed in almost five years earlier. The major plaza lay about halfway between, and even Stephens was unable to render its great charm, saying, *The print opposite will give an idea, which I cannot, of the beauty of this scene. The great volcanoes of Agua and Fuego look down upon it. In the center is a noble stone fountain, and the buildings which face it, especially the palace of the captain general, displaying on its front the armorial bearings granted by the Emperor Charles the Fifth* and [down the way] *the ruined cathedral, three hundred feet long, one hundred twenty broad, nearly seventy high and lighted by fifty windows, show at this day that La Antigua was once one of the finest cities of the New World.*[2]

Antigua is loaded with ruined colossuses, as befits what today is still one of the world's more romantic spots. Some of the devastated edifices had amenities that many of the city's current residents lack, such as flush toilets in cells of certain of the convents (provided by diverting a mountain freshet to run through the building's cellar). The gutters of its cobbled streets still run down the middle as Stephens described. The sidewalks are alive with golden-complexioned, aquiline-nosed, extremely short Maya Indians in traditional garb peddling trinkets or vegetables—or washing their clothes, as they were that day at the lavandería at the minor plaza a block or so beyond the main square. *With good government and laws, and one's friends around, I never saw a more beautiful spot in which man could desire to pass his allotted time on earth* was Stephens's assessment.[3]

A few blocks beyond the minor plaza, I came to the "old neighborhood." Even though it was mid-afternoon, Julio himself answered the door. For a moment he stood looking at me with a blank expression. Although less than five years had passed since I had seen him, he had aged ten years. He was heavier now and balder, with worry lines about his eyes. He appeared to be in his late forties, or perhaps early fifties, rather than the forty-three I knew him to be. Finally, his eyes sparked with recognition but before his face lit up, the fire went out. "Estick," he said, with as much enthusiasm as a man bowed down with some leaden preoccupation could.

He gave me an abrazo, and brought me into the compound. The most important structure in the Spanish courtyard house is the wall. It runs completely around the property line and functions as one of the interior walls for the rooms that are built along its perimeter. Sometimes the rooms are elegant, with overhanging roofs and fronting verandas, and sometimes they are rudimentary, as was the case with Julio's house. Four rooms ran along the wall, the last and smallest being the kitchen. His daughter, Alejandrina, hearing us, came out of one of the rooms. She was now a spectacled, very sweet eleven year old. She came right to me and put her arms around me. "Estick," she said. I was not sure whether the two younger boys remembered "Stick," but I'm pretty sure the fifteen-year-old son, Ariel, did. Ariel was in his room lying on the bed on a bare mattress, a black-and-white TV going. Even with Julio's urging he refused to get up and acknowledge me, rolling over on his side instead, which seemed to me a pretty normal response for a teenager and which I took as a sign of recognition.

Julio led me into the tiny kitchen where once he had me to dinner in what were obviously better times. Back then we had black beans and some sort of corn meal mush in which was embedded one or two small, fatty pieces of meat. All this had been prepared by Milagro, his attractive twenty-five-year-old wife, over a modest cooking fire in the corner. Now there was no fire in the hearth. The kitchen seemed very cold.

We had become close friends four and a half years before because Julio wanted to learn English. "My name is Jules Morales, and I study English at five o'clock sharp every day," is how he introduced himself after an unsolicited knock on the door. Julio did not think the streets in the United States were paved with gold; he knew it for a fact, because he had once illegally emigrated. He had done the underground Cook's tour of the country, but was subsequently nabbed by the INS in Boston and repatriated gratis. His favorite presidential candidate was Ross Perot because he thought (mistakenly, of course) that Perot, unlike the candidates of the established parties, would throw the border open to immigrants.

The only complaint Julio had with the United States was our pesky immigration laws. Sometimes he would get quite feisty, telling me it was not fair that any American could come to Guatemala, but he could not travel just as freely to the States. Julio had made $20 a week driving a light truck for the local parish. His wife brought another $10 home as a seamstress. But they had a fifty-gallon drum full of corn in the pantry—he showed it to me with great pride—and so they had as much as most of their countrymen and, what with his lovely family and their life together, a lot more than many Americans.

Now in that cold kitchen, as Julio took the shoebox down and passed photos of his family and me around, I asked, "Why aren't you working?"

He intimated that he had lost his job.

"Where's Milagro?" I asked.

"In Texas," he said.

He showed me a picture of Milagro in Houston with a refrigerator in the background, presumably at the house where she worked as a housekeeper. Like Julio, she was heftier, but in her case she was sassy looking, if a bit sly, it seemed. Or perhaps my impression was colored by the photo of her with a heaping plate of food and a sleazy-looking fellow with his arm around her.

Julio said the man was her brother. There was another photo of her seated around a table with other latinos, all eating.

In the dirt courtyard, as I was leaving, Julio said, "When you get back to the States, you send me a check."

I had known him quite closely for several months and sometimes he had been a pest about coming to the States, but he had never begged. We were standing by a nearly dead fruit tree. He pointed to the deadwood on the tree attacked by lichens. He seemed to see something symbolic there, which I affected to overlook.

10 / A Market Bus to Wayway

Once back in Guatemala City from his southern sojourn, Stephens posted a note to the authorities in Washington, "After diligent search, no government found." Immediately he *commenced making arrangements for* [his] *journey to Palenque. There was no one in the city who had ever made the journey. The archbishop, on his exit from Guatemala eight years before, had fled by that road, and since his time it had not been traveled by any resident of Guatemala. The whole mass of the Indian population of Los Altos was in a state of excitement, and there were whispers of a general rising and massacre of the whites. General Prem and his wife, while traveling toward Mexico, had been attacked by a band of assassins. He himself was left on the ground for dead, and his wife murdered, her fingers cut off and the rings torn from them. Every friend in Guatemala urged us not to undertake the journey. We felt it was a most inauspicious moment, and almost shrunk, but we had set out with the purpose of going to Palenque and could not return without seeing it.*[1]

Hope for safe passage lay in only one person, the twenty-three-year-old José Rafael Carrera. A full-blooded Indian (according to Stephens; others claimed he was a mestizo) and former pig driver, Carrera began his military career *with thirteen men armed with muskets that they were obliged to fire with cigars.* Ultimately he became the archetype for banana republic strongmen, remaining head of state, de facto or otherwise, for more than thirty years. In Stephens's day he was still a bit astonished to find himself at the head of the rabble that rose up against the reforms of the Liberal Party, being called by his followers *el rey de los Indios,* or The King of the Indians. At the moment he had just returned from Quezaltenango where he had summarily executed eighteen leading functionaries on the suspicion of trafficking with his political enemies. Although the youth's hands were still red with blood, and he was preceded by a fearful rumor that he intended to bring out two or three hundred prisoners and shoot them, Stephens was compelled to call on him for a safe conduct pass through the highlands.

When I entered he had [a gold chain] *in his hands which had formed part of the contents of those trunks of my friend, the captain* [Stephens's companion on the trip back from the south], *and which often adorned his neck. I feared* [Carrera] *had forgotten me, but he recognized me in a moment. He had an indefinite idea that I was a very great man in my own country, but he had a very indefinite idea as to where my country was.* He agreed to personally make out a pass for Stephens, which was more than Stephens expected. *In a few minutes he brought back the passport signed with his own hand, the ink still wet. It had taken him longer than it would have done to cut off a head, and he seemed more proud of it.*[2]

The side road from Antigua joins the Pan American Highway at Chimaltenango, a thriving crossroads community almost as full of surging humanity as it was of diesel exhaust. An old school bus painted in outrageously bold colors, the roof piled high with baggage of all sort, screeched to a halt, the conductor croaking, "Wayway?"

"Huehuetenango?" I asked.

He jerked his thumb and told me to get aboard. The driver, with a thinning widow's peak and a cigarette in his mouth, motioned at me impatiently, so Sally Duncan—my companion on this trip—and I pushed our way into the interior, and someone barked at us to sit. Every seat on the bus was occupied by at least two full-grown adults, who though not particularly tall were in many cases quite broad. Toward the back seven persons were seated, three on each seat and one squatting in the aisle, this in a vehicle that had started off hauling elementary school children somewhere in the icy North. We were pushed back toward the area where the aisle was clogged with people and Sally sat, one cheek supported by thin air. Looking out the window, I saw the porter struggling toward the bus with Sally's suitcase. My bags were still on the ground.

Wondering how I could have been so foolish as to board before my bags had been taken care of, I heaved bodies out of way and ran around to the back of the bus to find the conductor hoisting my bags aloft. I told them the cloth duffel bag needed protection from the elements. The porter who rode on top of the bus amid his freight, nodded and said he would wrap it in *plástico*. The conductor then hustled me aboard, and the driver, who had been gunning the engine, let out the clutch and we were under way. From the first squeal of the brakes until the tired old vehicle began limping up the highway, not more than sixty seconds had elapsed.

Shortly we were in the fabulous scenery of the central highlands. At every turn there was a different vista—of cultivated fields going right up to the top of mountains, other times of pine trees up a hilly slope, sometimes a shot of a valley entirely under cultivation. Seeing those almost-vertical plots worked on the mountain peaks reminded me of the old joke—except it was actually a news report—of a man falling out of his cornfield to his death. Obviously possible here. On the slopes was a patchwork quilt of small plots of cabbage, corn, wheat, and peas. Potatoes were being harvested. Calla lilies grew in the margins of the fields, and poinsettia plants—taking up valuable space—were allowed to grow into huge red bushes to help celebrate the Christmas season. Towering above were high mountains. This was *los altos, where the whole mass of the Indian population was in a state of excitement, and there were whispers of a general rising and massacre of the whites.*[3] A century and a half later, the situation had reverted to the more normal one of the times since the Conquest, and it was the whites who were massacring the Indians, although of course that was supposed to be at an end now with the signing of the peace accord about to occur.

Rigoberta Menchú is a Quiché Maya who grew up in a village in the central highlands. In her as-told-to autobiography, she documents the oppression of the Indians by the system in general, and the military in particular.[4] Some of her earliest memories were of being herded like cattle into the back of a truck, along with her family and many of her neighbors, and being hauled to a coffee, cotton, or sugar plantation at lower elevations. The wages for which she and her family worked were literally next to nothing, and frequently were nothing at all, as the overseer would assess damages for real or imagined infractions. For instance, when her baby brother died, her mother was charged money to bury the boy and was docked for missing work. In childhood, Rigoberta learned the hard verities of Indian life. She lost a second brother and a playmate. The latter was sprayed by a crop duster while she was working in the fields. The plantation owner took no responsibility for the young girl's death.

Menchú shows the self-sustaining communal spirit of a Quiché village. Her own particular highland village was a fairly recent settlement. The Indians had taken wilderness and made pastures for their animals and had broken turf for their corn *milpas*. Once the land was improved, greedy plantation owners began all kinds of government-backed maneuvers to take over the land, many of which were reminiscent of the tricks played by nineteenth-century Americans to gain control of Indian territories. For instance, Menchú's father, as the village headman, was asked to sign a document that would ensure the community's independence. Instead, the paper passed ownership to others. Later, everyone in the village—man, woman, and child—was made to sign (mark or fingerprint) a document, after which the government workers went peacefully off and left the village to itself. Two years later, however, the government was back, claiming that the agreement they had signed stipulated the villagers would leave in twenty-four months. Since no one in the village spoke or read Spanish, no one knew what they had agreed to.

These and other stratagems (such as the on-again off-again jailing of the father) radicalized the entire family. The father, Vicente, was one of those who stormed the Spanish Embassy in 1980—and thus was one of those who perished (along with all the embassy personnel) in the fiery reclamation of the compound by the military. The mother and Rigoberta both went off to work elsewhere. Only the sixteen-year-old brother stayed in the village. True to the family's leadership role, he functioned as the town's secretary, despite not being able to write. However, his inflammatory rhetoric attracted the attention of the military. He was kidnapped and tortured. His fingernails were pulled out, part of his tongue was cut off, and his pate was scalped. Then all the local Indians were ordered to assemble. The brother and many other torture victims were put on display. An army officer harangued the crowd about the evils of Communism, the brother and the others all being proclaimed as such. Then the suspects were doused with gasoline and set ablaze. Rather than pacifying the Indians, these tactics—according to Menchú—inflamed their sense of injustice.

Menchú's narrative (which was actually authored by a woman with the suspiciously left-wing name of Debray, in reality the ex-wife of the famous French Communist thinker Regis Debray, later a special and then somewhat right-wing advisor to President Mitterrand) has been criticized both for a left-wing political bias and for factual imprecision. For instance, it is claimed Menchú could not possibly have been an eyewitness at her brother's execution.[5] Notwithstanding all that, Menchú was awarded the Nobel Peace Prize in 1992, and whether absolutely faithful as a chronicle of events in any simplistic, empirical way, the narrative is, unhappily, a chillingly accurate portrayal of the life of the highland Maya during the 1980s in particular, and since the Conquest in general.

The bus pulled over for what I at first thought was an ordinary bus stop, but it turned out to be a traffic snarl—road work ahead. Vendors, understanding the problem, were lying in wait, and suddenly they swarmed aboard, screaming, "chorizos calientes," "agua fría," "papas fritas," or, in other words, hot sausages, cold water (soda), and french fries, the latter wrapped in paper, dusted with salt, presqueezed with ketchup, and stuck with a toothpick for convenience in eating. The vendors—youths and matrons or an occasional maiden—squeezed through the aisles—each row of which seated seven or more, barking at the top of their lungs.

The passengers swilling sodas or small cans of juice or dispatching a tamale and using the cornshuck wrapper for a napkin represented the full range of Guatemalan society. Men in city clothes—shirt, slacks, windbreaker jacket— women in huipiles and peasant men dressed any which way. One lady sported a necklace of three live chickens. Many had on used American sporting clothes—Chicago Bulls' sweat clothes, especially caps, seemingly the most favored. Although many of the men wore caps, some still wore the traditional broad-brimmed hat with what we would call a Western cut, all this giving a very colorful look to the passenger compartment. The bus's appearance was enhanced by the tinsel shrine to the Virgin above the driver's head. Likewise, the windshield was adorned with rainbow-colored curtains and plastic flowers and the motto "Amor de Dios" in gold letters.

A half-hour wait and then the signal came that the road was open. It was like hearing the opening shot of a grand prix race. Those lounging on the shoulders, some quite far away, dashed to their vehicles, and as soon as the drivers were seated their conveyances roared off. No check was made of passengers on our bus by anyone except me. Surprisingly enough, I counted seven or more heads per row. The highway too looked like a grand prix opening as cars, being smaller and more maneuverable, made jackrabbit jumps into the oncoming lane, but shortly the buses were over there too, passing everything in sight. A portable EPA monitoring station—had it been on the roadside— would have melted down from the billowing cloud of blue exhaust suddenly loosed into the atmosphere.

The driver was absolutely relentless. There was only one position for his foot, mashed down tight on a pedal. Whether gas or brake was immaterial. The important thing was that the vehicle be put to the existential test every moment it was rolling. (Any self-respecting school bus, if it had an inkling of what was in store for it south of the Río Grande, would take a suicide plunge into the river.) When a passenger was spotted on the shoulder, the driver sped up to make sure another bus did not beat him to the fare, then stomped on the brake pedal while the conductor leaped from the vehicle, accosting all standing around while croaking, "Wayway," sounding like a Budweiser amphibian, in the hope of generating additional customers. While the passengers shuffled aboard the conductor hustled the passenger's freight, which could entail most of a household, barnyard, or merchant's inventory, into the hands of the porter atop. Once, the driver himself, cigarette smoking away, had to debus to help shove aloft a net bag of pottery, which stood, I swear, four feet high and must have weighed in the hundreds of pounds. Then a bang on the roof and the bus would be rolling again, after a motionless interlude of only seconds. Frequently the conductor would enter the moving bus through a rear hatch and return to the front, by slipping between aisle-seated passengers like a knife through water. Sometimes, he would just hang on to the rear ladder until the next stop. One time we heard him, like a squirrel on the roof, coming forward along the top of the vehicle, while the bus was barreling down a mountain slope. He descended the ladder on the side of the bus. The driver without taking his eye off the road or foot off the accelerator flicked the lever that opened the accordion door. The conductor popped into the bus and immediately began croaking "Wayway" at potential passengers on the wayside.

Almost all of the guidebooks mention the gigantic pair of military boots and helmet that is used as the gatehouse for the military base just outside Sololá. It looked like a huge piggy bank with the eye slots being places where the coins should go. Traffic flowed by—no checkpoint here now—the soldiers in their fatigue-green uniforms marching around the compound looking as harmless as toy soldiers. Enterprising vendors were hawking predipped ice cream cones for half a quetzal (eight cents). The man on the bench seat in front of us, a grizzled gent in the rough togs of an Indian farmer, bought a cone without asking whether his wife or two kids, seated nearby, wanted one. He ate half and gave the rest to his five-year-old son who seemed to have no idea the cone would come his way. The wife, in huipil, took all this in with a slight flicker of gratitude at her son's receiving the cone, but otherwise showing no indication of considering that perhaps she could have been in line for a lick or two.

Of Quetzaltenango, Stephens says *there was no place we had visited except ruined cities, so unique and interesting and which deserved to be so thoroughly explored.*[6] The city is very high, almost seven thousand feet, with a no-fooling

temperate-zone climate—the countryside having a blighted, wintry look—
and some big buildings and the sort of eccentric pretensions, as Stephens
notes, that make provincial cities interesting. Stephens recounts a truly horri-
fying incident here when a mob, egged on by friars, tore a Liberal politician
limb for limb in the city's cathedral where the man had sought refuge—the
same cathedral to which Stephens later devoted pages while describing a
Catholic rite. But very little of note actually happened to Stephens here except
his visit to a hot spring where Indian men and women bathed together.[7] We
rolled past the spur road that runs into the city, being pleased to note that a
military checkpoint at this excellent location was conspicuous by its absence.

It was apparent we were approaching Huehuetenango, at a mere five thousand feet, when Day-Glo–colored sprays of tropical bougainvillea began to
appear. At the market next door to the bus terminal, pigs and cattle were
staked out for sale. Add the market folks to the bus folks, and there were
hundreds congested in the area. We were lucky to grab a cab to a hotel. The
taxi driver said the market goods would shortly end up on Christmas tables.
The ruins we wanted to see were a dusty fifty-minute walk away.

The site of the ancient city, Stephens says of the ruins of Zaculeu, *was chosen
for its security against enemies. It was surrounded by a ravine, and the general
character of the ruins is the same as at [Utatlán]. The principal remains are of
two pyramidal structures. They are not of cut stone as at Copan, but of rough
pieces cemented with stucco and painted. At the foot of the structure was a vault,
faced with cut stone, in which were found a collection of bones and a terra cotta
vase. The owner of the ground, a Mestizo, had bought the land from the Indians.
For some time after his purchase, he was annoyed by their periodical visits to
celebrate some of their ancient rites on the top of this structure. This annoyance
continued until he whipped two or three of the principal men and drove them
away.*[8]

Stephens concluded a deal with this sensitive chap that allowed him to
excavate the site, keeping only *the skulls, vases and other curiosities* and giving
the owner all the treasure. This work was rewarded with a great many bone
fragments and several now priceless vases and ornamental pots, all of which
were recovered in pieces or broken in the process of extracting them. Stephens
intimated a belief that Zaculeu was contemporary with Utatlán, and in this
belief he was correct.[9] Indeed, Zaculeu, though occupied by the Mam Maya,
appears to have been a vassal state to Utatlán's Quiché Maya, and it fell to the
same Spanish juggernaut. The Mam still inhabit the highlands about Zaculeu.
The work of the Conquest has not yet been completely effected as the recent

civil war, the last iteration of which was about to be officially ended in a couple of days by the stroke of pens at a peace table in Mexico City, was merely the most recent attempt to break the Maya to the invaders' will. In recent years, with the deciphering of the Maya hieroglyphic code, scholars were dumbfounded to learn that the Mam, like the other extant Maya, still worship the same gods and harbor the same belief systems (including the keeping of a rude version of the old calendar system) as the inhabitants of the great Classic sites of Copán, Tikal, and Palenque.

Zaculeu was cut down by the Spanish eight hundred years after those magnificent sites were in their glory. By the Conquest, many of the finer points of the Maya culture had been lost. No longer were monuments erected celebrating honored dates, and writing had become a lost art. Still, the longitude of Maya cultural history, reaching as it did into the huts of many of the folks coming to view the ruins with us that sunny afternoon, boggles the mind.

We took the first-class bus from Huehuetenango to the Mexican border. The journey reminded me a lot of Wright Morris's *Field of Vision*. In that novel, a family of Nebraskans goes to Mexico to warm up one winter and learn among other things that the most expensive in Mexico is not always the best. I had the day before thoughtfully, I believed, procured two tickets on the first-class coach, known as the Pullman, to the Mexican border. Just as brilliantly I had made arrangements with a cab driver to be at the hotel at the appointed time to carry us to the terminal. There was some mix-up and the cabbie was waiting impatiently as Sally and I returned from breakfast. He thought the Pullman departed at 10 A.M. I showed him the tickets with 10:30 plainly printed on them. Nevertheless, the taximan terrified the local populace as he tore through the streets at panic speeds to the station. The cabbie was correct. Departure time was officially scheduled for 10:00 on the dot—despite what was printed on the tickets. But that point was immaterial as the Pullman had not yet arrived from Guatemala City. Ten-thirty came and went. In the meantime a couple of market buses departed for the border.

A disreputable-looking fellow who seemed to function as a freelance porter suggested we take the 11:15 market bus. This fellow had a round, dark, somewhat unpleasant face made even more unattractive by a skin disease. He had befriended me the day before, and I had rewarded him with a handsome tip, a dollar and a half, as I remember it. He told me he was unmarried and had no children, and I supposed he was some sort of quasi outcast.

My strange friend had just hefted our bags to lug over to the market bus, when the Pullman turned into the lot. He greeted it with a shout, and then he shouted again at some fellow. Our bags were dropped in the dirt and he took off running. In the meantime, our luggage was quickly stowed in the Greyhound-style coach's bay and the Pullman, to make up for its late arrival, gave a diesel snort and was off. The last I saw of my friend the porter, his fingers were around the throat of a man, and they were both rolling in the dust.

Shortly after reentering the Pan American Highway, the bus displayed the behavior that made it late. The driver dawdled, sometimes parking and getting off for a snack, and once disappearing indoors with a painted-face hussy for what could have been a romp in the hay. A Guatemalan market bus, which must be among the world's most efficient means of transportation, would have been infinitely faster, although a bit less comfortable. On the way from Quetzaltenango, Sally had counted more than nine people jammed in some rows of our market bus.

The countryside outside of Huehue was dry scrub. The slopes were quite arid with a lot of oaks and mesquite and, in other spots, pines. We saw plenty of oranges, the fruit in full color on the trees, something you do not often see this far south where the oranges are usually green when they are harvested. Lots of bananas too. The houses here were still constructed of adobe, sometimes plastered and whitewashed and sometimes just the brown earth color. Sometimes the side facing the road got whitewashed while the side believed unviewable was left in its natural state.

It was not long before we were seriously heading down the mountain. I saw a mango tree, too sensitive to cold to fruit at the higher elevations, and then after a time mangoes became common. Their flower panicles were budding, looking like Christmas candles. More importantly, here and there, the sides of the hills were worked and planted to bananas, and under the bananas were small coffee plants. Larger bushes were loaded down with cheery red fruit—like Christmas ornaments—and even better than ornaments were the berries spread to dry on tarps in the yards. The houses looked more prosperous, and, judging by the small plots, it seemed likely these folks actually owned the coffee they raised and picked.

Running through the valley was a rapids-filled stream, clear and rather broad, and on all sides were mountains. Trees grew all the way down the mountain, but in spots the slopes were partially cleared, with the top in pasture and the lower reaches in coffee and bananas. At crossroads, there were mining and other activities. Always men were waiting around for nothing, it seemed, as the women sold a few *antojitos* (snacks), *churrascos* (char-broiled beef), peanuts, and packaged chips. As the bus continued to descend, the stream broadened and deepened, still quite clear and green. It was a beautiful country, smitten with poverty.

Stephens's freedom from border checkpoints allowed him to take a more direct route to his first stop in Mexico, the town of Comitán, over the highest country in Guatemala, much of it over ten thousand feet in altitude. Once he camped in an open-sided hut where water froze a quarter of an inch thick, and he was told that frost formed every night of the year when the sky was clear. *The descent was by a broad passage with perpendicular mountain walls, rising in rugged and terrific peaks, higher and higher as we descended. A stream of water was dashing down over rocks and stones, hurrying on to the Atlantic. We crossed the stream itself perhaps fifty times on bridges wild and rude as the stream and the mountains between which it rolled. As we descended the temperature became milder. On the right, far below us, was a magnificent table cultivated with corn, and bounded by the side of the great sierra and in the suburbs of the village were apple and peach trees covered with blossoms and young fruit. We had again reached the* tierra templada, *and in Europe or North America the beauty of this miserable unknown village would be a theme for poetry. A couple of days later we reached the Río Lagertero, the boundary line between Guatemala and Mexico, a scene of wild and surpassing beauty, with banks shaded by some of the noblest trees of the tropical forests, water as clear as crystal and fish a foot long playing in it as gently as if there were no fishhooks.*[10]

La Mesilla, on the Guatemalan side of the border, stood in stark contrast to Stephens's idyllic description. It was a large shanty village of thousands, clinging to the shoulders of the road. Peddlers were hawking petty things at petty rates. The trash underfoot, the confusion of vehicles parked every which way, and the fumes—along with the heat—was dispiriting. The immigration facility and the restaurant on the Mexican side gave an impression of order and relative cleanliness. The people also looked cleaner and healthier.

If the tidiness and godliness of the Mexican side far surpassed that of the Guatemalan, in one very important respect the Guatemalans nowadays had their house in better order. A report called "Guatemala: Never Again," issued by the Interdiocesan Project to Recover the Historic Memory, registered the testimony of 55,000 people in the period from 1960 to 1996. The report noted that four-fifths of the violence occurred in the early 1980s, 75 percent of it against Maya Indians. The army, either directly or through death squads, was held responsible for 79.2 percent of the pillage and the guerrillas were responsible for 9.3 percent. Altogether the war accounted for 150,000 dead, 50,000 disappeared, 200,000 orphaned and 40,000 widowed.[11] Going by the evidence of our sojourn through Guatemala and the ability of a report such as this to be developed, Guatemala seemed to be returning to a sort of uneasy peace, even if the cleric responsible for the report, Bishop Juan Gerardi, was assassinated by a paramilitary hit squad on its issuance.

Once in Mexico, we boarded a *colectivo,* a Volkswagen minibus jitney, which would depart for Comitán as soon as all the seats were occupied. Finally, a family of Guatemalans boarded and we were off, but not for long. Dead ahead loomed—oh no—a military checkpoint. *Federales* checked the papers of all foreigners in the vehicle. Our passports were given a perfunctory look, but the Guatemalan family in back caused some delay. Then we were conducted to a line of waiting vehicles while soldiers headquartered in a reinforced bunker—in flack jackets and helmets—went carefully through a pickup two vehicles ahead. Our driver tooted, hoping to shortcut the process, but he was made to wait. After a while the truck driver was asked to open the cargo area for a cursory inspection of his freight. The professionalism and courtesy of the Mexican soldiers was notable, compared to the way these inspections were carried on in the countries to the south. Nevertheless, submitting to a military search was galling, especially in Mexico, a country that thought of itself—with a great deal of justification—as light years more advanced than its Central American neighbors. I needed to learn to get used to military searches because this was just the first of many to come.

11 / Chiapas

How did it happen that in December 1996, years after the collapse of the Soviet Union, armed rebellion was still occurring in the mountains of southern Mexico? The first flush of this outburst occurred on New Year's Day 1994, four years after the demise of Nicaragua's Sandinista regime, and during a period when the region's longtime exporter of revolution, Cuba, had switched from automobiles to pedal-power because it could not afford to import gasoline. Had the Zapatista rebellion broken out at any time prior to 1990, the most Pollyannaish of critics could have been forgiven for suspecting those formidable stockpiles of supplies had been smuggled in from the Eastern Bloc. As it was, not even the most incorrigible of hard-line cynics could make that claim.

So how to account for the Zapatistas? Could it possibly be that many of the rebellions in Central America and elsewhere since 1917 have been bankrolled by the local peasants donating the equivalent of their egg money to the revolution? Oddly, the root cause of the Zapatista uprising can be found to rest squarely on the shoulders of Pope John XXIII. As far as that goes, much of the revolutionary sentiment in Latin America in the past few decades can also be traced back to him, or rather to the "liberation theology" movement he inspired, even if in actual practice the more successful of these movements ended up with a blatantly Marxist patina. In the particular instance of Chiapas, Mexico, the pope's local representative, Samuel Ruiz, is the agency most responsible for the armed rebellion. Known as Don Samuel or *Tatic,* an affectionate term for "Father" in the local Mayan language of Tzeltal,

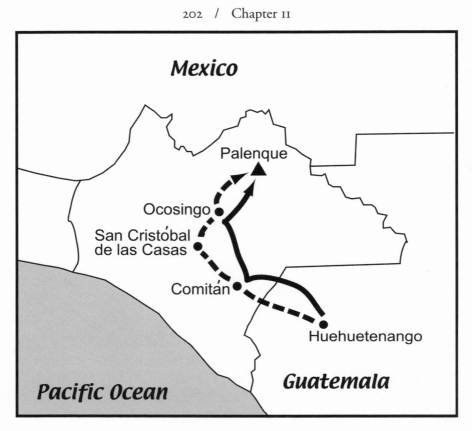

Huehuetenango to Palenque
Solid line shows Stephens's route by crude trail from Huehuetenango across the highlands to Comitán, Chiapas, Mexico, then on to Ocosingo and Palenque.

The author followed the modern highway to Comitán. He went on to San Cristóbal de las Casas (known as Ciudad Real in Stephens's time). He then continued on Stephens's trail to Ocosingo and Palenque.

Bishop Ruiz was not personally in favor of taking up arms on 1 January 1994. But more than anyone else, he put in place the mechanism that led to the rebellion.

The story whose title became liberation theology started in the late nineteenth century with Pope Leo XIII. His immediate predecessors, Pius VII and IX, tried to counter the materialism of the modern industrial world of big capital by ignoring it, according to the Euro-Brazilian José Comblin.[1] Leo XIII, to the contrary, confronted the modern world eyeball to eyeball. He encouraged the Church to make its peace with science. His goal was to keep the church vital in a world in which it was fast becoming an anachronism—like the crowned heads of Europe, one of which was the pope. Politically, Leo XIII eschewed the arch-conservative position the Church had come to represent. In 1891, he released the encyclical *Rerum Novarum,* in which the "undeserved poverty of workers" was treated. He encouraged the formation of center or center-left Catholic or Christian Democratic parties. According to Comblin, "The new 'Catholic' parties participated actively in states that were fully secularized or on their way to secularization. They contributed toward the working out of a new society, ultimately leading to social democracy or the welfare state. Leo XIII's evangelization provided the basis for a new Catholic praxis that lasted over a century."[2] We saw, earlier in this narrative, how Leo XIII's vision played out as late as the early 1960s in El Salvador. Duarte and others founded the Christian Democratic Party to appropriate the political middle between the revolutionary left, supported by the Communists, and the rightist conservatism of the landowners and the military.

The pope in the 1960s, John XXIII, showed by his example more than his words—according to liberation theologian Comblin—a rededication of the Church to the poor. "An option for the poor . . . circulated widely behind the scenes at Vatican II [the 1962 conclave of Catholic clergy and thinkers called by Pope John XXIII]. It was cultivated by a group of bishops from all continents who at the end of the Council committed themselves to promote a new episcopal style, one poorer and more committed to the causes of the poor."[3]

One of these was the newly appointed bishop of Chiapas, Samuel Ruiz. Liberation theology came to the fore at the Second Council of Bishops in Medellín, Colombia, in 1968. (In Church and Socialist circles Medellín is not code for an illegal drug cartel; it refers to the founding of liberation theology.) Bishop Ruiz was in attendance. Citing the Church's long-held belief in just wars, the liberation theologians called for a "peaceful" struggle to resolve the issues of the poor. Liberation theology adopted certain aspects of Marxist social analysis.[4] For example, Marx's class struggle was deemed an undeniable fact, as the poverty of the Third World was considered an inevitable byproduct of the industrial northern world. "God's plan," it was asserted, could be determined by biblical study, which itself would activate transforming energy. In view of the Marxist elements of liberation theology as formulated at Medellín, it would have been surprising had the "peaceful" aspects of these views held long-term sway. As it happened, armed rebellion was breaking out all over Latin America—both with and without the support of "God's Plan." In 1979, Somoza was driven out of Nicaragua by a coalition of armed resistance led by the Sandinistas. El Salvador, where Bishop Romero was gunned down in the national cathedral while saying Mass, seemed a lost cause. In Guatemala the poor had only two choices, armed struggle or oppression of the direst sort. The "working priests" of the Church had long been leaders in these struggles. After Medellín, many rightists considered the line between the Church and Communism erased. A number of priests, for instance, served in the higher echelon of the Sandinista regime. Elsewhere, as we have seen in Guatemala in particular, open season was declared on the clergy, whether socially active or not.

Conditions in Mexico's state of Chiapas, which abuts Guatemala on the north and west, were somewhat different. A state approximately the size of South Carolina, in 1996 Chiapas had a population of somewhat less than four million, slightly more than a quarter of whom were Indian.[5] About half the population was undernourished, and three-quarters earned less than $1,500 a year. In the highlands and the Lacandón forest areas of Chiapas, the parts Stephens (and I) traveled through, Indians made up about four-fifths of the population. As a part of the Mexican republic, Chiapas was much more stable than its neighbors to the south, thanks to the one-party rule of the PRI (the Institutional Revolutionary Party). PRI had managed to cling to power from 1930 until the time of this narrative, 1996, in two ways. (Finally, in 2000 PRI lost the presidency with the election of Vicente Fox.) First, the Mexican collective memory seems to have an image etched firmly in mind of the chaos and anarchy of the Mexican revolution during the second and third decades of the twentieth century. In Chiapas, up to 97 percent of the vote was regularly delivered to the PRI. Those too-impressive figures illustrate the second method the "official" party used to stay in office: outright fraud—buying ballots and sometimes the simple stuffing of the box in out-of-the-way rural areas. It was the self-confidence of the central government that allowed, and even unwittingly funded the post-Communist rebellion.[6]

Bishop Ruiz was responsible for the evolution of three of the four organizations of revolutionary action that developed in the Chiapas highlands and forests. The first, his diocesan organization, "Word of God," was an outright projection of liberation theology. The plight of the Chiapas poor was likened to events in the Bible. For instance, many peasants (mestizo and Indian alike) were forced out of work by cheaper Guatemalan labor in the coffee groves or from their haciendas by the government-sponsored transition from raising field crops to stock ranching. These folk thronged to the lowland Lacandón forest, the last great rain forest reserve in Mexico, to squat and form their own communities—with a fair amount of opposition from the government and private interests. This great migration, according to the tenets of liberation theology's radical Bible study, was held up as the equivalent of the Exodus—and imbued with the same sort of heaven-ordained right to the promised land. These doctrines, along with a native tendency to a parochial mindset, as Stephens found, heightened revolutionary consciousness among Ruiz's catechists.

In 1976, Ruiz invited a group of Maoists to Chiapas. Their leader, Adolfo Orive, had actually been trained in Beijing, but his group generally eschewed violence in favor of peasant social action—on the model of, say, a highly radicalized Peace Corps. Thirty young Maoists began working with Ruiz's social activists to bring modest programs, roads, water, hygiene, and electricity to the villages when possible. The *brigadistas* were successful enough to form an organization called *Unión de Uniones.* The government supported Unión de Uniones with grants and loans to found a credit union, among other things. Although generally law-abiding, the brigadistas kept their revolutionary credentials up-to-date by occasionally occupying unused lands of haciendas. By then, of course, Ruiz had lost control of Orive and this movement.

The third group was the remnants of a failed northern Mexico revolutionary army formed in Monterrey in 1969. In 1974 the Mexican army all but wiped it out, but a ragtag band found its way south to the fastness of the Lacandón forest, where it was left more or less in peace to lick its wounds and make the most of the growing revolutionary consciousness of the local inhabitants. This group came to be called the EZLN, or the Zapatista Army of National Liberation.

The last group was a revolutionary army with the (unhappy in English) acronym of SLOP, which was founded in 1980 by Bishop Ruiz himself. His motivation was partly to counteract the Zapatistas and partly a natural response to what at that time seemed the winning ticket in the great lottery of social reform in the area, namely armed rebellion. After all, in 1980 violent revolution was the going thing in Central America; the Sandinistas had just wrested control of Nicaragua from Somoza and there seemed no other option in Guatemala and El Salvador. During the 1980s all four Chiapas organizations cooperated; indeed, there was a sort of interlocking leadership among many of them. And all were funded, to one extent or another, by Mexican government monies diverted from social programs.

After the fall of the Eastern Bloc, the agendas of the organizations diverged. Ruiz no longer believed armed rebellion viable. The Zapatistas, under the leadership of Subcomandante Marcos (who was born in Tampico in 1957 and university-educated as Rafael Guillen Vicente), became profoundly anti-religious. On 1 January 1994 Subcomandante Marcos, acting on his own (but representing several thousand Chiapas peasants), rose up. His forces occupied the towns of Ocosingo and San Cristóbal de las Casas. The Mexican army responded, giving no quarter. After two weeks of extremely bloody fighting, a truce was called as Ruiz, among others, rushed in to mollify the authorities. Now, in late 1996, almost three years later, while fighting was minimal or nonexistent, the army still occupied all of lower Mexico. Checkpoints were manned, and an appearance, at least, of searching all cargo was maintained.

To return to Sally and me just entering Mexico on Christmas Eve 1996 and eager to be on our way toward more settled parts, the soldier finally completed his search of the colectivo's cargo. The driver put his foot through the floor and it was off to Comitán. The country here was like scrub country near the Río Grande in Texas—with hills and mountains in the distance. We passed a grove of low spreading trees completely without leaves. They looked like fig trees. I asked the man next to me what they were and was told the trees were *jocotes,* a term of some plasticity that in this case seemed to indicate a fruit sparingly grown in Florida where it is known as the purple mombin. My new friend told an older woman riding behind him that my Spanish was very good. I pulled out my Spanish book and showed him what I was studying. This pleased him. He said his name was Lionel. He was twenty-five. When I told him I was from Florida, he said he had been there working as a picker of truck produce, around Jupiter. He now lived on a small farm with his mother where he grew corn. Shortly, the colectivo stopped. Lionel and his madre headed off, by shank's mare, down a dusty road. At last look, Lionel was still waving.

It was about forty-five miles from the border to Comitán. We stashed our bags at a refreshment kiosk and headed off for a quick look around. *Comitan, the frontier town of Chiapas, contains a population of about ten thousand. It has a superb church and well-filled convent of Dominican friars. It is a place of considerable trade and has become so by the effect of bad laws, for most European goods consumed in this region are smuggled in from Belize and Guatemala. The markets, however, are but poorly supplied. We sent for a washerwoman, but there was no soap in the town. We wanted our mules shod, but there was only iron enough to shoe one.*[7]

The population of Comitán now is eighty thousand and the Pan American Highway, where we were discharged by the minibus, was hopping with parts shops, banks, and other perfectly legitimate commercial enterprises. The *zócalo,* as the central plaza is known in most Mexican towns, lay half a mile or more to the east, and it was well tenanted the day before Christmas, with families lounging in the sun, as well as the usual village loafers. A light bar thirty feet long with a serious number of impressive klieg lights was set up for Christmas festivities. One corner of the zócalo housed the local university of the arts, and down the block was a museum named after a local dignitary. Three churches fronted the square, and a block or so south there was a larger church, whose interesting architecture included a double spire in front and a St. Peter's–like dome in back. Painted white, in the late afternoon sunlight, it looked very appealing.

The streets around the zócalo were shoulder to shoulder with shops stuffed full of goods and almost as full of Christmas shoppers, despite the recent devaluation of the peso, and in contrast to Guatemala where (as in Stephens's time) the shops had fewer and less interesting things. Restaurants and cafes vented the pleasant smells of cookery, and they were full of people having a late afternoon cup and a chat. In any case, the place was a far cry from the sleepy village on the brink of terror that Stephens found.

Sally and I elected to spend Christmas in San Cristóbal de las Casas, the local administrative center in earlier times, which Stephens did not visit, nor wanted to get anywhere near, for fear of finding himself interned for lack of travel documents. A jacket was welcome but not necessary in Comitán. However, the Volkswagen *combi* began a steady upward climb, and shortly we were up in the pine trees again and a coat became a necessity, even snuggled between two hefty passengers. Women bundled in colorful huipiles were drawing water from wells and pouring it into clay pots. Firewood was stacked in huge ricks near houses, some of which were frame. Once, looking down into a valley from the road high above, I saw a church standing out starkly in the flat-streaming late afternoon sun. The opposite slope was covered with pine trees, and above fluffy cumulus clouds were tinged pink. It was a grand sight.

At 7:15 the day after Christmas, Sally and I were at our busline's dingy station in San Cristóbal, cattycorner from the Cristóbal Colón terminal. The coaches of the other line put to shame any bus I've ever seen plying the highways of the United States with the exception of a few lavishly appointed RVs. These things were huge and shiny and impressively clean looking. It was hard to believe anything that big could be made to go down a regular two-lane road. The two coaches in our station—terminal is too impressive a word for it—were dirty and ratty. The less grubby coach was driven off and the other pulled around in front. A barker hollered "Tuxtla," a city in the wrong direction. In the meantime the p.a. system from the Cristóbal Colón station across the way announced the pending departure of its second-class coach to Ocosingo, our destination. I began to wonder whether I had pulled another Wright Morris, that is, paying for the best that was not really the best as I had bought first-class tickets on this line instead of second-class tickets on the Cristóbal Colón. Seven-thirty arrived with no bus in sight as I watched the Cristóbal Colón bus depart. But at 7:31 an impressive-looking coach pulled in, our bags were loaded, and in a blink of the eye we were under way.

This bus was the first I had been on in Mesoamerica that was not dedicated to god. Almost all Guatemalan buses bear a shrine, or at least a written motto, such as "Jesús es único." To make up for it, the station had in a corner an altar dedicated to the Virgin. When the cleaning lady, a young woman in her twenties, passed the shrine, she crossed herself and kissed her thumb and forefinger forming a cross.

Our coach lumbered a few miles back toward Comitán and then turned toward the Gulf of Mexico onto the road to Ocosingo and Palenque. The pine forest gave the impression of being pretty much untampered-with at first, but, as I looked closely, I saw cornfields planted amid the pines, and within a few short miles the trees had been chopped down on the lower elevations and houses and *milpas* (corn plots) were intertwined with the few remaining pines. I was cogitating on the problem of environmental destruction versus an adequate lifestyle and income for the resident Indians—who inhabit these precincts at a density of seventy-six per square kilometer—when static growled in the front of the coach and the TV set came on. A stupid-seeming film called *Max,* about a dog that was nabbed from an experimental lab by animal-rights activists. Besides, I was more interested in the environmental question outside the window. Also, there was the fact that this route is one of the most spectacular mountain roads I've ever traveled, rivaling the Pan American Highway through the Quiché highlands. Shortly, however, I learned that this Max dog has been genetically engineered and, if not deprogrammed, would turn into a killing machine of King Kong proportions. Now the movie had me hooked, and not without my apprehending the irony of watching a story about a first-world environmental catastrophe in the making while riding through a real third-world one, while in a bus that would put the Greyhound line to shame through some of the most beautiful scenery in North America.

Stephens's journey to Ocosingo required three days. The coach rolled to a stop before the movie ended. Ocosingo is a frontier town three thousand feet up in a mixed tropical hardwood-pine environment. It gives the impression of being much smaller than its population of twenty thousand. The bus halted on the road, not even pulling off the pavement. The town is as lonely, romantic, and forlorn as its name, Ocosingo. The great Lacandón forest, or what's left of it, stretches from Ocosingo to the Guatemalan border, a distance of one hundred miles, without a single through road. In Stephens's time *In the center of the square was a magnificent ceiba tree.*[8] Nowadays the center of the town was notable for trees that, while smaller, were impressively shorn into topiary shapes.

War was again in our way. While all the rest of Mexico was quiet the points in our journey, were in a state of [unrest].[9] The ruins of Toniná lay fourteen kilometers behind Ocosingo, and on the taxi ride out we passed an army camp that had been established after the Zapatista rebellion. When I had passed through here in the Ranger, I would have picked Ocosingo as the last venue in Mexico, perhaps the globe, to end up on the world's front page. But two years later the Zapatistas, in their stocking-cap-like hoods, descended from the hills and took civil control of the town. The Mexican army, after initially being caught with its pants down, counterattacked. The streets of Ocosingo were stacked with bodies of dead Zapatistas for the citizenry to admire or take as a cautionary tale, as the case required.

A row of ordinary barbed wire fencing—more appropriate for keeping cattle in than Zapatistas out—protected the perimeter of the base. A furrow a few inches deep had been plowed twenty feet behind the fence, and a truck was rolling along deploying Mexican soldiers who dropped into the trench and pointed the muzzles of their rifles at the road—where our taxi was driving. We came under the trained sights of a company of soldiers with, no doubt, live ammunition, all of whom scowled fiercely as though to scare the enemy off.

At nearly a mile distant, we saw on a high elevation one of the buildings of Tonina, the Indian name in this region for stone houses. We rode on to the foot of a high structure, probably a fortress, rising in pyramidal form with five spacious terraces. [One of the buildings occupying a terrace] *is fifty feet front and thirty-five feet deep; it is constructed of stone and lime, and the whole front was once covered with stucco, of which part of the cornice and moldings still remain. In one of the apartments was the same pitchy substance we had noticed at Copan. The lintel was a beam of wood. Our guide said it was of the* [sapodilla or chewing-gum] *tree. It was so hard that, on being struck, it rang like metal.*[10]

Each Maya site is impressive in its own way, and Toniná, normally considered one of the lesser sites from both the tourist and the archaeological perspective, was to my mind one of the most intriguing. Stephens would no doubt have been astonished to learn that one of the last dated monuments from any Classic Maya site was found here. It was dated A.D. 909, almost a full century later than Copán's last long-count stela, and only a year before the very latest (yet discovered). Also, Kan Xul, a king of Palenque, Stephens's true destination in Chiapas, was captured and sacrificed by Toniná's Ruler 3 in or about A.D. 711, which surely for a time put Toniná at or near the top of the AP-Coaches poll of the time.[11]

Those dry archaeological facts meant less to me than the incredible effect of the setting of modern Toniná, which is really just a huge five-story staircase set into a small mountain. Making it to the top kept me fully occupied. I did not bother to look about until I arrived at the small pyramid at the very apex of the hill. Turning around, I saw far below two toylike horses picketed among some stood-on-end-feather-dusters that were cohune palms, the signature tree of lowland Central America, which reappeared here for the first time since we left the lowlands of the Río Dulce. In the distance was range upon range of green-clad mountains and, in the middle distance, a vast checkerboard of Lacandón rain forest and cleared pasture. It was a grand sight, and if the Maya designed their cities chiefly to be appreciated in the way of landscape architecture, which probably in part they did, Toniná would have to rate as a Salzburg or Santa Fe.

Stephens, being a serious archaeologist, could not settle for anything as facile as a view. He had to poke into every fissure and cranny, not the least being a subterranean building that supposedly provided an underground shortcut to Palenque. *I took off my coat and, lying down on my breast, began to crawl under. When I had advanced about half the length of my body, I heard a hideous hissing noise, and starting back, saw a pair of small eyes, which in the darkness shone like balls of fire. The precise portion of time that I employed in backing out is not worth mentioning. My companions had heard the noise, and the guide said it was "un tigre." I thought it was a wildcat. But whatever it was, we determined to have a shot at it. We took for granted that the animal would dash past us, and in a few moments our guns and pistols, swords and machetes, were ready. Taking our positions, Pawling, standing close against the wall, thrust under a long pole, and with a horrible noise out fluttered a huge turkey buzzard, which flapped itself through the building and took refuge in another chamber.*[12]

From the ruins I walked back to town. I wandered through the valley, which smelled blessedly of warm grass and clematis from virgin bower vines growing on the fences. The signs on billboards proclaimed this year to be one of peace and reconciliation, because of the peace accord signed with the Zapatistas that called for the demilitarization of the area. The government reneged on the deal—hence the base on the road—but it made for good publicity. All this seemed to have worked a magic spell. No dog so much as barked at me, although once a gigantic bull peacefully munching grass in the ditch startled me.

As I approached the army camp, I looked off and saw the photograph I had been trying to take all afternoon—black mountain with cumulus clouds above and green pasture land in blazing sunlight. The best shot was toward the camp—a line of parked trucks and some black plastic tarps—but I shot across the grain of the pastureland because the army camp would have ruined the bucolic effect I wanted. I smiled to myself, though, thinking how cute it would have been to take a photo of the base, like a spy. The grin was still on my face when I saw a soldier walking toward me with his rifle at port arms. End of my cleverness. I waved and smiled an altogether different kind of smile and said "hola," and he slung his rifle. I told him I was taking a photo of the pastureland, not one of the army camp. He warned me against taking a picture of the base. The young man's name was Gabriel. He was a pleasant, friendly fellow from Sinaloa. Such was the state of war-torn Chiapas, that day after Christmas 1996, where you ride in buses showing pretty good Hollywood movies and walk along the valley without even a dog barking at you and had you not read the newspapers—or noticed the soldiers in flak jackets and helmets—you would be sure this must be one of the most peaceful places on earth.

My inclination would have been to dine at the Hotel Central on the zócalo, the only place in this sleepy burg that appeared busy and interesting. Not withstanding the guidebook's recommendation for a hotel, which turned out to be a classic Mexican dive complete with overflowing toilet, blaring radios and TVs, and squalling kids running the halls, I continued to put my trust in it. We walked two or three blocks west of the zócalo down an unpromising and unlighted street of tumbledown buildings to what the book claimed to be the best restaurant in town. Sure enough, there was a sign saying the Restaurant Rafsha. To get to it we had to go down a little path and loop around into the basement of a private residence. The place was cute, with a wine rack about six feet long, a dozen wine glasses hanging upside down above it, and a fifteen-gallon keg of tequila next to it. The cocina was stashed in a corner of the room and an open fire was blazing—supervised by a middle-aged woman. The proprietor was a man of similar age in a guayabera. One couple—very young, the girl quite attractive, with short coiffed hair, makeup, lipstick, and jewelry, all this on a very cute traditionally Mexican face—were nursing Cokes in the corner. Just after we walked in, a middle-aged man in fatigues, sporting a sidearm, arrived. With him came the whole family, grandma, assorted kids, and two middle-aged sisters. The one with flaming red hair—dyed—showed a proprietorial interest; presumably she was the wife.

The menu featured Negra Modelo beer (not easily found in provincial areas in the country of its origin). I ordered *queso fundido,* or Mexican fondue, and an avocado salad. Another young couple arrived. The guy in a long leather coat had a rough peasant face, and the girl was plump and good-looking in an uninteresting way. If she had not been angry for a reason I tried to puzzle out—slowness of service or her boyfriend's obstinacy—she would have not piqued a second look. In any case, everything came together, and this was the first good meal we had had since arriving in Mexico—and who could have expected it in a place like Ocosingo.

After dinner we took a stroll through Ocosingo. We saw neon lights off to the east and headed for them. We were astonished to see shops open for business. This place had been a ghost town when I strolled through here during the siesta period. The front wall of each small establishment was now completely open to the street. Each cubicle was stuffed with a single domestic product—cowboy hats, mops, hardware, or what-have-you. Down the street was a department store with chic dresses hanging on mannequins in the display windows. We strolled along peeking into offices at girls in dark skirts and white blouses—and, less often, at guys in dark trousers and white shirts—banging away at typewriters or at least sitting behind them.

The *zócalo,* or town square, was hopping. A line of pushcarts was strung out on the street in front of the church, selling popcorn, hot dogs, ice cream, *pollo frito* (fried chicken), and papas fritas, the deep fryer powered by propane. Beneath the topiaried trees of the zócalo, the young folks were getting down to the serious business of he-ing and she-ing, and the boys a bit younger all seemed to be running around with a shoe kit, giving each other shines. I was told later by a family who had lost land to the Zapitistas that this new found prosperity was a direct result of the boom occasioned by the rebellion and the army's occupation.

We left Ocosingo at a quarter past eight [A.M.], Stephens wrote.[13] Sally and I took our leave at pretty nearly the same time. The bus driver was a swarthy man who had not been introduced to the joys of underarm deodorant. His ten-year-old son was the conductor. The two, the boy being a miniature of the father, discussed matters relating to business as equals with great if somewhat disconcerting seriousness. Only occasionally did the father pull rank. Once we got on the open road, the boy claimed his duty seat, a Coleman cooler tucked up against the windshield and next to the door, which occasionally slammed open for no discernible reason. An open-faced carton of four dozen eggs sat on the motor housing, the vibrations of which pushed them toward the edge. One of the young man's tasks was to intercept these eggs before they crashed to the floor. After a while the kid nodded off, but, each time, just as the eggs were about to slip over the side, he jerked awake and pushed them back to the center of the console. Then the kid dozed off again, his head lolling against the windshield in what seemed the constant threat of tumbling off the ice chest and out the accordion door. An orange crate with a pineapple, a papaya, some bananas, and other comestibles completed the furnishings in the front of the bus. Three hours of this and we were in Palenque.

The same journey took Stephens and Catherwood five days on a route that *lay through an Indian country, in parts of which the Indians bore a notoriously bad character.* The topography too was a challenge. *We commenced ascending the steepest mountain I ever knew. Riding was out of the question. It was very hot, and I can give no idea of the toil of ascending these mountains. Our mules could barely clamber up with their saddles only. We disencumbered ourselves of sword, spurs, and all useless trappings* [and] *came down to shirt and pantaloons and as near the condition of the Indians as we could.*[14]

Now, of all times, Stephens suffered a bout of malaria and was forced to mount a *silla*, a chair carried on the back of an Indian, something he was loath to do for humanitarian reasons. *My face was turned backward. I could not see where he was going but I sat as still as possible. Looking over my shoulder I saw we were approaching the edge of a precipice more than a thousand feet deep. Here I became anxious to dismount but the Indians could or would not understand my signs. My carrier moved along carefully, with his left foot first, feeling the stone on which he put it. I rose and fell with every breath, felt his body trembling under me and his knees seemed to give way. The precipice was awful and the slightest irregular movement on my part might bring us both down together. He started again and with the same care ascended. To my extreme relief, the path turned away but I had hardly congratulated myself upon my escape before he descended a few steps. This was much worse. If he fell nothing could keep me from going over his head.*[15]

It hardly needs to be said, but the bearer did not fall. And Stephens, like Sally and I, arrived in due time at Palenque, the best known of all ruins in lower Mexico at the time of Stephens's trek, in spite of its great isolation. Indeed, Palenque is still quite far distant (although no longer truly isolated) from the closest urban center, prosaic Villahermosa in neighboring Tabasco state. However, today the small village of just a few thousand can accommodate the tourist quite comfortably. In Stephens's time, few amenities were available in the village. In any case, the Maya explorer made directly for the ruins some distance away.

12 / Palenque

We spurred up a sharp ascent so steep that the mules could barely climb it, to a terrace covered, like the whole road, with trees, that it was impossible to make out the form. Continuing on with this terrace, we stopped at the foot of a second when our Indians cried out "el Palacio," and through the openings in the trees we saw the front of a large building richly ornamented with stuccoed figures on the pilasters, curious and elegant, trees growing close against it, and their branches entering the doors; in style and effect extraordinary, and mournfully beautiful. We had reached [Palenque,] *the end of our long and toilsome journey. The first glance indemnified us for our toil.*[1]

For no obvious reason, fate selected Palenque to be the first Maya city to come to the attention of the outside world. Fifty-three years before Stephens, an officer in the colonial administration at Guatemala City, Antonio del Río, led an expedition there. Imbued with a sense of mission by a demand for information from the royal historiographer in Spain, del Río commanded the destruction of the woods around the site and, according to his report and to the great horror of modern archaeologists, "ultimately there remained neither a window nor doorway blocked up."[2]

Some years later, in 1804, a retired captain of dragoons, Guillermo Dupaix, was detailed to make another survey. We have already discussed Juan Galindo's contribution to Stephens's ultimate understanding of the Maya. Stephens's most interesting precursor, and the one who supposedly spent up to two years at the site, was the putative nobleman, Count Waldeck, a veritable Munchausen who claimed as intimates both Robespierre and Marie Antoinette. According to him, he visited the latter frequently in her cell as she awaited her date with the guillotine. Although subsequent historians have accepted few of Waldeck's assertions, including his claim to nobility, he really does seem to have lived to the ripe age of 109, going to Mexico at the tender age of fifty-six. His favorite avocation in his golden years was girl-watching from the sidewalk cafes of Paris. His biographer claims he died from complications of an injury received from a sudden shift to get a better view of the charms of a young woman.[3] Too bad that more of the man's creative energy—technically his artistic ability challenged Catherwood—could not have been channeled into legitimate scholarship. Instead, he frequently drew pictures of how he wished the ruins to have looked rather than the way they did appear. Little of value regarding the Maya was added by Walker and Caddy, sent out from the Belize colony by Colonel MacDonald after Stephens told of his own plans to visit the site.[4]

Of the ancient city's admirers, only del Río was able to view the city in anything like its full extent, thanks to being able to command the local Indians to clear the forest. Stephens found *the trees, beaten down and heavy with rain, hanging so low that we were obliged to stoop constantly, and very soon our hats and coats were perfectly wet. From the thickness of the foliage the morning sun could not dry up the deluge of the night.*[5] Despite all this, Stephens could still take a moment to observe: *Amid all the wreck of empires, nothing ever spoke so forcibly of the world's mutations as this immense forest shrouding what was once a great city. Once it had been a great highway, thronged with people who were stimulated by the same passions that give impulse to human action now. They are all gone, their habitations buried, and no trace of them left.*[6]

Del Río had claimed that the city of Palenque extended for miles in all directions. Stephens felt that his first task, after making camp in the Palace, was to verify this claim. Owing to the thick growth it was impossible to see another building from the Palace. Making a survey of the ruins promised to be an extremely arduous task. As it turned out, an even more difficult one was simply surviving. The country roundabout was in a near-famine situation; corn for tortillas was difficult to procure. But even worse was the insalubrious location. *Rains, hard work, bad fare, seemed nothing. But we could no more exist without sleep than the "foolish fellow" of Aesop, who at the moment when he had learned to live without eating, died. The next night the mosquitoes were beyond all endurance. The slightest part of the Body, the tip end of a finger, exposed was bitten. With the heads covered the heat was suffocating, and in the morning our faces were all in blotches.*[7]

The Palace at Palenque. Note the tower with the blind staircase that mystified Stephens.

We expected at this place [eight miles from the nearest village] *to live upon game, but were disappointed. A wild turkey we could shoot at any time from the door of the palace. After trying one, we did not venture to trifle with our teeth upon another. Besides these, there was nothing but parrots, monkeys, and lizards, all very good eating, but which we kept in reserve for a time of pressing necessity,* [Stephens joshed]. *Besides mosquitoes and garrapatas, or ticks, we suffered from another worse insect, called by the natives* niguas *which we are told, pestered the Spanish on their first entry into the country, and which says the historian, "ate their Way into the Flesh, under the Nails of the Toes, then laid their Nits there within, and multiplied in such manner that there was no ridding them but by Cauteries, so that some lost their Toes, and some their Feet, whereas they should at first have been picked out; but being as yet unacquainted with the Evil, they knew not how to apply the Remedy." We had escaped them until our arrival at Palenque, and being unacquainted with the evil, did not know how to apply the remedy. I carried one in my foot for several days, conscious that something was wrong, but not knowing what, until the nits had been laid and multiplied.* Pawling [an American who left Guatemala with Stephens and Catherwood] *undertook to pick them out with a penknife, which left a large hole in the flesh. Unluckily, from the bites of various insects my foot became so inflamed that I could not get on shoe or stocking. I was obliged to lie by, and sitting an entire day with my foot in a horizontal position, uncovered, it was assaulted by small black flies, the bites of which I did not feel at the moment of affliction, but which left marks like the punctures of a hundred pins.*[8]

Stephens and Catherwood did not stay at Palenque as long as they intended—they were chased away by the inhospitable conditions. They left saying that one day they would return, as is the way of disappointed travelers. By the time Stephens penned the Palenque passages in his book, it was apparent he was not going back (even as he was making preparations to return to drier and more hospitable parts of the Yucatán peninsula). However, Stephens did not leave without first making a major contribution to future understanding of the site. *In regard to the extent of the ruins, even in this practical age the imagination of man delights in wonders. In a series of well-written articles in our own country they have been set down as ten times larger than New York. It is not in my nature to discredit any marvelous story. I am slow to disbelieve, and would rather sustain all such inventions. But it has been my unhappy lot to find marvels fade away as I approached them. The whole extent of ground covered by those as yet known is not larger than our* [Central] *Park* [which was considerably smaller in 1840 than today] *or Battery. In stating this fact I am very far from wishing to detract from the importance or interest of the subject. It is proper to add, however, that considering the space now occupied by the ruins as the site of palaces, temples, and public buildings, and supposing the houses of the inhabitants to have been, like those of the Egyptians and the present race of Indians, of frail and perishable materials, and as at Memphis and Thebes, to have disappeared altogether, the city may have covered an immense extent.*[9]

From the palace no other building is visible. Passing out by what is called the subterraneous passage, you descend the southwest corner of the terrace, and at the foot immediately commence ascending a ruined pyramidal structure, which appears once to have had steps on all its sides. These steps have been thrown down by the trees, and it is necessary to clamber over stones, aiding the feet by clinging to the branches. The ascent is so steep, that if the first man displaces a stone it bounds down the sides of the pyramid, and woe to those behind. About half way up, through openings in the trees, is seen the building [or temple topping the pyramid]. *The height of the structure on which it stands is one hundred and ten feet on the slope. The building is seventy-six feet in front and twenty-five feet deep. It has five doors and six piers, all standing. The whole front was richly ornamented in stucco. The corner piers are covered with hieroglyphics, each of which contains ninety-six squares. The interior of the building is divided into two corridors, run-*

ning lengthwise, with a ceiling rising nearly to a point, and as in the palace, and paved with large square stones. In [the first] *corridor, on each side of the principal door, is a large tablet of hieroglyphics, each thirteen feet long and eight feet high, and each divided into two hundred and forty squares of characters or symbols. The impression made upon our minds by these speaking but unintelligible tables I shall not attempt to describe. There is one important fact to be noticed. The hieroglyphics are the same as were found at Copan and Quirigua. The intermediate country is now occupied by races of Indians speaking many different languages, and entirely unintelligible to each other. But there is room for the belief that the whole of this country was once occupied by the same race, speaking the same language or, at least, having the same written characters. From some unaccountable cause* [the hieroglyphics in this temple] *have never before been presented to the public. It is my belief* [that del Río and Dupaix] *did not give them because in both cases the artists attached to their expedition*[s] *were incapable of the labor, and the steady determined perseverance required for drawing such complicated, unintelligible, and anomalous characters. As at Copan, Mr. Catherwood divided his paper into squares. The original drawings were reduced, and the engravings corrected by himself, and I believe they are as true copies as the pencil can make: the real written records of a lost people.*[10]

The building Stephens described is now known as the Temple of the Inscriptions. Although displaced as the number one destination for Maya-seekers by ruins closer to the populous tourist meccas such as Cancún, Palenque, in general, and the Temple of the Inscriptions, in particular, have contributed much to modern man's understanding of the ancient Maya. The temple is notable for two great discoveries that advanced Maya studies. As Stephens would not be surprised to learn, the temple's hieroglyphics are the most extensive of any useful text yet discovered. They are only exceeded by the hieroglyphic staircase at Copán, which unfortunately was scrambled by natural and manmade disasters.

It was at Palenque that the last stage of the decipherment of the Maya language occurred, and the helpfulness of these tablets in that process speaks for itself. Stephens noticed that the interior chambers of the temple were "paved with large square stones." For more than one hundred years, no investigator seems to have wondered what was under those stones. No one, including Stephens, noticed that one of the flagstones had large notches that could allow for levering devices. Presumably Stephens overlooked this due to the quantity of rubble that had accumulated in the one thousand years since the temple was last maintained. The intervening investigators missed the obvious because they were blinded by the received wisdom of Morley and Thompson which held that, unlike the Egyptians and almost all other public-monument-erecting peoples, the Maya temples were not used—or so the conventional wisdom of the early twentieth century ran—for crass political or social purposes, such as tombs. Now it is known that the Maya behaved much like other peoples in similar circumstances, particularly in regard to their public buildings, which *were* used for funerary purposes.

Notwithstanding all this, the Cuban-Mexican archaeologist, Alberto Ruz Lhuillier, lifted the floor stones. He found a rubble-filled passage. For three years, workers under his direction removed rocks and dirt. Finally, in 1952, the object at the bottom of a one-hundred-foot staircase was revealed—a tomb. A single male lay inside. The body was adorned by jade beads. His face was covered with a priceless jade mask, the opulence of the jade being exceeded only by the craftsmanship of the mask. On the wall above the sarcophagus were nine figures in stucco. The sarcophagus lid depicted a man stripped down to basics falling into the open maw of Xibalbá, the Maya underworld, a really scary place that makes our hell seem a not-bad choice for a vacation home by comparison. Just below the depiction of the deceased is the mask of the sun god, half of which is shown as a skeleton. It is presumably that of the interred descending into the underworld to rise again as a resurrected god—as the sun rises daily. The Maya tree of life is also depicted, with the celestial bird and the two-headed sky serpent in its top. Clearly, the fellow in the tomb had the power—not to mention the wherewithal with the jade beads and mask—to buy his way out of Xibalbá.[11]

Just five or six years before the uncovering of this burial, murals were discovered at nearby Bonampak that showed the supposedly peaceful Maya engaged in ritual warfare and sacrifice. Those Bonampak murals and the suggestion that the Temple of the Inscriptions had been erected for funerary purposes set the stage for a massive reevaluation of the Maya in the coming decades. Among the first item unscrambled twenty years later by pioneer epigraphers, Schele and Mathews, was the name of the man in the tomb. It was Pacal (formally K'inich Janaab' Pakal I), sometimes referred to by the English equivalent, Shield. He was also the man responsible for the erection of the Temple of the Inscriptions, much of the Palace, which extends over a space larger than a football field, and other lesser buildings.[12]

Pacal was born in A.D. 603 and assumed the throne in A.D. 615. He was the first in his dynastic line, which stretched through seven more rulers until the last copal fire at Palenque flickered out in A.D. 799 or thereabouts. So, what moved Pacal to erect the giant hieroglyphic tablets, as well as to become something of an overachiever in tomb and temple building? The answer is that he was, after a fashion, a bastard—at least as far as Maya kings were concerned. As we have seen, by the early seventh century any normal Maya king, such as Copán's 18 Rabbit, should have been able to trace his lineage back for a couple hundred years. Pacal's royal predecessor was his mother, Lady Zak Kuk, or "White Macaw." Normally, the royal lineage descended from the father. In short, the combination of royal mother and nonroyal father was an embarrassment to any pretender to Maya royalty.

Pacal strove to hide this blot in the way of political strongmen since time immemorial, by erecting vast public monuments and by rewriting history. Hence the need for the large stone hieroglyphic tablets that so impressed Stephens. The hieroglyphics tell two stories, one presumably a simple recounting of historical record, the other a highly personalized version of Maya cosmology. The first story relates back just a few years to the reign of Lady Kanal Ikal, A.D. 583–604, when power was transferred to a woman before being passed on to her son. The second story highlights the Maya creation myth of the First Mother. She was born in the third creation and was the motive force behind the present or fourth creation. In what in our day would be considered going over the top, Pacal equated his mother, Lady Zak Kuk, with the First Mother. Bringing this closer to home, Pacal's claim would be the equivalent of a seventeenth- or eighteenth-century European emperor claiming his mother was a reincarnation of the Virgin Mary. As we saw with 18 Rabbit at Copán, who was a comfortable thirteenth in dynastic succession, such claims to supernatural provenance were routine among Maya kings. The populace would probably have felt something was amiss if such assertions were not made. Nevertheless, Pacal's inscriptions argue his case more fully than any similar treatise yet discovered.

Stephens gave a complete description of only five buildings at Palenque. The first two, the Palace and the Temple of the Inscriptions, were the work of Pacal. The others were built by his immediate heir, Chan Bahlum II, A.D. 684 to 702. Those three buildings, the temples of the Sun, the Cross, and the Foliated Cross, conform to Maya convention. The triad represents the sacred three stones of the hearth, on which Maya cooks even today place a clay or metal griddle to bake their tortillas.[13] After Chan Bahlum II's death, Pacal's next-eldest son took power. Kan Xul II made further improvements in the

Palace. His most notable achievement was the erection of a tower that amused and mystified Stephens. *This tower is conspicuous by its height and proportions, but on examination in detail it is found unsatisfactory and uninteresting. The base is thirty feet square, and it has three stories. Entering over a heap of rubbish at the base, we found within another tower, distinct from the outer one, and a stone staircase, so narrow that a large man could not ascend it. The staircase terminates against a dead stone ceiling, closing all farther passage, the last step being only six or eight inches from it. For what purpose a staircase was carried up to such a bootless termination we could not conjecture. The whole tower was a substantial stone structure, and in its arrangements and purposes about as incomprehensible as the sculptured tablets.*[14]

The purpose of that dead-end staircase is today still a mystery. The tower itself seems to venerate and commemorate Pacal's descent and resurrection from the underworld. On the winter solstice the sun sets directly behind the Temple of the Inscriptions, when viewed from the platform atop the tower, just as Pacal last sank down the shaft in the building to his final resting place—from which he would have us believe he, like the sun, was resurrected. Kan Xul II is best remembered for something other than his building program. When raiding Toniná for captives to sacrifice at the dedication of his tower, he was taken prisoner. The king at Toniná appears to have felt he had a jaguar by the tail. Kan Xul II was held in captivity for two years. He was probably tortured for a good deal of that time before finally being put to death.

Stephens would no doubt have sympathized with Kan Xul's plight. Palenque had the honor of being the only stop on his itinerary that was too much for the energetic Maya explorer. He hauled himself to the village of Palenque to recruit his health after his bot-fly infected toe was attacked by simulid flies. He returned ready to pull up stakes. *There was a marked change in* [the Palace] *since I left. The walls were damp, the corridors wet. The continued rains were working through the cracks and crevices and opening leaks in the roof. Saddles, bridles, boots, shoes, &c., were green and mildewed, and the guns and pistols covered with a coat of rust. Mr. Catherwood's appearance startled me. He was wan and gaunt. Lame like me from bites of insects, his face was swollen, and his left arm hung with rheumatism as if paralyzed.*[15] Stephens and Catherwood showed Palenque a light heel with no sense of regret, remarking only that *in the romance of the world's history nothing ever impressed me more forcibly than the spectacle of this once great and lovely city, overturned, desolate and lost, discovered by accident, overgrown with trees for miles around, and without even a name to distinguish it. Apart from everything else, it was a mournful witness to the world's mutations.*[16]

My travel mate, Sally Duncan, had visited many of the major Yucatán sites, including Calakmul, one of the most remote and least visited of all major Maya ruins, just miles north of the Petén boundary. Like Stephens—but for different reasons—Palenque had been her ideal of Maya achievement, and her first glimpse of the Temple of the Inscriptions, as we passed by the ticket kiosk into the grounds, brought tears to her eyes. "My god, it's gorgeous," she croaked out.

Despite a potentially cracked rib there was no keeping Sally from climbing the sixty-nine (by her count) very steep steps that led to the shoe-box structure housing the hieroglyphics panels that give the Temple of the Inscriptions its name. At the top Sally stopped and, like Pacal in days gone by, surveyed all before her. Almost all Maya sites seem to fit into their environment in a way that makes the setting enhance the awe felt by the visitor. The Maya inhabited (and still inhabit) an area as diverse as any spot on the face of the globe. However, the lowland rain-forest habitat has come to typify the Maya homeland, and Palenque, thanks to its characteristic mansard roof combs and to its taking advantage of the foothills on which it is built, manages to call attention to the lushness and splendor of its jungle setting while giving the impression of not being swallowed by it. It was Stephens's great misfortune not to have been able to appreciate the site as it is today, no doubt more similar to Palenque in its heyday than the rainy-season Xibalbá (hell) he endured.

Modern epigraphers have furnished the answer to some of the questions Stephens asked at Palenque. Lakam Ha' (Big Water) is the city's original name; the larger kingdom was called B'aakal (Bone).[17] Some questions still have the epigraphers confused. According to the inscriptions, Pacal's reign lasted from A.D. 615 to 683, sixty-eight years, dating from his twelfth birthday until his death at eighty. Strangely, the bones found in the tomb were judged to be those of a forty-year-old man.[18] It may be worth mentioning that Stephens's claim to publishing the first reproductions of Palenque's inscriptions was incorrect. Waldeck had rendered a copy of some of the tablets, although the utility of his presentations to scholars was questionable. An elephant's head appears in one of the glyphs, for example. As Stephens asserted, Catherwood's reproductions were the best to be had during most of

Waterfall at Palenque. In classical times the center was known as Lakam Ha' or Big Water.

the nineteenth century. It was not until the very end of that century that the Englishman Alfred Maudslay, working with a large-format camera, superseded him. Maudslay's images made serious study of the hieroglyphs possible. Nevertheless, the work Stephens and Catherwood did at Palenque stood as the benchmark for sixty years and is still studied by serious archaeologists today.

13 / Yucatán

There was a stir at one end of the plaza, and an object presented itself that at once turned my thoughts and feelings homeward. It was a post-coach, from a Troy, New York, factory, exactly like those seen on every road in our country. It was one of a line of diligences between Campeche and Mérida and had just arrived from the former place. It had nine persons inside, and had an aspect so familiar that, as the door opened, I expected to see acquaintances get out.[1]

We too exited a coach in Mérida, an ADO-buslines coach, which was built by Mercedes Benz presumably in far off Germany. We too had come by way of Campeche, having started in Palenque, which was somewhat more than three complete American movies—plus a fair amount of very loud salsa music and very cold air conditioning—distant.

We celebrated that New Year's Eve with a cross section of middle Mérida, mostly the adult members of families, by no means spiffily turned out. There were also quite a few small fry, some young couples with grandparents, a few singles, and one table of four college-age young women, who, whether purposefully or not, were seated near a party of young men. The guys made a lot of noise whenever one of the women got up but, in truth, they were more interested in their free *cervezas,* none asking the girls to dance or engaging them in conversation. Midnight was announced and women pulled out their hatpins and started popping the balloons that decorated the room. Males, young and old, flicked their Bics and proceeded to wreak havoc on the balloons, causing me a fair amount of distress given the well-known propensity of nightclubs to go up in flames and the lack of exit signs in this place.

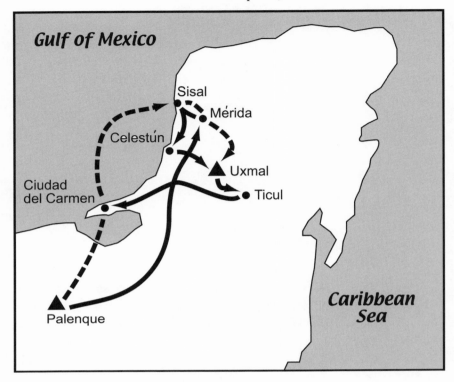

Chiapas-to-Yucatán Express
Stephens's journey is indicated by dotted line, the author's by solid line. The latter covered much the same route via the roadways as Stephens, who went down the Usumacinta River from Palenque and on to Sisal by boat, but in a somewhat different order.

Everyone consumed twelve grapes—celebrating the Spanish hope for twelve fruitful months. Sedate kisses and hugs were traded among friends. Strangers were saluted with *sidra*, a bubbling, lightly alcoholic cider. There was none of the kissing and grabass that Americans try to get away with, at least not at La Tocha.

The city of Mérida contains about twenty thousand inhabitants. It is founded on the site of an old Indian village, and dates from a few years after the conquest. The houses were well built, with balconied windows, and many had two stories. The streets were clean, and many people in them well dressed, animated, and cheerful in appearance. [Coaches] fancifully painted and curtained, having ladies in them handsomely dressed, without hats, and their hair ornamented with flowers, gave it an air of gaiety and beauty that after the somber towns through which we had passed, was fascinating and almost poetic. No place had yet made so agreeable a first impression. Most of all there was that unwonted luxury, *a hotel in a large building kept by Donna Michaele, driving up to which we felt as if by some accident we had fallen upon a European city.*[2]

As the capital of the powerful state of Yucatan, it had always enjoyed a high degree of consideration in the Mexican confederacy. It was the eve of the fete of El Corpus Christi. Two sides of the plaza were occupied with corridors, and the others were adorned with arbors of evergreens, among which lights were interspersed. Gay parties were promenading under them, and along the corridors and in front of the houses were placed chairs and benches for the use of promenaders. There was a large collection of Indians, both men and women, the best-looking race we had seen, and all were neatly dressed.

But the great attraction was in the ladies kneeling before the altars, with white or black veils laid over the top of the head, some of them of saintlike purity and beauty, in dress, manners and appearance realizing the pictures of Spanish romance. Indeed, the Spanish ladies appear nowhere so lovely as in church. The Indian women were really handsome. All were dressed in white, with a red border around the neck, sleeves, and hem of their garments, and their faces had a mild, contented, and amiable expression. The higher class were seated under the arbors before the doors of the houses and along the corridors, elegantly attired, without hats, and with veils or flowers in their hair, combining an elegance of appearance with simplicity of manners that made almost a scene of poetic beauty. They had an air of gaiety and freedom from disquietude, so different from the careworn faces of Guatemala, that they seemed as if what God intended them to be, happy.[3]

Nowadays, Mérida contains a population of about a half million, and it seems to be two cities, one of which is the old-fashioned part of walled courtyard houses around the central plaza that Stephens described. The sidewalks were still conspicuous with Indian women in their lowland-style huipiles, which amount to a white cotton shift, with a bit of colorful embroidery on the breast and hem, just as Stephens described more than a century and a half ago. The main plaza was decorated during our visit too, but with the tinsel ornaments and colored lights of the Christmas season; old hands tell me that the arrival of these decorations is a fairly recent thing, going back less than two decades.

We celebrated New Year's Day by hiking to the newer part of Mérida, the Paseo de Montejo, named for the Spanish conqueror of the peninsula, whose house is still pointed out on the main plaza. The paseo, which dominates the north-central part of the town, actually dates to about the turn of the twentieth century when flush times in the sisal trade motivated planters to erect palaces along this boulevard. If you are looking for a sports bar, a mansion turned into a museum, a fast food eatery, a bank, a high-rise hotel, or the American Consulate, this is the place to go. Because it was New Year's Day and everyone seemed to be sleeping one off, we settled for Reese's Pieces Blizzards at the Dairy Queen.

Later that night, we took in an inadvertent nightclub act. It was at an outdoor restaurant on a closed-off street near Hildalgo Plaza just off the main square. We seated ourselves and tried to attract the attention of one of three waiters in greasy aprons and Mac the Knife caps who talked in a surly manner among themselves. These guys looked more likely to mug us than to wait on us, and, after too long a time, it became apparent they were going to do neither. It was a little cool for outdoor dining anyway, and a nasty wind was blowing. As we were about to hoist ourselves out of our chairs, a little chap in apron and flat cap shot out of the kitchen balancing a tray above his head. This fellow—the right lens of his eyeglasses was starred—rushed over to our table and said, "Un momento," delivered the dish on his tray to another table, rushed back, shoved menus in our hands, took our drink orders, and shot across the patio to pick up another order, and was back in a jiffy with our drinks.

Seated at the table in front were a young Mexican couple and, from the adoring looks shot the young man's way, the guy's parents. They were laxative-ad kinds of people. He was a self-assured, silver-templed senior partner type and she was the sort of attractive, unassuming woman out of whose mouth a disagreeable word had never fallen (in public). The son was good-looking, handsome even, in his late twenties. He wore a leather coat and was cocky in a way that pleased mom and dad. He offered his father a large and expensive-looking cigar. The men sipped coffee and tried to enjoy their smokes in the breeze. I had admired the daughter-in-law from time to time all evening. She was patrician from the word go—or at least that was the air she projected for mom and dad. Her dark hair was lovingly coiffed with a couple of careless-on-purpose curls spilling onto her forehead. She struck a series of lovely and well-bred poses that were becoming of a daughter-in-law, not too haughty, but sophisticated and loving.

The table to the left was occupied by four Italians. Two of them called for Coffee Royales. In the blink of an eye, the little chap was back. He set up a tray table and deposited two large empty snifters, two smaller ones full of brandy, a banana-split dish of ice cream, a pot of coffee, and an assortment of paraphernalia. He lighted a can of sterno, sugared the rims of the snifters, and warmed them over the uncertain flame flickering in the stiff breeze. Then he splashed half a small snifter of brandy into each glass, swirled the liquor to vaporize it, and lighted the brandies. One of the bluish flames flickered out. Undeterred, the little chap removed the coffee pot from the sterno, reheated the snifter, and ignited the liquor. Then, working quickly but methodically, he added scoops of ice cream to the larger snifters, topped them off while still flaming with coffee and the contents of the smaller brandy snifter, and—with a workaday flourish—plopped each drink in front of the waiting Italians. It was a virtuoso performance—done in a brisk wind and with incredible speed—and the foreigners looking on, including Sally and me, broke into spontaneous applause. The poor daughter-in-law, though, was as unnerved as a campesino might have been at this spectacle. Her eyes popped and her mouth dropped. She not only had never seen anything like that, she had not even conceived of the possibility of such a display. Let's hope her in-laws, for whom she had striven so hard to project just the right blend of sophistication and haughtiness, did not hold it against her.

Heading out the next morning in a rented Honda, we came up on the *bomberos,* a company of firemen in red berets and wide leather belts, each with a bugle. They were marching into the town square, their bugles blaring. This ritual occurs at 7:30 each morning, and is part of the reason Mérida is one of my favorite spots on the globe. Stephens, too, was fond of the town. He regretted not being able to spend more time there and vowed to come back, which he did the following year for an extended study of the ruins of Yucatán. On his first trip, though, he was weary after his grueling journey, and he settled for a quick march inland to the site of Uxmal (pronounced Ooshmol) before returning to the port of Sisal for a ship home. For ourselves, we had—due to the vagaries of modern transportation—reversed the order of Stephens's march through the Yucatán. We were now bound for Sisal, from whence we would journey to Uxmal and ultimately, Ciudad del Carmen, where Stephens and Catherwood arrived on their boat trip down the Usumacinta from Palenque, and where we would finish retracing Stephens's epic journey.

The first community of any significance was Hunucmá, *pleasantly situated, embowered among trees, with a large plaza, at that time decorated with an arbor of evergreens all around. Here we took three fresh horses.*[4] The horse stable has been replaced by its modern-day equivalent, a Pemex filling station. Walking down the road, as I was preparing to turn into the gas station, were two men with cages on their heads with cardinals inside. Had I not been preoccupied with getting gas, I like to think I would have stopped and bought the song-birds and freed them, and even now I feel a tinge of regret at leaving those beautiful birds cooped up.

At the gas station, I took the usual precaution, stationing myself facing the dial on the pump before I told the attendant to fill it up. While I watched the numbers on the dial to make sure they were rung back to zero, the assistant brought a hose around and began filling. Trouble was the hose was attached to another pump. Immediately I followed the hose to its source and saw eighty pesos were already racked up. After a time the nozzle tripped off and the attendant told me the tank was full, the price being 120 pesos. I gave him forty pesos. The proprietor and the pumper got in my face, claiming I owed eighty more. I laughed at them. These boys had obviously graduated from the old school of Mexican gas stationry, where tricks like this could be expected every time you filled up. I called them *ladrones,* or thieves, to the astonishment of a patron, who had just arrived, and of the proprietor, who evidently had sel-dom been caught in his petty cons. Finally, the proprietor told the pumper to take my tag number, which they did, and I drove off, having gotten only about a quarter of a tank. I'm happy to say that I estimate I actually gained more than forty pesos in gas and so had effected a minor reverse sting.

Not a stream flows in all the northern part of the Yucatán peninsula—from Campeche to Chetumal. This fact stems in part from the porous limestone soil and in part due to the aridity of the country, which was covered with low but thick-growing semi-desert scrub. However, country as unpromising as this, agriculture-wise, can produce a crop that got its name from the one-time-flourishing port of Sisal. In its finished state as cordage, the product is called henequén, sisal, or hemp. Botanically it is known as *Agave fourcroydes.* Hor-ticulturally, it is called the century plant—because it blooms at great intervals, usually about every ten years. Its close relative *Agave americana,* also known as century plant, is a common feature of the landscape in the Deep South. The sisal resembles a large aloe vera plant, and the small fields we motored by, usually bounded by stone fences, looked like plantations of very large pineapple tops, the bottom spikes or leaves having been harvested. On the northern outskirts of Hunucmá, trucks were unloading bundles of century-plant leaves into a building, known as a *desfibrador.* After crushing and drying, the product would be sent on to a cordage mill. The building was minuscule, an indication of the present-day scale of a once-mighty industry, all this owing to the development of more cheaply produced synthetic fiber.

Twenty-four scrub-filled kilometers brought us to a mangrove swamp and then a brief stretch of open water and Sisal, which Stephens described *as prettily situated on the seashore and a thriving place. Near the shore was an old Spanish fortress with turrets. A soldier, barely distinguishable on the battlements, challenged us. Passing the quartel, we were challenged again. The answer, as in Central America, was "Patria Libre."*[5]

Our guidebooks said Sisal—having long since been supplanted by Progreso as Mérida's port—was a sleepy little town. Not true. The place snored. We had planned to eat breakfast there, but nothing resembling a restaurant was to be found. The only commercial enterprise was the *tortillería.* A line of a dozen women stretched outside the entrance as one woman exited munching a fresh tortilla and holding three or four dozen tortillas wrapped in a piece of newspaper. In the distance the Gulf of Mexico showed turquoise, blue, and green. On the outskirts down along the gulf there were a few summer homes and many lots with "Se Vende" (for sale) signs. If you want to go to a really-get-away-from-it-all beach, Sisal is the place for you. Just do not forget the picnic hamper.

Sisal is merely the depot of the exports and imports of Mérida. There was nothing to detain us at Sisal. At two o'clock we set out for the capital.[6] Rather than return to Mérida, we wended our way to Celestún—retracing the twenty-four kilometers to Hunucmá, which I was happy to slip through without having intercourse with the gendarmerie vis-à-vis the disputed gas bill. On achieving the road from Mérida, we turned right toward the gulf. Celestún is famous for its flamingos, being only one of two places in the Yucatán to harbor permanent populations. After crossing the causeway to the island of Celestún we turned off at the village end of the bridge where we were accosted by a tall, rather impatient fellow who offered to take us out in his boat for twenty-five dollars. The price was all right, and, since there were no other offers, he had a deal. He loaded us and two other men into the boat and opened the throttle full bore. We tore under the bridge into the river. The water here is shallow, muddy, and has a perceptibly greenish hue. Mark Brenner, a University of Florida biologist I had met in the area earlier, had told me that the greenish cast was caused by a buildup of nutrients. The causeway, which had been completed a few years before, prevented a tidal flush of the basin, and so bit-by-bit the waterway was dying.

Even though the tide was going out, the boatman kept the throttle cranked on high as he snaked the boat through the narrow channel between emerging sandbars. The boat shot out into the open lagoon, and, yonder to the tune of seven or eight thousand birds, vivid pink lines were stretching in front of the distant mangroves. Still, the boatman went flat out, cutting in front of other boats.

When close enough that the individual birds could be made out, he throttled the engine back a bit, but still he went hell-bent, flushing flocks of the awkward yet strangely graceful birds with hook noses and double-hinged knees. He circumnavigated the entire lagoon, then asked for an additional few pesos to show us the saltwater spring boiling up in the red mangroves. I told him we were from Florida and had seen all the bubbling springs and mangroves we needed to see and for him to take us back to the car. This can be translated as meaning we still had not had anything to eat that day.

Stephens had visited the other colony on his second trip to the area. *Toward the end of a sandy beach I noticed on the water what seemed to be a red cloud of singular brilliancy, and, at the same time, delicacy of color, which on drawing nearer, I found to be a flat covered with flamingoes.*[7] Stephens had traveled with an ornithologist, a Dr. Cabot of the Boston Cabots, who needed to collect specimens of the beautiful pink birds. *For two hours we toiled, struggled, floundered and fired, a laughing stock to the beautiful roseate spoonbills,* which they had to settle for in lieu of the more elusive flamingos. Finally Stephens *shot one, which fell at the other side of a stream. As I rushed in, the water rose above all my mud stains, and I fell back, and hastily disencumbered myself of clothing. A high wind was sweeping over the bay. Having no stone at hand with which to secure them, my hat and light garments were blown into the water, and at the same moment the roseate bird stood up, opened its large wings, and fluttered along the beach. Distracted between the bird and the fugitive clothing, I let the latter go, and gave chase to the bird, which after securing it, kicking, under my arm I pursued my habiliments, now some distance apart.*[8]

Sally, not feeling well, stayed in the room in the evening. I had a crab and shrimp *relleno* at a pedestrian restaurant that had suspended water-filled balloons to ward off houseflies. When I asked about the practice, the owner shrugged and said it seemed to work. My order came, a deep-fried fish fillet stuffed with crab and cocktail shrimps with a raisin or two thrown in for the hell of it. After eating, I strolled through the poorly lighted village streets. A few kids were abroad in the cool night air, playing or shooting fireworks. Older folks sat in chairs watching the world pass by, which in this case was me. The doors of many houses, never minding the chill, were thrown open and I could peek in and take a mental snapshot of the inhabitants' lives. Sometimes there would be clothes hanging on a line around a cook fire in a courtyard. Other times there would be neatly arranged sitting rooms, with wooden furniture and bookshelves. Always there would be a hammock, usually with someone swinging in it watching a blaring color TV. Dogs barked but otherwise pursued a policy of peaceful coexistence. Corner *tiendas* (shops) and bakeries were open, often with a patron passing a few idle moments chatting with the clerk. Such was life in Celestún village, not roaringly exciting but pleasant enough in its way.

We left Celestún early in the morning before a morning fog had burned off. Going over the bridge I chanced to notice a line of pink in the fog. As we parked and got out of the car, a flight of birds came in from the gulf and landed on a bar behind the first rank of flamingos. The birds on the bar gobbled like fowls in a barnyard. In the foreground, a flock of gulls roosted on a closer sandbar toward which three barking dogs were swimming. The gulls spooked and rose, circling over the water. In the meantime, just below the bridge, a fisherman rigged his gear and began to paddle his rowboat toward the flamingos. I was expecting an eruption into the sky at any moment, but no, the birds just continued feeding. Although they keep an edgy distance from tour boats, the pink birds paid the fisherman no heed at all. I got my binoculars out, and, suddenly, the blobs of distant color snapped into focus. The birds became individual entities, three lines of them with some egrets and a cluster of other white birds, maybe wood ibises, and staggered among the flamingos were five fishing boats, flat-bottomed, the men as busy with their fishing as the birds were with their feeding. Even those crazy dogs on the foreshore with the gulls circling overhead contributed to a pleasant and unusual scene, which unfortunately could not be photographed, given the distance and poor light.

The map showed three alternative roads leading away from Celestún. Two of them would take us back to the outskirts of Mérida. We were bound for Uxmal, no more than eighty miles all told. We took the third option, turning south off the main road onto a very narrow lane—two cars could not pass abreast. A roadrunner jumped out of the scrub, ran ahead for a few yards, then ducked into the brush on the other side of the road. Seventeen miles from the turn a giant smokestack glared boldly through the trees, and shortly we came to a village. There was one miserable-looking tienda with the usual Coke sign and a few thatch or cinderblock houses—and several massive buildings with a large grassy area between them. It could have been the campus of a small private college—an abandoned and ruined small private college—as these buildings were hulking wrecks. A concrete apron in front of one building had been appropriated as a basketball court, and parts of some of the buildings appeared to be occupied by squatters and perhaps the village government. At the far end of the plaza stood a relatively small, extremely graceful structure; an architect of classical training and some skill was responsible for this building. A herd of goats came running out its gaping doors. Dating these ruins required little cerebral effort, as the building the smokestack rose from bore four numbers, "1908." A few villagers bestirred themselves to gawk at us. They wore dirty, ragged clothes and seemed dispirited, almost imbecilic, giving an even stranger feeling to our coming upon these immense and splendid ruins after seventeen miles of complete wilderness.

A few miles down the road, we came to another ruined hacienda, the buildings, if anything, even grander than the first. Altogether we passed five such places, some marked on the map as villages and some not. These were old sisal plantations from the salad days of the industry, which developed in the period after 1880. In Stephens's time the haciendas were less opulent and devoted to cattle and corn raising. The labor situation, however, was the same: *When the bell of the church is struck five times, every Indian is obliged to go forthwith to the hacienda, and, for a real a day and three cents' worth of maize, do whatever work the master or his delegate, the majordomo, may direct. The authority of the master or his delegate over these is absolute. He settles all disputes between the Indians themselves, and punishes for offenses, acting both as judge and executioner. If the majordomo punishes an Indian unreasonably, the latter may complain to his master. And if the master refuses to give him redress, or himself punishes an Indian unreasonably, the latter may apply for a discharge. There is no obligation upon him to remain on the hacienda unless he is in debt to the master, but, practically, this binds him hand and foot.*[9]

The market for natural fiber was strong up through World War II. But by then these mills were in ruin due to events that started with the overthrow of Mexican dictator Porfirio Díaz in 1910. The proletarian and peasant upboiling of the Mexican Revolution that followed spelled the end of the sisal barons and the seat of their economic power, the institution of debt peonage, which is the fancy way of saying the workers' souls were owned by the company store. The absolute death knoll of the haciendas came in 1937 when President Lázaro Cárdenas confiscated them and assigned them to Maya groups as *ejidos,* which unhappily have not been brilliantly managed.

A brig bound for Havana and New York lay at anchor at Sisal. It was only with great perseverance and fortitude that Stephens and Catherwood turned their backs on it. They were fatigued after nine months of the most rigorous traveling through a most trying territory. But, as luck would have it, months before, Stephens had met in New York a Don Simón Peón, the proprietor of the ruins of Uxmal. *I soon found that everybody in Merida knew Don Simon. In the evening we called at his house. It was a large, aristocratic-looking mansion of dark gray stone, with balconied windows, occupying nearly the half of one side of the plaza. Unfortunately, he was then at Uxmal. Donna Joaquinna, his mother, promised to make all necessary arrangements for the journey.*[10]

We were treated to a tour of the town of Muna, on the north face of the Puuc hills, due to the usual expedient of a couple of wrong turns. It was an active, pleasant town, where life seemed to have purpose and regulation in stark contrast to the torpid sisal villages. According to archaeologist Michael K. Smyth, the Puuc hills are a low ridge of upthrusting, forest-clad limestone that runs diagonally toward the northeast across the Yucatán. Because of the deep mollisoils (dark, rich soils usually associated with grasslands as in the U.S. corn belt), field agriculture can be practiced here—the area had been a breadbasket in historical times and probably in prehistorical ones as well.[11] Farmers on tractors were tilling large plots or setting out winter crops such as cabbages, greens, and the like, all this being responsible for Muna's prosperity. We turned south and in the blink of an eye went over the escarpment that anywhere but in a perfectly flat place like the Yucatán would go completely unremarked.

That strange moniker, Puuc (which simply means "hills"), was given to the characteristic architectural style at Uxmal. The hallmarks of the Puuc style are a richly ornamented upper story of a generally geometric pattern with plain stone surfaces below. This style was not apparent at the first building we sighted, the Temple of the Dwarf, sometimes called the Pyramid of the Magician, or, if you really want to get esoteric, of the *Adivino,* by the local folk today and in Stephens's time. This edifice falls into the category of ugly to the point of beautiful, being both tall and squat.

As Stephens pointed out, it is not really a pyramid in the sense that a pyramid must start at ground zero with a square. This building has an oval base, being approximately 240 feet long and 120 broad, and the ascent up the face fronting the entrance is challenging without the aid of the chain running up the steps. A descent down the back side, the one with a view of the ruins, without recourse to the chain is practically foolhardy, as a sort of lean-to room is tucked near the top, just below the summit. The out-thrusting of that room makes for a very steep slope indeed—sixty degrees or so—and it also gives this temple a quite anomalous, almost grotesque, hunchback look. As it happened, I spent a fair amount of time on the roof of the lean-to, where in

Uxmal, Yucatan, from the vantage point of the Palace of the Governor. The Pyramid of the Magician is on the right. Parts of the east and north wings of the Nunnery Quadrangle are visible to the left of the pyramid.

another day priests and kings practiced interesting and unspeakable rites. I merely viewed the ruins.

At the foot of the Pyramid of the Magician lay the *Casa de los Pájaros,* a courtyard of small buildings decorated with birds, little of which had been in evidence in Stephens's time, or, as far as that went, in my earlier trip to these ruins ten years before. Just beyond this court and a bit to the right was a far larger courtyard, surrounded by the famed Nunnery Quadrangle, which consists of four long, narrow buildings set on an elevation of about fifteen feet above the surrounding plain. These buildings form a square about 250 feet on a side. In the distance, across a shallow wooded ravine and above the level of the Nunnery, are the House of the Turtles, the Grand Pyramid, the House of the Doves, and the Palace of the Governor. And then beyond the ruins, as far as the eye could see, there was a solid mass of greenery, the scrub forest, here considerably thicker and taller than along the littoral. This view was very much the same as the one Stephens gazed out on. In fact, this was probably the only view of Classic lowland ruins that I apprehended that was remotely similar to that which Stephens took in.

By happenstance, the area around the Uxmal ruins had been cleared by the

UXMAL.

HOUSE OF THE DWARF AND HOUSE OF THE NUNS.

F. Catherwood.

H. Jordan.

Uxmal as seen by Stephens and Catherwood.

hacienda owner in Stephens's time because it had been discovered that the grounds were fertile for planting corn. So where I saw lawn, Stephens saw young corn plants peeping above the ground. Similarly, the forest here was still in pristine condition; at most other ruins a view from the highest building now showed the forest razed, whereas in Stephens's time the trees overgrew the sites and were a great detriment in taking observations and making diagrams and drawings.

We entered the Nunnery Quadrangle, so called because it reminded the local folk of a domicile for nuns, through an elegant corbeled archway in the south building. On attaining the courtyard, we turned around and looked south through the arch and saw the Palace of the Governor. Many a procession of Uxmal notables started here and went there or vice versa. In any case, at either end of the *sacbé,* or ceremonial walkway connecting these buildings, are two of the highest expressions of Maya architecture. Both exemplify the Puuc style. Two of the greatest of contemporary Mayanists, Linda Schele and Peter Mathews, have provided a lengthy explication of the meaning of the Nunnery's stonework in their book, *The Code of Kings.*[12]

The southern tier of the Nunnery Quadrangle has four doorways, above each of which is a stone replica of a thatch house. On top of the roof, like the roofcomb on temples at Palenque, Tikal, and even on the Temple of the Dwarf visible at about eleven o'clock from my vantage point, was a monster with corn leaves for hair. These temples are set in a field of stylized "itz" hieroglyphs. In the contemporary Yucatec Mayan, "itz" is the word for flower nectar. The word also means to make magic. Therefore, according to Schele and Mathews, the imagery on the south building pays homage to the life-sustaining grain of the Maya, the dough from which in Maya origin myths the First People were made. Also, it puts the knowledgeable viewer on notice that the edifice is devoted to the important business of sorcery, without the unforgivable gaucherie of coming right out and saying so, as Pacal did at the Temple of the Inscriptions at Palenque. To the naive tourist not conversant with Schele and Mathews, the buildings in the quadrangle, and those erected in the Puuc style generally, are pleasing because they strike a mean between a complete lack of ornamentation and the incredibly busy—almost garish—decoration of some Maya stonework.

The east and north wings show considerably more sophistication in their imagery while still maintaining—thanks to the geometrical repetition and the plain stone walls beneath—that pleasing and relaxing quality. Latticework is used on the east building and stylized cloud patterns among others on the

Detail from the Nunnery. The scarified penis indicates self-sacrifice.

more ambitious north tier, the building that is higher than the other three in homage to its greater importance. My favorite is the west wing. The statuary presented in plots of arabesques is more or less understandable to the viewer, or at least so I thought before consulting Schele and Mathews. Between the first and second door and the last two doors there are figures of human males.

Sally Duncan with Chac (Tláloc) mask at the base of the reconstructed Pyramid of the Magician.

That these figures are male is obvious because they are nude, and their penises and thighs are scarified in ritual sacrifice. Flanking the humans in both instances are rattlesnake heads, above each of which is a serpent's tail, the rattles distinct. In the crook of the snake's tail is an object that very much resembles a pineapple with a leafy top, and which I had assumed was a sacrificed human heart and the associated vein work. All this is framed by a stack of monsterlike Chac (rain god) masks on the corners of the building and over the second and next to last door and set in quads of more intricate geometrical design, most being diamond-shaped, with a repeated internal design and also larger maze-like squares.

Schele and Mathews show that these seemingly straightforward images actually require a bit of interpretation. They start with the stacked masks, which they identify as the central Mexican rain god, Tláloc, because of the elephantine nose, which they insist is not a common incarnation of the Maya rain god Chac. In many of the masks, Tláloc's eyes are shown using the bar and trapeze glyph, the symbol of Venus, which represented war to the Maya—as Mars did for the Romans. Tláloc wears in many of his iterations a flower serpent headband, which again indicates a house of sorcery, flowers like nectar indicating magic. The rattlesnake wears a feather headdress, and is in fact intertwined in a pose of mating with the tail of the snake from the opposite end of the building. The pineapple-like affair in the tail is actually what archaeologists call the drum major headdress, which denotes royal power. In short, the mating feathered snake imagery, presumably with the Mexican rain god, lets us know this is a house of sorcery of a royal line that traces its heritage back to the ancient central Mexico city of Teotihuacan, the only other place where dominant feathered snake imagery was known. As an interesting side note, the large square mazelike design indicates clouds, which serve the dual purpose of reinforcing the notion of magic (clouds being another indicator) and lightening up the busyness of the arabesque patterns. In conclusion, Schele notes that the south and west wings are devoted to corn and creation themes. The beauty of the west and north buildings is dedicated somewhat chillingly to war, specifically to the Tláloc-Venus and human sacrifice motifs. Not only is there the auto-sacrifice of the west wing—probably used to induce hallucinations to commune with ancestors and so on—but the back side of the north shows the figures of nude captives who were sacrificed, permanently memorializing the victims, who died that the rains might fall and the universe be kept in harmony, a touching if grisly tribute.

At the present time, scientists cannot say when Uxmal came on the Maya scene. In days gone by it was supposed that Uxmal was founded perhaps as late as A.D. 700, but recent research by Smyth shows the area was populated much earlier.[13] In any case, it is known to have collapsed about A.D. 1000. Uxmal's contributions to Maya, Mexican, and, yes, even world culture, have been enormous. The ruler responsible for the erection of the Nunnery was Chan-Chak-K'ak'nal-Ahaw, better known as Lord Chac, the various wings of which he dedicated in A.D. 906 and 907.

Lord Chac was also responsible for the erection of the Palace of the Governor. Stephens, who took up residence in the building, thought it the most noble of all Maya structures. *There is no rudeness or barbarity in the design or proportions. If it stood at this day on its grand artificial terrace in Hyde Park or the Garden of the Tuileries, it would form a new order, I do not say equaling, but not unworthy to stand side by side with the remains of Egyptian, Grecian and Roman art.*[14] He was seconded in the opinion that the Governor's Palace was the finest building at Uxmal by Frank Lloyd Wright. No doubt one of the reasons the Puuc style appeals to modern-day Americans is that Wright and his protégés designed many a courthouse, theater and other large public building in its image. The style was dubbed the Maya Revival.[15] In fact, it might not be too much of a stretch to say that the geometrical designs on the concrete edifice that was the Salvadoran border post and Father Napoleón's church in Sonsonate, El Salvador, were inspired by Lord Chac's Puuc style, coming by way of the twentieth-century Maya Revival.

From the Nunnery we crossed to the Palace of the Governor, which is raised, as Stephens noted—in three levels—fifty feet above the bank of the ravine it looks into. The monumental amount of earth moved—considering the Maya employed no draft animals and were unfamiliar with the wheel—boggled the mind, especially since it is believed Lord Chac erected this gargantuan edifice, 320 feet long by about forty feet wide and thirty feet high containing twenty thousand sculpted pieces of stone, almost simultaneously with the Nunnery. In addition, Lord Chac dedicated a ballcourt in A.D. 905, and the Maya stadiums were every bit as expensive, given the enormous amount of masonry, as their often community-divisive modern counterparts. On the far side of the Governor's Palace there is a raised platform with a double-headed jaguar throne at its center. I took a seat on the stone molding surrounding the earthen platform of the jaguar throne and examined the Governor's Palace, which in conjunction with the roofcomb of a distant pyramid lined up with Venus at its southernmost declination.

It seemed a fitting spot to reflect on Stephens's conclusions regarding the strange civilization he was the first to systematically study. Because of the prevailing notion that the ruins were the work of peoples from more accomplished lands, he felt it necessary to strike a defensive stance. *As yet we perhaps stand alone in these views, but* [in] *my opinion we are not warranted in going back to any ancient nation of the Old World for the builders of these cities. They are not the work of people who have passed away and whose history is lost, but that* [they are] *the same races who inhabited the country at the time of the Spanish Conquest or some not very distant progenitors. It was not until our arrival at the ruins of Uxmal that we formed our opinion of their comparatively modern date. Some are beyond doubt older than others. Some are known to have been inhabited at the time of the Spanish Conquest, and others perhaps were really in ruins before.*[16]

It was not until his return the following year that Stephens ventured the opinion that the builders of the cities were the forefathers of the present Indian inhabitants of the area and that he applied the name Maya to a larger cultural entity.[17] Coming to these conclusions was not easy for Stephens (or for Catherwood, who, it can never be forgotten, was his constant companion and confidant). He had not only the conventional wisdom, but also his own prejudices to overcome. He once noted that not a single Indian *mozo* had impressed him enough to remember his name, and the political situation did not help any, as the Indians represented in Stephens's mind either rabble and anarchy, or blind partisans of the Church party and rank conservatism. Stephens, a Jacksonian Democrat, was a liberal of the economically and socially progressive kind.

But Stephens possessed native Yankee sagacity and was heir to the British empirical tradition. He took the evidence and arranged it as reason dictated. Today, the conclusions he drew may seem obvious, but, I was reminded, sitting by the jaguar throne, of what the great British mathematician and Harvard philosopher Alfred North Whitehead said of the Greek discoverers of the basis of mathematics and philosophy. Whitehead claimed that laying the foundations was more difficult than the impressive edifices built on them. In some instances, such as the belief Stephens expressed as a possibility at Copán that the monuments were erected by temporal rulers exulting in their glory, it would be more than one hundred years—until well after World War II—before a new generation of professional Mayanists agreed with him. Still, as I watched an iguana scuttle into the Governor's Palace where Stephens and royalty had slept, I could not help but reflect that Stephens had a fair amount of intuition, and luck, too.

Had that appointment as U.S. minister to Central America not fallen his way, the expedition would have been doomed. More particularly, on occasion he drew the right answer from the wrong evidence, such as his dating the ruins as being of no great antiquity, meaning not contemporaneous with the Egyptian or even classic Greeks. In that he was correct, but he made that judgment on the basis of the wooden lintels at Uxmal, some of which had still been in a fair state of preservation. He assumed, correctly, that sapodilla wood could not stand up to the tropical elements for thousands of years, but he would have been surprised to learn that it had done so for more than a millennium—and that the buildings he so much admired at Uxmal had been erected more than a thousand years before. In other ways, he was just plain lucky. For instance, he dug a hole and found the jaguar throne I was sitting beside. In any case, the concrete detail and levelheaded reasoning he left in his two books on the Maya provided future archaeologists with a solid base on which to build.

Ticul, not far from Uxmal and the largest town in the central part of the state of Yucatán, is famous for the three-wheeled bike carts that are used to haul cargo from warehouses to corner tiendas. With the insertion of a board seat and a small canopy they become bikeshaws, and Sally had her heart set on touring the city in one of these vehicles, which are workaday taxis and not geared to the tourist trade. After that, hunger dictated our next move, so we headed downtown to Los Almendros, a locally famous restaurant that has spawned clones in Mérida and Cancún. I ordered the specialty of the house, *poc chuk,* which turned out to be a pork tenderloin, which you eat fajita style by cutting off a slice and rolling it up in a tortilla.

After all that grease, I needed some ice cream to help take the edge off. The restaurant had none in stock so I stopped at a "supermarket," which was more reminiscent of an old-fashioned corner grocery. None of the clerks seemed to understand my request in Spanish for ice cream. Finally the manager was called and he caught on. He gave me instructions to the town's ice cream parlor, fronting the zócalo. The streets, though unlighted, were choked with parked cars, due to a political rally in the town square. I told Sally, who stayed in the car, that if I did not succeed in finding my ice cream at the hole-in-the-wall store a block away I would return immediately. I hiked to that establishment. I could not make myself understood to the bagboy there. When he finally understood me, he said, "No hay" (there is none), and looked at me as though I was some kind of moral degenerate to think a grocery store would carry ice cream. However, he gave me directions—one block and to the left—to another grocery store.

Hoping Sally would not panic by herself in the dark, I headed for that store. I arrived, but before I opened my mouth, a man said in English, "We have no ice cream. You have to go to the zócalo." What the hell was going on here? At that I gave up and went to the zócalo and found the supposed ice-cream parlor was really a candy store that looked singularly unpromising. Still, it held a small freezer with one kind of prepackaged ice cream cup, which incidentally turned out to be the tastiest treat I had consumed in a long while.

We had now touched all the dots on Stephens's map—at least all we were going to touch—except for Ciudad del Carmen, which was a fairly long haul of 250 miles, much of the way by back road. Although far inland, we motored parallel with the gulf through pristine forest, and with every mile south the trees seemed to grow taller and nobler. Old friends began to show their faces. Here was a gumbo-limbo with its flaking reddish-green bark and there a ceiba, the lord of any tropical American forest and the sacred tree of the Maya. It gave a strange feeling, going through virgin woods in an area that any Cancún tourist with a little determination could reach in a matter of hours. Naturally, it brought to mind the question of what happened to the great Classic Maya civilization that once flourished in the lowlands.

The answer to that is easy. Nobody really knows. But the minds of the best Mayanists have been engaged in speculation on that matter from the very beginning. Not surprisingly, many of their guesses have mirrored the preoccupations of the times. During the cold war era and before, when revolt and revolution was on the minds of Westerners, the idea that the peasant class rose up against their overlords was looked on with favor by some, notably J. Eric Thompson. Later, when the environment first became a top priority for intellectuals, ecological degradation was fingered by many as the number one culprit. Now we live in an age when diversity is the buzzword of choice, and it should not be surprising to learn that many—perhaps even most—scholars now favor multiple causes for the fall.

To take some of the romance out of the idea of a collapse, it would be a good idea to keep in mind a basic law of physics, that all ordered systems tend with time to become disordered. The independent Maya "civilization" existed in many areas for as much as 2,000 years, starting at 400 B.C. or before. I live in Florida, the most recently settled state east of the Mississippi, and often on outings I come on ruins—old hotels, homesteaders shacks, crossroads named for communities that no longer exist—in woods that are as impressively wild as those we were now motoring through. Two millennia is a long time.

It may come in handy to remember too that the term "civilization" is used in a special way in relation to the Maya, and that they did not have the same command of the environment as moderns do. The meat the elite consumed was to a great extent wild game—deer, rabbit, armadillo, turkey, and various rodents. Jaguars and other large animals roamed their forest preserves. Although their art and architecture were sophisticated and subtle, the Maya practiced ritualized warfare and human sacrifice between population centers frequently no farther removed than the team your local high school played last Friday night. In short, they were a people more akin to Homer's heroes than to Plato's philosopher-kings. Given all of that, it is a tribute to the resiliency and conservatism of their culture that they were able to sustain themselves in great ceremonial centers for as long as they did, which was a long, long time indeed.

Of the several causes for the collapse that modern archaeologists take seriously, the most amusing has to be the possibility of self-fulfilling prophesies based on the catastrophic predictions dictated every 256 years by the long-count calendar.[18] Almost everyone is familiar with the gloomy forecast for circa A.D. 1500. The Aztecs and others were supposedly waiting for blue-eyed gods to sail in from the east. The Spanish being taken for these gods and the subsequent easy victory of hundreds of Europeans over hundreds of thousands of indigenous warriors was, therefore, due in part to the fatalism of the Indians. Similar predictions were forecast for the end of the 256-year cycle in the mid–thirteenth century when Chichén Itzá fell, in the mid–sixth century during the so-called Middle Classic Hiatus (when Tikal and perhaps other sites suffered catastrophic declines due to war losses), as well as in the third century at the beginning of the Classic period and a quarter millennium earlier at the beginning of the Late Preclassic era. However, the most significant change occurred in the ninth century, when the great central Classic sites at Copán, Palenque, Yaxchilán, Tikal, Calakmul, and elsewhere foundered, possibly aided by a belief in dire times to come. In short, the belief that the end was upon them itself could have helped bring on the doom all were expecting.

The Maya practiced intensive agriculture, but their technology must have been stretched very thin to support the large numbers of specialized workers of their increasingly urbanized states, where artisans, warriors, and royalty snuggled up to the tit—rather as the declining number of workers in the future must support a greater number of retirees supping at the Social Security trough. Bone samples show even royal personages suffered malnutrition during Late Classic times. On top of this, add the incredibly labor-intensive public works projects undertaken in the Late Classic period, such as Pacal's erection of the Palace and the Temple of the Inscriptions and his successors' building of the crosses complex at Palenque. These great works may have been a last-ditch attempt to mollify the gods and forestall the already impending doom, or they may have been mere human vanity brought on by keeping up with rival classic centers. In any case, scholars believe the massive economic disruption these great projects brought about left the classic communities so bankrupt that a single fairly unimpressive cause or a number of them may have tipped the balance. The cause or causes could be many things: the sudden arrival of an epidemic; meteorological catastrophes, such as a series of hurricanes or floods (unlikely) or to a long-term drought (which a team of University of Florida researchers has shown did indeed occur);[19] the invasion of an outside group, such as the Putun Maya, taking advantage of already weak systems (which is known to have occurred at several sites); or perhaps some other as-yet-undetermined reason or reasons. In any case, the population centers of the southern lowland regions declined dramatically—if unevenly—throughout the ninth century, finally becoming completely deserted a century or so later. The vast forest remained a trackless waste until very recent times.

The Maya did not disappear, even though the great Classic centers fell into ruin. Remnant populations moved north into the Yucatán, sometimes founding new city-states, sometimes merging with preexisting communities. As we have already noted, when Montejo's conquistadors invaded the peninsula, impressive Maya towns were still in the center and, also, running along the Caribbean coast as far as Belize. The Quiché, Cakchíquel, and Mam Maya in the mountains of Guatemala—as Stephens showed us—were subdued by Spanish arms. As we have already noted—the Maya folk culture, the *hombres de mais,* endured for a period of three millennia and is still going strong in the Yucatán and the highlands.[20]

We passed the boundary into the state of Campeche and the first village we went through, Bolonchén, known for its great caves, was neat as a pin and clean as any New England town. We took a back road that bypassed the city of Campeche, which Stephens never visited because the town was in a state of rebellion against the central government, skirted the ruins of Edzná, and then suddenly we were in an agricultural area. A citrus grove—the leaves dark green and large, sure signs of health—was bounded by a white board fence. Farther on, citrus or mango groves flanked us on both sides of the road and there were all kinds of signs that scientific agriculture was being carried on.

Then the groves gave over to vast sugar cane plantations. The fields had recently been fired, and the sabal palms in the peripheries had had their fronds burned off. New palm shoots had emerged and they were growing fiercely. Tractor-drawn wagons were piled high with cane. Set in these agricultural precincts—and announced by signs—were barracks of Maya who had fled to Mexico from the mountains of Guatemala. It made me think of the laughing bishop of Santa Cruz del Quiché. Raphael had told me in a recent letter that Bishop Cabrera was still there, I hope still laughing, but not for the same dire reasons as when we visited him years before. Judging by the cleanliness and order of the barracks housing the members of his flock in Campeche, his parishioners appeared to have landed on their feet.

We came out on the Gulf of Mexico at Champotón, which has a wide sandy beach that extends almost a hundred miles to Ciudad del Carmen, with only one commercial establishment, a proletarian tourist stop at Sabancuy, where a road cuts across the swampy delta to intersect the coast highway. The drive was lonely along probably one of the longest stretches of unspoiled coasts left anywhere. Like most such stretches, it did not exactly meet the Disney ideal of a tropical beach. It was littered with sargasso weed, and a tropical storm a couple years before had torn up the interface vegetation. Added to those fairly pedestrian woes was the lethal yellow disease, a mysterious ailment that appeared in Florida about twenty-five years ago and decimated certain species of palm trees. You can tell if the lethal yellow has struck by a spindly trunk sticking up with a few dead fronds. The inland side was one vast coconut grove of the susceptible Jamaican Tall variety. Most trees were either dead or slowly dying. So we motored through a forest of naked trunks, the fronds gone or yellowing. Here and there sabal palms were doing their part to replace them, or small plantations of the resistant Malaysian Dwarf coconut had been set out.

We had no idea what to expect of Carmen, a town of eighty thousand inhabitants. To the right was the Gulf of Mexico and off to the left and seemingly just as large, the Laguna de Términos, where Stephens sailing in from the Usumacinta almost had his life terminated on a flat-bottomed sailing vessel called a bungo. *In front but a little to the left, and barely visible, a long line of trees, marked the island of Carmen, our port of destination.*

At two o'clock we saw clouds gathering, and immediately the sky became very black, the harbinger of one of those dreadful storms which even on dry land were terrible. The hatches were put down, and a tarpaulin spread over for us to take refuge under. The squall came on so suddenly that the men were taken unaware, and the confusion on board was alarming. The patron [or master] *with both hands extended, and a most beseeching look, begged the senores to take in sail. The senores, all shouting together, ran and tumbled over the logwood, hauling upon every rope but the right one. The mainsail stuck halfway up, and would not come down. While the patron and all the men were shouting and looking up at it, the sailor who had* [earlier] *been upset in the canoe, with tears of terror actually streaming from his eyes, and a start of desperation, ran up the mast by the rings, and, springing violently upon the top one, holding fast by a rope, brought the sail down with a run.*

A hurricane blew through the naked masts, a deluge of rain followed, and the lake was lashed to a fury. We lost sight of everything. At the very beginning, on account of the confusion on board, we determined not to go under the hatch. If the bungo swamped, the logwood cargo would carry her to the bottom like lead. We disencumbered ourselves of boots and coats, and brought out life-preservers ready for use. The deck of the bungo was about three feet from the water, and perfectly smooth, without anything to hold on by, and, to keep from being blown or washed away, we lay down and took the whole brunt of the storm. This continued for more than an hour, when it cleared off as suddenly as it came up, and there was now a dead calm.[21]

After a while another storm came up and the bungo made it to the harbor. *There were breakers between us and the shore. We saw a fine jolly-boat, with a cockswain and four men, coasting along the shore against a rapid current. We hailed them in English, and the cockswain answered in the same language that it was too rough, but after a consultation with the sailors they pulled toward us, and took Mr. Catherwood and me on board. As soon as we struck* [the beach], *we mounted the shoulders of two square-built sailors, and were set down on shore, and perhaps in our whole tour we were never so happy as at that moment in being rid of the bungo.*[22]

Once on shore, Stephens presented himself to the American consul, Charles Russell, who was known as Don Carlos Russell by virtue of long residence and marriage to a great fortune. He also met a New Yorker, a Captain Fensley, *who asked news of me, which I was happy to give him in person. At the moment I did not recognize him and in my costume from the interior, it was impossible for him to recognize me.*[23]

We motored along the coast highway, paralleling the route Stephens had taken in luxury in Captain Fensley's ship. The captain had deposited him at Sisal, and after a short visit to Uxmal, Stephens and Catherwood had boarded a Spanish ship for the trip homebound to New York, where as we have already learned, their work met an enthusiastic reception.[24] All told, Stephens may have earned as much as $50,000 from the royalties of his book in the first year after its publication. The return trip to the Yucatán brought a maturation in his understanding of the Maya culture—and even more literary and pecuniary success. After that, Stephens turned to the normal occupations of a man pushing middle age. He resumed his career as a lawyer—and politico. He was a delegate to the New York constitutional convention in 1846, the year he turned forty. The following year he became an officer in the Ocean Steamship Navigation Company, and then a rather strange thing occurred. Stephens dropped completely out of sight. Had he taken up travels to distant lands again? His family refused to say a word.

When he reemerged, it turned out he had been to Bogotá to negotiate for rights to a railroad—and canal—across the Panamanian isthmus. His partner in this venture was William Aspinwall, the shipping magnate, and Stephens had been included—one supposes—as much for his presumed political skills as his tropical savvy. The next few months found him in Washington, where he jawboned members of Congress as to the strategic necessity of an American railroad across Central America. And he convinced the congressmen who then approved a fat subsidy for the railroad that would run across the isthmus. The only possible stumbling block was James K. Polk, Andrew Jackson's protégé and a benefactor of Stephens's campaigning during the last election. Polk is also the first president to project American influence in Central America—or so claims Walter LaFeber, the historian, who asserts Central America is a mere dependency of the United States. Be that as it may, Polk vetoed the measure Stephens worked so hard for. He cited his belief that subsidies for extranational works were unconstitutional. For all that, the rail link across the isthmus bound the United States's west coast to the east, and, later the completion of this vital link was deemed a chief reason for California not declaring its independence from the northern states during the Civil War; the defection of that state would have sealed the fate of the Union.

Undeterred, Stephens took charge of the building of the road on the site in Panama. His title was president of the Panama Rail Road Company. Within five months half the laborers, who had been lured to the tropics by posters advertising "Money, Adventure, Women," were dead. More laborers were to be had—in the usual way, by ponying up more money. In a year and a half, seven miles of track were laid, at a cost of more than a third of a million dollars a mile, and the company was nearly bankrupt.

But Stephens's luck, as usual, held. Swarms of gold-mad prospectors descended on the railhead, demanding to be transported those seven miles across a stretch of swamp with a nasty reputation for a particularly virulent disease called for want of more accurate nomenclature, Chagres fever. Seeing money coming in, investor confidence rose, and rightfully it may have, because, by some reckonings, Stephens's company was considered the most successful nineteenth-century venture undertaken outside the United States. It paid a dividend of 24 percent per annum. However, none of that was to do the Maya explorer any good. His mule slipped while on a second trip to the highlands; Stephens fell and was dragged. The accident left him little better than an invalid. Recuperation came slowly, and, when it did, his old malady, malaria, came with it. Stephens returned to New York where he died in 1852. He was only forty-six. By coincidence, Catherwood had also become a railroad engineer, in nearby British Guyana. Fearing for his health, he—after an extensive visit with Stephens—relocated to California. He too died prematurely, being lost at sea in 1855, having passed fifty-six years on the planet.

Stephens's corpse was inadvertently laid to rest in the wrong tomb in an unmarked vault in New York. After a remarkable life, the ignominy of his burial pretty much summed up his reputation for the next one hundred years. In short, he was almost entirely forgotten. The Panamanian railway was identified with the tycoon Aspinwall. Maya studies went out of fashion. A lone tramp steamer plying the waters between northern cities and, fittingly, the banana ports, bore his name. By mid–twentieth century the critic Van Wyck Brooks tried to resurrect Stephens's literary reputation with mixed results. He inspired Victor Wolfgang von Hagen to do a full-fledged (and interesting, and according to the archaeologist Michael Coe, who obviously admires factual precision over poetic charm, not always stunningly accurate) biography.

In terms of his literary legacy, Stephens's Mesoamerican books have been in print in many editions for many years. Many of his readers have been referred to Stephens from encountering his name in their travels or by archaeologists or historians in college classes. In short, though professional literary critics have generally continued to ignore his considerable literary contributions, the public at large has rediscovered Stephens, and is paying homage to his great works. For instance, recently a San Diego museum mounted a show of Catherwood's prints and Stephens's text. A website is devoted to a retracing of Stephens's trail, a sort of electronic version of this book. The National Geographic recently ran a series of articles on the Maya devoting a couple of issues to Stephens and Catherwood.[25] Dozens or hundreds or perhaps even thousands set off every year on the Ruta Maya with Stephens's book in hand. Even the odd English professor pens a paper now and then about Stephens, but so far those have only touted him as a remarkable "find," owing to the lack of entries in the Modern Language Association bibliography—this about a literary figure whose books are in print a century and a half after his death and which can be found on the shelves of bookstores throughout the country.

I was hoping that for our last night on the Stephens's trail we could stay in a hotel more sentimentally tied to Stephens's age and time. But we had been a month on the trail, and as modest as our travails had been compared to Stephens's, we were worn down. We had no idea what to expect of Carmen, a town of eighty thousand inhabitants. The guide book did not offer much by way of encouragement, claiming it was an expensive, muggy oil town. We arrived near dusk on a Saturday night, and though muggy, little was in evidence of the vast offshore oil industry in the Bay of Campeche that the town serviced. In fact, the mugginess was welcome, after the cold snap that had struck Mérida on New Year's Day and had lingered through the week. I was determined to find what the book claimed was a good non-air-conditioned hotel. We spent forty-five minutes going back and forth trying to locate a supposed rational address in a grid-style street system that a waterfront and navy base, plentiful small plazas, and age had conspired to skew. Finally, several blocks away from the center of the town, as though designed to nab weary lodging seekers, we saw a nice looking building with a sign, "Hotel." No name. Sally rented a room for 150 pesos. There were no windows, but it had air conditioning, and was very modern and clean, with about six movie channels in English with Spanish subtitles.

Resigned to a quiet evening, I stepped out of the hotel to check out the Flame Steakhouse down the street—and was attacked by a woman from the beauty parlor next door. She actually jumped out of the doorway, where she was lurking, and insisted vehemently that I needed a beard cut, which she was prepared to give. Talk about hard sell. The way she went on, you would think it was a matter of life and death. I suppose it goes without saying that she was young and attractive—why else would anyone put up with such a strange harangue? She had a strong face, very swarthy, and she was tallish with a nice build and an extremely deep, throaty, sensual voice. She was wearing a sort of leotard bodysuit with a blue vest.

And she just would not take no for an answer. As usual in situations like this, my Spanish failed and most of the discussion took place via gesture. By now I was inside her shop, where she grabbed a pair of scissors and was snipping away in the air and I was protesting, Samson-like, that I could not convey to her the look I really wanted. She kept shouting, "espejo, espejo," mirror, mirror, meaning, I suppose that I could look in the mirror and guide her. She dragged me from the salon through a back room with an unmade poster bed (that under the circumstances was equal parts suggestive and unsettling) to a poorly lighted, dirty courtyard. She grabbed a piece of dark plastic that could have been used as a mirror and said again, "espejo." I wondered what the hell I was doing back there looking at a mirror, an object that lined the walls of the shop.

Even more disturbing was her fellow beautician, a tall creature with long hair that fell down the back, but with about as much hair on top as an onion. He (or she) had on an androgynous pantsuit and sported the nicest set of falsies I had seen since high school. Now in the back courtyard, the normal male homophobia kicked in, and I figured this person who had dragged me back here was as swish as the pantsuit guy, and that they wanted me to have my beard cut in front of some kind of two-way peepshow mirror, behind which somebody would be stationed and getting their kicks. I did what any right-thinking American would do. I panicked and ran, bursting away and hotfooting through the bedchamber and into the salon. The person in leotards came running right behind me, screaming that I should not go. The bald-headed guy in the phony bra in the front room folded his arms and laughed at our carrying on. Sally told me later that I arrived at the room looking white and shook up. No matter what, it was a very weird incident.

In the morning we sun-oiled and went for a stroll. Being January, it was pleasantly cool, but the sun had a tropical intensity and I was plenty thankful that I had oiled up. We stopped by the market, always one of my favorite places, and I admired the vegetables and haggled for some stuff I did not need and then found the Roma Hotel, which we had searched for diligently but fruitlessly the day before. It was on the only part of the street blocked to car traffic. It was a flophouse and was full up to boot. Once out of the courtyard houses of the downtown area, Carmen resembled a Florida town more than any we had been to—a lot of sand, and a lot of water, which surrounded the city on three sides. The sun was hot and by now the atmosphere had warmed and it was muggy, and there was lots of nice tropical vegetation. Even the wild palm of choice, the sabal, the state tree of Florida, reminded me of home. We crossed the main drag by the old ferry station and came to a village separated from the mainland by a tidal creek. An old guy in a twenty-foot dory ferried people across the creek. A little stand made from a shipping pallet was the dock on both sides. The creek was about three lengths of the boat wide. The patrons did not pay the ferryman, the service was evidently provided by the state.

Back downtown we had coffee and juice at an open-air seaside restaurant. Four parrots in small cages set on cement blocks were being tormented by a male child. The kid would stick a leaf in a cage and a parrot would grab at it. After a while the kid's mother and toddler sister came over, and joined him in poking leaves into the cages. I figured someone was about to lose a finger or an eye. But my fun was spoiled when the family's interest waned and they drifted away. Then the parrots started squawking in Spanish. Evidently the birds enjoyed the attention and wanted the people to come back.

The parrots were not the only fowl in evidence. Brown pelicans were diving into the water just off the sea wall. The water was a lovely aquamarine. After loading the luggage into the car, I went over to the beauty salon, which was open even though it was Sunday, and got a haircut. The name of that oh-so-insistent pitchman was Maxita. In the clear light of morning there was no doubt she was female. Hormone treatments might generate breasts as impressive as hers, but they could not produce that fecund swelling of the hips. She told me she was twenty-five and had been a hairdresser for two years. She worked with the intensity and concentration of a brain surgeon and had the gentle touch female barbers often have. She seemed rather subdued today, perhaps because of Sally's occupation of a chair in the waiting area. Or perhaps I had just had a hallucination and that strange scene had not really occurred the day before. In any case I gave Maxita a handsome tip to let her know that I appreciated the attention, even if I did not exactly understand the purpose of it. She surprised me by being confused and perhaps even a bit put out by the gratuity.

Our problem as we coasted along the Gulf was finding the proper spot for a picnic—a not inconsiderable quandary when you have one hundred miles of beach, each area just as eligible as the next, and the American inclination to put the pedal to the metal and keep it there. Barreling down that long empty reach of road, I happened to look up and see a flock of huge white birds. Even a glance showed these were no ordinary chin-tucked-into-neck, wings-winking egrets, or the more interesting curved-bill ibises. I pulled the car over onto the shoulder and got out, putting a hand up to shelter my eyes from the sun.

As though on cue, the birds wheeled and began to spiral, one behind the other, up into the sky. They were white pelicans. Unlike their clownish cousin, the brown pelican, common to subtropical coasts, the white pelican is a stately bird, befitting its status as the largest self-sustaining avian in North America, now that breeding colonies of California condors have disappeared from the wild. I watched as the birds spiraled and flapped and spiraled some more. They had caught a thermal and were riding it up into the heavens. Unlike those complete boobs, their brown relatives, white pelicans know how to have fun without losing dignity. Taking a clue from them, we laid out our picnic repast on a downed log and thought how appropriate it was for those birds to appear as we were taking leave from Stephens. He knew how to maintain his dignity and have his fun too. The pelicans, like Stephens, denizens of northern climes who spend a good deal of their time in tropical environs, wheeled and soared, spiraling farther and farther up into the heavens. Finally, I lost sight of them.

Notes

Introduction

1. The sobriquet "Father of American Archaeology" is sometimes applied to Thomas Jefferson. Jefferson published a monograph on the results of his excavation of an Indian mound in Virginia. This work showed the same kind of good sense Stephens's later investigations in Central America demonstrated. A better appellation for Stephens could perhaps be the Father of Mesoamerican Archaeology.

2. "Despite past claims that Classic Maya societies were organized as theocracies, that is, as states ruled by priests, there is not the slightest evidence for the existence of priests in Classic times!" (Michael D. Coe, *The Maya*, 6th ed. [New York: Thames and Hudson, 1999], 210). "It appears that warfare among these little city-states was almost incessant" (Michael D. Coe and Justin Kerr, *The Art of the Maya Scribe* [New York: Harry N. Abrams, 1998], 35).

3. William L. Fash, *Scribes, Warriors and Kings: The City of Copan and the Ancient Maya* (New York: Thames and Hudson, 1991), 10. It would be well to keep in mind that all of Stephens's archaeological surmises were no doubt vetted by and perhaps even coauthored by his artist companion, Frederick Catherwood. I do not much discuss Catherwood's contributions because the main academic thrust of the present volume is directed at Stephens's literary accomplishments. There is no record of the exact nature of Catherwood's contributions and hence there is very little of a concrete nature to say about them, at least to one of my background.

4. Richard Preston, "America's Egypt: John Lloyd Stephens and the Discovery of the Maya," *Princeton University Library Chronicle* 53 (spring 1992): 243–63; Richard O'Mara, "The American Traveller," *Virginia Quarterly Review* 74 (spring 1998): 221–

33. In the period 1963–2002, the Modern Language Association Bibliography lists only two sources of critical works in which Stephens is discussed (along with other writers): David E. Johnson's "'Writing in the Dark': The Political Fictions of American Travel Writing," *American Literary History* 7, no. 1 (1995): 1–27 and Richard McCann Preston's dissertation, "The Fabric of Fact: The Beginnings of American Literary Journalism," *Dissertation Abstracts International* 44, no. 1 (1983): 170A.

5. See chapter 4, note 27.

6. All specialized fields are difficult to maneuver in for the nonspecialist. Maya archaeology and Central American history are especially swampy. After slow progress during the past two centuries, the state of Maya archaeology is in rapid flux; even the specialist can hardly keep up with developments. Likewise, Central American history, thanks to the cold war irruptions of the 1980s, is even more fraught with political quagmires for the unwary. I offer what I perceive to be the conventional, middle-ground position in most instances.

7. Van Wyck Brooks, *The World of Washington Irving* (Philadelphia: Blakiston, 1944), 475, 478, 480.

8. Quoted in William Wasserstrom, "Van Wyck Brooks," in *The Makers of American Thought: An Introduction to Seven American Writers,"* ed. Ralph Ross (Minneapolis: University of Minnesota Press, 1963, 1974), 185.

9. Ibid., 190.

Chapter 1

1. John Lloyd Stephens, *Incidents of Travel in Central America, Chiapas and Yucatan,* 2 vols. (1841; reprint with Publisher's Note from 1854 edition, New York: Dover, 1969), 1: 11. Because Stephens's text is used as an adjunct to my own, I have taken certain liberties. The spelling has been modernized (changing the British spelling then in use to Noah Webster's suggestion for American orthography used today but *generally* leaving Stephens's idiosyncratic misspellings), the punctuation is exactly as I would do it (which is better than his archaic punctuation but probably not good enough), and I occasionally take license with his prose by joining passages from different contexts, eliminating words and so on. For instance, the word "actual" appeared before beauty in the original passage. Added words, with the rare exception of an article or other short word, are marked in the usual way by enclosing in brackets. In a series of quotes from the same general location, I give the page number of the first quote.

2. For these and most other biographical details, I follow von Hagen. Victor Wolfgang von Hagen, *Maya Explorer: John Lloyd Stephens and the Lost Cites of Central America and Yucatán* (1947; San Francisco: Chronicle Books, 1990).

3. Stephens, *Central America,* 1: 12.

4. Ibid. "Sable" omitted before the term ladies.

5. State Department, Bureau of Public Affairs, "Background Notes: Belize, August 1987" (Washington, D.C.: GPO, 1987), 1–6.

6. Stephens, *Central America,* 1: 14.

7. Tim L. Merrill, ed. *Guyana and Belize: Country Studies,* 2nd ed. (Washington, D.C.: GPO, 1993), 164.

8. William David Setzekorn, *Formerly British Honduras: A Profile of the New Nation of Belize* (Athens: Ohio University Press, 1981), 134.

9. Stephens, *Central America,* 1: 18–19.

10. Ibid, 15. Stephens's attitude about race is confusing and at times seems confused. A recent master's thesis (Michael Daum, "Modernity's Ethnographer: John Lloyd Stephens in Belize" [University of South Florida, 1999]) castigates Stephens for not maintaining a politically correct (as seen from the 1990s) view of race. If we put aside the rather high requirement this critic heaps on a man who lived when slavery was practiced in his homeland, we must admit that he is correct in saying Stephens shared many of the racist viewpoints, if perhaps not the prejudices, of the time. Even though he was among the first to accept the idea that the Maya ruins were the work of the ancestors of present-day Indians, Stephens rarely had a kind word for the local populace, perhaps in part due to its general hostility to whites at the time.

11. Merrill, *Guyana and Belize,* 168.

12. Stephens, *Central America,* 1: 16.

13. Ibid., 19.

14. Ibid., 23–24.

15. Anne Sutherland, *The Making of Belize: Globalization in the Margins* (Westport, Conn.: Bergin and Garvey, 1998), 77.

Chapter 2

1. See chapter 1, note 2 for bibliographical information on von Hagen. All quotes in this chapter taken from von Hagen.

2. Stephens, *Central America,* 1: 20.

3. Ibid., 26–31.

4. Wayne M. Cleghorn, *British Honduras: Colonial Dead End, 1859–1900* (Baton Rouge: Louisiana State University Press, 1967), 40–46.

5. Stephens, *Central America,* 1: 28.

Chapter 3

1. Stephens spells this name "M'Donald." Most other sources use "MacDonald."

2. Clifford D. Conner, *Colonel Despard: The Life and Times of an English Jacobin* (Conshohocken, Pa.: Signpost, 1999), 10.

3. Setzekorn, *Formerly British Honduras,* 151.

4. H. C. Allen, "Border Disputes (1823–60)," in *Great Britain and the United States: A History of Anglo-American Relations (1783–1952)* (New York: St. Martin's, 1955), 382–451.

5. Stephens, *Central America,* 1: 14.

6. Ibid., 21–22.

7. Stephens tells us that "on the third of March, 1835, a resolution passed the Senate of the United States, 'that the president be requested to consider the expediency of opening negotiations with the governments of Central America and Grenada.' . . . A special agent was appointed by General Jackson who was instructed to proceed without delay" to survey the best site for a trans-isthmus canal (*Central America,* 1: 415). Stephens reported to Secretary of State Forsyth that he visited the site of a possible Nicaraguan canal "at his own expense," 17 August 1840 (William R. Manning, ed. *Diplomatic Correspondence of the United States: Inter-American Affairs, 1831–1860,* vol. 3: Central America 1831–1850, documents 723–995 [Washington, D.C.: Carnegie Endowment for International Peace, 1933], 160) and that he had procured a copy of the Central American Federation's survey of the canal which he offered the Secretary of State on 6 April 1840 (*Diplomatic Correspondence of the United States,* 158–59). See chapter 9 and especially note 4 for specifics on the attempts of British Foreign Secretary Lord Palmerston to exact intelligence of American efforts to obtain rights to a canal from Central American emissary Juan Galindo.

8. David M. Pendergast, ed. and comp., *Palenque: The Walker-Caddy Expedition to the Ancient Maya City, 1839–1840* (Norman: University of Oklahoma Press, 1967), 177.

9. Stephens, *Central America,* 1: 23.

10. Cleghorn, *British Honduras,* 98, 118.

11. Setzekorn, *Formerly British Honduras,* 228–29.

12. Thomas P. Anderson, *Politics in Central America: Guatemala, El Salvador, Honduras and Nicaragua* (New York: Praeger, 1983), 13.

13. Linda Schele and Mary Ellen Miller, *The Blood of Kings: Dynasty and Ritual in Maya Art* (London: Thames and Hudson, 1992), 1. The view of "blood as mortar" seems to be losing currency among Mayanists.

14. Anderson, *Politics,* 14.

15. David Crystal, ed. *Cambridge Fact Finder* (Cambridge: Cambridge University Press, 1993), 251.

16. Walter LaFeber, *Inevitable Revolutions: The United States in Central America,* 2nd ed. (New York: W. W. Norton, 1993), 8.

17. Generally, the term "mestizo" means mixed blood, "latino" means of Spanish descent, and "ladino" means participating in Spanish culture. There is a great deal of latitude in usage. For instance, ladino as used in Guatemala has been defined as anything from "an Indian who wears shoes" to a person of European blood. In short, my use of these concepts is elastic—as it frequently is in Central America.

18. Lesley Byrd Simpson, *The Encomienda in New Spain: The Beginning of Spanish Mexico* (Berkeley: University of California Press, 1966), viii–ix.

19. "The Indian side was taken by the Dominican priest Bartolomé de Las Casas who had served as the Bishop of Chiapas. His extensive defense of the Indians contains aggressive discussions of such categories as 'barbarians,' 'city,' 'Christian,' 'language,' and 'natural slavery' as a means to argue that preconquest Indian societies met all the Aristotelian criteria for a civil society. On [the other] side of the debate was the Spanish philosopher Juan Ginés de Sepulveda. He argued in a five-hundred page treatise that the Indians were 'as inferior to Spaniards as women to men, as monkeys to men'" (Davíd Carrasco, *Religions of Mesoamerica: Cosmovision and Ceremonial Centers* [San Francisco: Harper and Row, 1990], 8). Bernal Díaz del Castillo and Bishop Francisco Marroquín were other important voices raised in defense of the Indians.

20. Thomas L. Karnes, *The Failure of Union: Central America, 1824–1960* (Chapel Hill: University of North Carolina Press, 1961), 82. Also see Ralph Lee Woodward Jr., *Central America: A Nation Divided* (New York: Oxford University Press, 1999).

21. Ronald H. MacDonald, "Civil-Military Relations in Central America: The Dilemmas of Political Institutionalization," in *Rift and Revolution: The Central American Imbroglio,* ed. Howard J. Wiarda (Washington, D.C.: American Enterprise Institute for Public Policy Research, 1984), 136.

22. "United Fruit built its Guatemalan empire on foundations laid during the first phase of the Liberal reform when the . . . [the Barrioses, 1873–97] pursued a modernization program that served the interests of the coffee planters. The Liberals believed that the expansion of the coffee economy would provide them the capital they needed to create a modern diversified economy. To this ambitious end, they seized communal lands, reimposed forced labor systems, confiscated church properties, and promoted infrastructural development" (Paul J. Dorsal, *Doing Business with the Dictators: A Political History of United Fruit in Guatemala, 1899–1944* [Washington, Del.: SR Books, 1993], 17).

23. Norman B. Schwartz, *Forest Society: A Social History of Petén, Guatemala* (Philadelphia: University of Pennsylvania Press, 1990), 10–30.

24. Stephens, *Central America,* 1: 36.

25. Ibid., 45.

26. This conversation with Ilsa actually occurred on the road from Punta Gorda to Placencia, Belize, where she chose to take a shortcut by boat rather than ride all the way with a representative of gringo imperialism, a possibility she briefly entertained. I changed the venue to the Petén because our discussion dovetailed with the material discussed here. The dialogue between us is a creative reconstruction.

27. LaFeber, *Inevitable Revolutions,* 81–82.

28. Anderson, *Politics,* 39–40, 43–44.

29. Stephens, *Central America,* 1: 88–89, 106.

30. Ibid., 125.

31. Ibid., 56–57.

32. Ibid., 52.

33. Ibid., 58.

34. Ibid., 49.

35. Ibid., 59.

36. Ibid., 91, 164–65.

37. Ibid., 107–8.

38. Schwartz, *Forest Society*, 12.

39. Stephens, *Central America*, 1: 21.

40. Robert J. Sharer, *The Ancient Maya*, 5th ed. (Stanford: Stanford University Press, 1994), 747–53.

41. Linguistic evidence indicates the Lacandón could not have evolved from the Itzá. The graph on page 48 of Michael D. Coe's *Breaking the Maya Code* (New York: Thames and Hudson, 1999), shows that the Itzá and the Lacandón Maya split about A.D. 1000, approximately seven hundred years before the conquest of Tayasal.

42. Letter from Barbara Tharp dated 17 May 1999.

43. Regarding "innkeeper Michael DeVine, a U.S. citizen detained and slain in Guatemala in 1990 in whose case [Guatemalan Colonel] Alpirez is suspected of involvement, the CIA has confessed that it failed to keep Congress fully informed of its activities in Guatemala, two top CIA officials have been fired, and at least eight others have been disciplined. Alpirez had been on the CIA payroll for a long time, but they had been furious with him for months because they believed he was responsible for the death of Michael DeVine," Eric Black, "Advocating for Human Rights," *Minneapolis Star Tribune*, 7 May 1996, 6A.

44. Stephens, *Central America*, 1: 80–83.

Chapter 4

1. Stephens, *Central America*, 1: 33.

2. Ibid., 20.

3. Ibid., 33–34.

4. Ibid., 32.

5. William B. Hatcher, *Edward Livingston: Jeffersonian Republican and Jacksonian Democrat* (Baton Rouge: Louisiana State University Press, 1940), 286–87.

6. Stephens, *Central America*, 1: 32–33.

7. Ibid., 40, 42–43.

8. Ibid., 46.

9. W. O. Lessard, *The Complete Book of Bananas* (Homestead, Fla.: [The author], 1992), 2–5.

10. Charles David Kepner Jr. and Jay Henry Soothill, *The Banana Empire: A Case*

Study in Economic Imperialism (New York: Vanguard Press, 1935; New York: Russell & Russell, 1967), 43.

11. LaFeber, *Inevitable Revolutions,* 120.

12. Stephen Schlesinger and Stephen Kinzer, *Bitter Fruit: The Untold Story of the American Coup in Guatemala* (1982; New York: Anchor Books, 1990). Also, some say a more balanced approach to the UFCO-Arbenz crisis is given by Richard H. Immerman, *The CIA in Guatemala: The Foreign Policy of Intervention* (Austin: University of Texas Press, 1982).

13. Stephens, *Central America,* 2: 123.

14. Sharer, *Ancient Maya,* 317–30. Also, Simon Martin and Nikolai Grube, *Chronicle of the Maya Kings and Queens* (London: Thames and Hudson, 2000), 215–25.

15. Stephens, *Central America,* 1: 59–60.

16. Ibid., 68–69.

17. Ibid., 420–21.

18. Richard F. Nyrop, ed. *Guatemala: A Country Study,* 2nd ed. (Washington, D.C.: GPO, 1983), 29–32. Also see Richard Newbold Adams, *Crucifixion by Power: Essays on Guatemalan National Social Structure, 1944–1966* (Austin: University of Texas Press, 1970).

19. Victor Perera, *Unfinished Conquest: The Guatemalan Tragedy* (Berkeley: University of California Press, 1993), 41–42, 335.

20. Susanne Jonas, *The Battle for Guatemala: Rebels, Death Squads, and U.S. Power,* Latin American Perspective Series, no. 5 (Boulder, Colo.: Westview Press, 1991), 70.

21. Stephens, *Central America,* 1: 174–75.

22. Ibid., 178.

23. Ibid., 170–71.

24. Ibid., 166.

25. Ibid., 169.

26. Ibid., 169.

27. Ibid., 169–70.

28. "Until the government instituted passport regulations some years ago, as many as 100,000 people annually sought the shrine of the Black Christ on 15 January" (Vera Kelsey and Lilly de Jongh Osborne, *Four Keys to Guatemala* [New York: Funk and Wagnalls, 1948], 45–46).

Chapter 5

1. "Central American Federation, 'Peace, Amity, Commerce, and Navigation,'" *Unperfected Treaties of the United States* (Dobbs Ferry, N.Y.: Oceana, 1976–94), 129–40.

2. "On the 14th day of July of last year a General Convention . . . was concluded at Guatemala and signed by Mr. DeWitt on the part of the United States. For causes

which remain unexplained it had not, at the period of Mr. DeWitt's departure from Guatemala received the required sanction of the Central American government. . . . It is not, however, the desire of the President that the negotiation should thus remain without a result; and he is disposed to apply to the Senate, in the event of the Convention meeting his and their approbation, for authority to proceed to the exchange of the ratifications, notwithstanding the lapse of the period within which that ceremony was to have taken place. Such a step, however, on the part of the President would be without a corresponding desire and action on the part of the Central American government. You are authorized, in your interview with the Minister for foreign affairs, to sound the disposition of his government in this respect, and, in case you should think it favorable, to propose that if the Convention shall have received or will receive the required sanction of the Central American Government, its executive will obtain the authority to extend the time," Aaron Vail, acting secretary of state of the United States to John L. Stephens, special agent of the United States to Central America, Washington, 13 August 1839, *Diplomatic Correspondence of the United States,* 24.

3. Stephens, *Central America,* 1: 194, 196–200.

4. Tim L. Merrill, ed. *Nicaragua: A Country Study,* 3rd ed. (Washington, D.C.: GPO, 1994), 10.

5. Stephens, *Central America,* 1: 196.

6. Ibid., 311–12.

7. Ibid., 114.

8. Crystal, *Cambridge Fact Finder,* 240.

9. Richard A. Haggerty, ed., *El Salvador: A Country Study,* 2nd ed. (Washington, D.C.: GPO, 1990), 11.

10. Haggerty, *El Salvador,* 9–14.

11. Sharer, *Ancient Maya,* 132. Martin and Grube do not credit the eruption with the extinction of cultural development in the highlands. There is evidence that the eruption of Ilopango occurred later than the dates Sharer gives.

12. Mark Pendergrast, *Uncommon Grounds: The History of Coffee and How It Transformed Our World* (New York: Basic, 1999), 45, 48.

13. Ibid., xv.

14. Thomas P. Anderson, *The War of the Dispossessed: Honduras and El Salvador, 1969* (Lincoln: University of Nebraska Press, 1981), 16–17. Rafael Zaldívar (1876–85), a pragmatic liberal, "ordered a survey of the common lands in 1879. This was seen as a prelude to their abolition; and those who were anxious to seize upon them had not long to wait, for on 26 February 1881 a decree came forth abolishing communal lands. Marco Virgilio Carías sees this as a critical step toward the situation which produced the war of 1969." Anderson could have added the abolition of common land led directly to *la matanza* of 1932 and the civil war of 1979 as well; "A February 24, 1881, decree, the Law of the Abolition of Communities, mandated that all communal prop-

erty be divided among co-owners or become property of the state. . . . The indigenous people were often evicted, sometime violently, from their ancestral lands. There were five popular uprisings in the coffee-growing area between 1872–1898" (Tommie Sue Montgomery, *Revolution in El Salvador: Origins and Evolution* [Boulder, Colo.: Westview Press, 1982], 42).

15. Haggerty, *El Salvador,* 14–16.

16. Stephens, *Central America,* 1: 326–27.

17. Ibid., 321–24.

18. Ibid.

19. Stephens, *Central America,* 1: 338–39.

20. Carl L. Hubbs and Gunnar I. Roden, "Oceanography and Marine Life along the Pacific Coast," in *Handbook of Middle American Indians,* ed. Robert C. West (Austin: University of Texas Press, 1964), 173.

21. Mario Lungo Ucles, *El Salvador in the Eighties: Counterinsurgency and Revolution* (Philadelphia: Temple University Press, 1996), 121.

22. Harold Jung, "Class Struggle and Civil War in El Salvador," *New Left Review* (London), July–August 1980, in *El Salvador: Central America in the New Cold War,* ed. Marvin E. Gettleman, Patrick Lacefield, Louis Menashe, and David Mermelstein (New York: Grove Press, 1986) 64.

23. Craig Pyles, "Roots of the Salvadoran Right: Origins of the Death Squads," in *El Salvador, Central America in the New Cold War,* 86–89.

24. Haggerty, *El Salvador,* 33–41.

25. Hugh Byrne, *El Salvador's Civil War: A Study of Revolution* (Boulder, Colo.: Lynne Renner, 1996), 169–94.

26. Philip J. Williams and Knut Walter, *Militarization and Demilitarization in El Salvador's Transition to Democracy* (Pittsburgh: University of Pittsburgh Press, 1997), 1.

27. Stephens, *Central America,* 1: 89–90.

28. Tom Buckley, *Violent Neighbors: El Salvador, Central America and the United States* (New York: Time Books, 1984), 105.

29. Stephens, *Central America,* 2: 22, 24.

30. Ibid., 24–25.

31. Ibid., 27.

32. William Oscar Scroggs, *Filibusters and Financiers: The Story of William Walker and His Associates* (New York: Macmillan, 1916). Walker's story has been retold many times since Professor Scroggs's wrote, but his book remains a classic.

33. Stephens, *Central America,* 1: 389–90, 391–92.

34. Crystal, *Cambridge Fact Finder,* 292–93.

35. Merrill, *Nicaragua,* 55–58.

36. David Close, *Nicaragua: Politics, Economics and Society* (London: Pinter, 1988), 17–20.

37. Conor Cruise O'Brien, "God and Man in Nicaragua," *Atlantic Monthly*, August 1986, 66–69.

38. Harry E. Vanden and Gary Prevost, *Democracy and Socialism in Sandinista Nicaragua* (Boulder, Colo.: Lynne Rienner, 1993), 26.

39. David Howard Bain, "The Man Who Made the Yanquis Go Home," *American Heritage* 36, no. 5 (1985): 50–61.

40. Stephens, *Central America*, 1: 404–5.

41. Merrill, *Nicaragua*, 25–38.

42. Shirley Christian, *Nicaragua: Revolution in the Family* (New York: Random House, 1985), 145.

43. Vanden and Prevost, *Democracy and Socialism*, 9–14.

44. Merrill, *Nicaragua*, 39–51.

45. Stephens, *Central America*, 1: 422.

46. Ibid., 396.

47. Ibid., 402.

48. Ibid., 413.

49. Ibid., 403.

50. David McCullough, *The Path between the Seas: The Creation of the Panama Canal, 1870–1914* (New York: Simon and Schuster: 1977), 261.

Chapter 6

1. Stephens, *Central America*, 1: 347–48.

2. Crystal, *Cambridge Fact Finder*, 230–31.

3. Richard F. Nyrop, *Costa Rica: A Country Study*, 2nd ed. (Washington, D.C.: GPO, 1983), xiii–xix.

4. Stephens, *Central America*, 1: 355–56.

5. Ibid., 352–53.

6. William Roseberry, Lowell Gudmundson, and Mario Samper Kutschback, eds., *Coffee, Society, and Power in Latin America* (Baltimore: Johns Hopkins University Press, 1995), 5.

7. Lowell Gudmundson, "Peasant, Farmer, Proletarian: Class Formation in a Smallholder Coffee Economy, 1850–1950," in *Coffee, Society and Power in Latin America*.

8. Stephens, *Central America*, 1: 362–64.

9. Ibid., 365–66

10. Nyrop, *Costa Rica*, 14.

11. Stephens, *Central America*, 1: 366–67.

12. Ibid., 368–69.

13. Ibid., 359–60.

14. Nyrop, *Costa Rica,* 22.

15. John Patrick Bell, *Crisis in Costa Rica: The Revolution of 1948* (Austin: University of Texas Press for the Institute of Latin American Studies, 1971), 42.

16. Charles D. Ameringer, *Don Pepe: A Political Biography of José Figueres of Costa Rica* (Albuquerque: University of New Mexico Press, 1978), 270.

17. Albert Z. Carr, *The World and William Walker* (New York: Harper and Row, 1963), 217.

18. Crystal, *Cambridge Fact Finder,* 254–55.

19. Anderson, *Politics,* 110.

20. Tim L. Merrill, ed. *Honduras: A Country Study,* 3rd ed. (Washington, D.C.: GPO, 1995), 48–49.

Chapter 7

1. Stephens, *Central America,* 1: 94–95.

2. Ibid., 101–5. All Stephens citations in this chapter come from this section of his text unless otherwise noted.

3. Robert L. Brunhouse, *In Search of the Maya: The First Archaeologists* (Albuquerque: University of New Mexico Press, 1973), 31. General information on Galindo and other early Mayanists in this section taken from Brunhouse.

4. William J. Griffith, "Juan Galindo, Central American Chauvinist," *Hispanic American Historical Review* 40 (1960): 37; Griffith cites the following correspondence: 15 January 1836 Galindo to Palmerston letter FO 15/18, fol. 199, and Admiralty to Galindo, 23 January 1836, ibid., fol. 212.

5. Brunhouse, *In Search of the Maya,* plate 14.

6. "As the 20th century advanced, the view became widespread that the main function of Classic Maya writing was to provide astronomical calculations, and to mark the passage of time. By extension, the individuals portrayed on the stone monuments must be either the gods themselves or the astronomer-priests who were charged with measuring the passage of time and prophesying the future based on auguries of the multitude of supernatural forces. The Classic Maya, according to conventional wisdom, was a theocratic society run by benevolent priests who exhorted the ingenious, peaceful farmers scattered in the countryside to build more temples at their 'vacant ceremonial center,' in honor of the high gods in their pantheon. Ironically, today's scholars have come to realize the wisdom of many of Stephens's original interpretations. Stephens correctly surmised that Copan and the other Maya ruins were the remains of indigenous New World peoples, that the human portraits on the monuments represented 'deified kings and heroes.' He also correctly guessed that the writing system recorded the history of the kings and their cities" (Fash, *Scribes, Warriors and Kings,* 10).

7. Stephens, *Central America,* 1: 140–42.

8. J. Eric S. Thompson, *The Rise and Fall of Maya Civilization* (Norman: University of Oklahoma Press, 1954), 79.

9. Fash, *Scribes, Warriors and Kings,* 24.

10. "The Great Stephens," Coe, *Maya,* 223; other information from Michael D. Coe, *Breaking the Maya Code,* rev. ed. (New York: Thames and Hudson, 1999). Discussion of the many false starts and the final unraveling of the Maya hieroglyphs follows Coe.

11. Coe, *Breaking,* 16–18.

12. Coe, *Breaking,* 121.

13. Thompson, *Rise and Fall,* 55.

14. Coe, *Breaking,* 171.

15. Sharer, *Ancient Maya,* 19–43. Background on the Maya comes largely from Sharer.

16. Thompson, *Rise and Fall,* 143.

17. Fash, *Scribes, Warriors and Kings,* 112–13.

18. Linda Schele and Peter Mathews, *The Code of Kings: The Language of Seven Sacred Maya Temples and Tombs* (New York: Scribner, 1998), 134.

19. Stephens, *Central America,* 1: 155.

20. Schele and Mathews, *Code of Kings,* 141–46. All material on Stela C from this source.

21. Sharer, *Ancient Maya,* 308.

22. Stephens, *Central America,* 1: 137.

Chapter 8

1. Stephens, *Central America,* 1: 187–88.

2. Ibid., 190–91.

3. Ibid., 192–93.

4. Sister Dianna Ortiz of New Mexico is probably the nun to whom they were referring.

5. Stephens, *Central America,* 2: 171. The extensive quotes from Stephens over the next several pages follow from here.

6. "Robert Carmack traces the [Quiché] elite to a much later incursion of the Tolecized Chontal-Nahua speakers from the Gulf coast [who were] completely Mexican down to the last . . . detail" (Coe, *Maya,* 188). In short, not only can Stephens's surmise regarding the difference in cultural genesis of the ruins at Utatlán be said to be not without some basis in fact, but also that the highland Maya were subject to at least two waves of massive outside influence prior to the Spanish Conquest, that of the Chontal-Nuhua speakers noted here and of the Mexican Teotihuacan rulers of the highlands in the middle classic period.

7. Stephens, *Central America,* 2: 180–81.

8. Ibid., 189.

Chapter 9

1. Stephens, *Central America,* 1: 273–75.

2. Ibid., 266–67.

3. Ibid., 278.

Chapter 10

1. Stephens, *Central America,* 2: 127.

2. Ibid., 135, 137.

3. Ibid., 131.

4. Rigoberta Menchú, *I, Rigoberta Menchú, an Indian Woman in Guatemala,* ed. Elisabeth Bugos-Debray, trans. Ann Wright, 1983 (London: Verso, 1984).

5. See the following for more information about this rather embarrassing imbroglio: *The Rigoberta Menchú Controversy,* ed. Arturo Arias, with a response by David Stoll (Minneapolis: University of Minnesota Press, 2001).

6. Stephens, *Central America,* 2: 219.

7. Ibid.

8. Stephens, *Central America,* 2: 229.

9. Sharer, *Ancient Maya,* 427.

10. Stephens, *Central America,* 2: 234–35.

11. Tom Roberts, "Truth Commission Report Details Years of Military Abuses," *National Catholic Reporter,* 12 March 1999, 13–16.

Chapter 11

1. José Comblin, *Called for Freedom: The Changing Context of Liberation Theology,* trans. Philip Berryman (Maryknoll, N.Y.: Orbis, 1998), 2.

2. Comblin, *Called for Freedom,* 8.

3. Ibid.

4. Enrique Krauze, "Chiapas: The Indians' Prophet," *New York Review of Books,* 16 December 1999, 68.

5. *Encyclopedia Britannica,* online edition.

6. Krauze, 71.

7. Stephens, *Central America,* 2: 252.

8. Ibid., 256.

9. Ibid., 250.

10. Ibid., 258.

11. Sharer, *Ancient Maya,* 295.

12. Stephens, *Central America,* 2: 260.

13. Ibid., 264.

14. Ibid., 264, 266, 274.

15. Ibid., 275–76.

Chapter 12

1. Stephens, *Central America,* 2: 291–92.

2. Brunhouse, *In Search of the Maya,* 8–9.

3. Ibid., 50, 82.

4. Pendergast, *Palenque,* 177.

5. Stephens, *Central America,* 2: 290.

6. Ibid., 291.

7. Ibid., 308.

8. Ibid., 320, 322–23.

9. Ibid., 304, 355.

10. Ibid., 337–38, 339, 341, 343.

11. "The elite caste may have considered itself immortal. In this case, the greater paradigm would have been the myth of the Hero Twins recounted in the pages of the Quiché Maya epic, the *Popol Vuh,* which tells of the descent of a pair of handsome brothers to Xibalbá the Underworld, their triumph over the lords of death, their resurrection of their father, and the apotheosis as the sun and the moon. In a tour-de-force of iconographic analysis, Karl Taube has shown that this myth of death and resurrection symbolically celebrates the planting of the maize seed in the earth sending it to Xibalbá, and its resurrection when the rains finally arrive and it sprouts on the earth's surface" (Coe and Kerr, *Art,* 34–35).

12. Discussion in the preceding two paragraphs and the following passage follows Schele and Mathews, *Code of Kings,* 95–128.

13. "The Preclassic triadic arrangement, seen at Nakbe and El Mirador, and the placement of the tallest building at the north, seen in the North Acropolis at Tikal and the initial temple at Cerros" (Sharer, *Ancient Maya,* 284).

14. Stephens, *Central America,* 2: 317.

15. Ibid., 334.

16. Ibid., 356–57.

17. Martin and Grube, *Chronicle,* 155, 157.

18. Sharer, *Ancient Maya,* 280. Professor Sharer in an informal chat at the Congreso Internacional de Copán conference at Copán Ruinas, Honduras, 14 July 2001, assured me that more recent tests have confirmed the epigraphical evidence by showing the bones in Pacal's tomb were much older than first believed.

Chapter 13

1. John Lloyd Stephens, *Incidents of Travel in Yucatan*, 2 vols. (1843; New York: Dover, 1963), 1: 115.

2. Stephens, *Central America*, 2: 396–98.

3. Ibid., 398–400.

4. Ibid., 396.

5. Ibid., 395.

6. Ibid.

7. Stephens, *Yucatan*, 2: 289.

8. Ibid., 289–91.

9. Ibid., 415.

10. Ibid., 397.

11. Smyth personal correspondence, 4 April 2001.

12. The following discussion taken from Schele and Mathews, *Code of Kings*, chap. 7, 257–90.

13. Smyth personal correspondence, 4 April 2001.

14. Stephens, *Central America*, 2: 429–30.

15. Sharer, *Ancient Maya*, 638.

16. Stephens, *Central America*, 2: 442–43.

17. "Who were the builders of these American cities? . . . some were probably in ruins but in general I believe they were occupied by the Indians at the time of the Spanish invasion" (Stephens, *Yucatan*, 2: 307); "among themselves [the natives] speak of their country only under its ancient name of Maya" (*Ibid.*, 1: 77). Stephens used the word "Maya" to denote the territory and language of the ancient league of Mayapán throughout the book. Penn State's David Webster traces the etymology of the term Maya. He concludes, "This brings us to the final meaning of the word Maya—essentially the one invented by Stephens and Catherwood" (*The Fall of the Ancient Maya: Solving the Mystery of the Maya Collapse* [London: Thames and Hudson, 2002], 46).

18. These speculations regarding the collapse of Maya culture reflect the views expressed in Sharer, *Ancient Maya*, 339–48.

19. According to Michael D. Coe, "three University of Florida scientists—Jason Curtis, David Hobell, and Mark Brenner . . . [determined on the basis of core samples of an area lake] that there had been an unusually severe drought that lasted from A.D. 800 to 1050, peaking at 862. Now we have solid evidence from a number of sources that by the ninth century the Classic lowland Maya had severely degraded their environment to the point that extremely high populations could no longer be sustained" (*The Maya*, 39).

20. David Webster makes the point that the Maya "collapse" can be likened to the

"collapse" of ancient Rome. Although the last emperor of Rome was executed by the barbarians in A.D. 476, the city and environs continued to be occupied by native Romans right up to the present time. These folk spoke a Latin that evolved into modern Italian and in other ways utilized cultural components of the defunct classic Roman empire (*Fall of the Ancient Maya*, 73).

21. Stephens, *Central America,* 2: 386–88.

22. Ibid., 389.

23. Ibid., 390.

24. Biographical information comes from von Hagen.

25. Two such articles appearing in the April 2002 issue of *National Geographic* were George E. Stuart's "Yucatán's Mysterious Hill Cities," 54–69, and Tom O'Neill's "Uncovering a Maya Mural," 70–75.

Bibliography

Adams, Richard Newbold. *Crucifixion by Power: Essays on Guatemalan National Social Structure, 1944–1966.* Austin: University of Texas Press, 1970.

Allen, H. C. "Border Disputes (1823–60)." In *Great Britain and the United States: A History of Anglo-American Relations (1783–1952).* New York: St. Martin's Press, 1955.

Ameringer, Charles D. *Don Pepe: A Political Biography of José Figueres of Costa Rica.* Albuquerque: University of New Mexico Press, 1978.

Anderson, Thomas P. *Politics in Central America: Guatemala, El Salvador, Honduras and Nicaragua.* New York: Praeger, 1983.

———. *The War of the Dispossessed: Honduras and El Salvador, 1969.* Lincoln: University of Nebraska Press, 1981.

Arias, Arturo, ed. *The Rigoberta Menchú Controversy.* With a response by David Stoll. Minneapolis: University of Minnesota Press, 2001.

Bain, David Howard. "The Man Who Made the Yanquis Go Home." *American Heritage* 36, no. 5 (1985).

Bell, John Patrick. *Crisis in Costa Rica: The Revolution of 1948.* Austin: University of Texas Press for the Institute of Latin American Studies, 1971.

Brooks, Van Wyck. *The World of Washington Irving.* Philadelphia: Blakiston, 1944.

Brunhouse, Robert L. *In Search of the Maya: The First Archaeologists.* Albuquerque: University of New Mexico Press, 1973.

Buckley, Tom. *Violent Neighbors: El Salvador, Central America and the United States.* New York: Time Books, 1984.

Byrne, Hugh. *El Salvador's Civil War: A Study of Revolution.* Boulder, Colo.: Lynne Renner, 1996.

Carr, Albert Z. *The World and William Walker.* New York: Harper and Row, 1963.

Carrasco, Davíd. *Religions of Mesoamerica: Cosmovision and Ceremonial Centers*. San Francisco: Harper and Row, 1990.

"Central American Federation, 'Peace, Amity, Commerce, and Navigation.'" *Unperfected Treaties of the United States*. Dobbs Ferry, N.Y.: Oceana, 1976–94.

Christian, Shirley. *Nicaragua: Revolution in the Family*. New York: Random House, 1985.

Cleghorn, Wayne M. *British Honduras: Colonial Dead End, 1859–1900*. Baton Rouge: Louisiana State University Press, 1967.

Close, David. *Nicaragua: Politics, Economics and Society*. London: Pinter, 1988.

Coe, Michael D. *Breaking the Maya Code*. Rev. ed. New York: Thames and Hudson, 1999.

———. *The Maya*. 6th ed. New York: Thames and Hudson, 1999.

———. *Mexico: From the Olmecs to the Aztecs*. 4th ed. New York: Thames and Hudson, 1982.

Coe, Michael D., and Justin Kerr. *The Art of the Maya Scribe*. New York: Harry N. Abrams, 1998.

Comblin, José. *Called for Freedom: The Changing Context of Liberation Theology*. Translated by Philip Berryman. Maryknoll, N.Y.: Orbis Books, 1998.

Conner, Clifford D. *Colonel Despard: The Life and Times of an English Jacobin*. Conshohocken, Pa.: Signpost, 1999.

Crystal, David., ed. *Cambridge Fact Finder*. Cambridge: Cambridge University Press, 1993.

Daum, Michael. "Modernity's Ethnographer: John Lloyd Stephens in Belize." Master's thesis, University of South Florida, 1999.

Diplomatic Correspondence of the United States: Inter-American Affairs, 1831–1860. Vol. 3: Central America, 1831–1850, Documents, 723–995. Edited by William R. Manning. Washington, D.C.: Carnegie Endowment for International Peace, 1933.

Dorsal, Paul J. *Doing Business with the Dictators: A Political History of United Fruit in Guatemala, 1899–1944*. Washington, Del.: SR Books, 1993.

Fash, William L. *Scribes, Warriors and Kings: the City of Copan and the Ancient Maya*. New York: Thames and Hudson, 1991.

Fox, John W. *Quiche Conquest, Centralism and Regionalism in Highland Guatemalan State Development*. Albuquerque: University of New Mexico Press, 1978.

Freidel, David, Linda Schele, and Joy Parker. *Maya Cosmos: Three Thousand Years on the Shaman's Path*. New York: Quill, 1993.

Griffith, William J. "Juan Galindo, Central American Chauvinist." *Hispanic American Historical Review* 40 (1960): 37.

Gudmundson, Lowell. "Peasant, Farmer, Proletarian: Class Formation in a Smallholder Coffee Economy, 1850–1950." In *Coffee, Society, and Power in Latin America*, edited by William Roseberry, Lowell Gudmundson, and Mario Samper Kutschback. Baltimore: Johns Hopkins University Press, 1995.

Haggerty, Richard A., ed. *El Salvador: A Country Study.* 2nd ed. Washington, D.C.: GPO, 1990.

Hatcher, William B. *Edward Livingston: Jeffersonian Republican and Jacksonian Democrat.* Baton Rouge: Louisiana State University Press, 1940.

Hubbs, Carl L., and Gunnar I. Roden. "Oceanography and Marine Life along the Pacific Coast." In *Handbook of Middle American Indians,* edited by Robert C. West. Austin: University of Texas Press, 1964.

Immerman, Richard H. *The CIA in Guatemala: The Foreign Policy of Intervention.* Austin: University of Texas Press, 1982.

Jonas, Susanne. *Rebels, Death Squads, and U.S. Power.* Latin American Perspective Series, no. 5. Boulder, Colo.: Westview Press, 1991.

Jung, Harold. "Class Struggle and Civil War in El Salvador." *New Left Review* (London), July–August 1980, in *El Salvador: Central America in the New Cold War,* edited by Marvin E. Gettleman, Patrick Lacefield, Louis Menashe, and David Mermelstein. New York: Grove Press, 1986.

Karnes, Thomas L. *The Failure of Union: Central America, 1824–1960.* Chapel Hill: University of North Carolina Press, 1961.

Kelsey, Vera, and Lilly de Jongh Osborne. *Four Keys to Guatemala.* New York: Funk and Wagnalls, 1948.

Kepner, Charles David, Jr., and Jay Henry Soothill. *The Banana Empire: A Case Study in Economic Imperialism.* New York: Vanguard Press, 1935; New York: Russell & Russell, 1967.

Krauze, Enrique. "Chiapas: The Indians' Prophet." *New York Review of Books,* 16 December 1999.

LaFeber, Walter. *Inevitable Revolutions: The United States in Central America.* 2nd ed. New York: W. W. Norton, 1993.

Lessard, W. O. *The Complete Book of Bananas.* Homestead, Fla.: The Author, 1992.

MacDonald, Ronald H. "Civil-Military Relations in Central America: The Dilemmas of Political Institutionalization." In *Rift and Revolution: The Central American Imbroglio,* edited by Howard J. Wiarda. Washington, D.C.: American Enterprise Institute for Public Policy Research, 1984.

Martin, Simon, and Nikolai Grube. *Chronicle of the Maya Kings and Queens.* London: Thames and Hudson, 2000.

McCullough, David. *The Path between the Seas: The Creation of the Panama Canal, 1870–1914.* New York: Simon and Schuster, 1977.

Menchú, Rigoberta. *I, Rigoberta Menchú, an Indian Woman in Guatemala.* Edited by Elisabeth Bugos-Debray. Translated by Ann Wright, 1983. London: Verso, 1984.

Merrill, Tim L., ed. *Guyana and Belize: Country Studies.* 2nd ed. Washington, D.C.: GPO, 1993.

———, ed. *Honduras: A Country Study.* 3rd ed. Washington, D.C.: GPO, 1995.

———, ed. *Nicaragua: A Country Study.* 3rd ed. Washington, D.C.: GPO, 1994.

Montgomery, Tommie Sue. *Revolution in El Salvador: Origins and Evolution.* Boulder, Colo.: Westview Press, 1982.

Nyrop, Richard F, ed. *Costa Rica: A Country Study.* 2nd ed. Washington, D.C.: GPO, 1983.

————, ed. *Guatemala: A Country Study.* 2nd ed. Washington, D.C.: GPO, 1983.

O'Brien, Conor Cruise. "God and Man in Nicaragua." *Atlantic Monthly,* August 1986.

O'Mara, Richard. "The American Traveller." *Virginia Quarterly Review* 74 (spring 1998): 221–33.

O'Neill, Tom. "Uncovering a Maya Mural." *National Geographic,* April 2002: 70–75.

Pendergast, David M., ed. and comp. *Palenque: The Walker-Caddy Expedition to the Ancient Maya City, 1839–1840.* Norman: University of Oklahoma Press, 1967.

Pendergrast, Mark. *Uncommon Grounds: The History of Coffee and How It Transformed Our World.* New York: Basic, 1999.

Perera, Victor. *Unfinished Conquest: The Guatemalan Tragedy.* Berkeley: University of California Press, 1993.

Preston, Richard. "America's Egypt: John Lloyd Stephens and the Discovery of the Maya." *Princeton University Library Chronicle* 53 (spring 1992): 243–63.

Pyles, Craig. "Roots of the Salvadoran Right: Origins of the Death Squads." In *El Salvador, Central America in the New Cold War,* edited by Marvin Gettleman, Patrick Lacefield, Louis Menashe, and David Mermelstein. New York: Grove Press, 1986.

Roberts, Tom. "Truth Commission Report Details Years of Military Abuses." *National Catholic Reporter,* 12 March 1999: 13–16.

Roseberry, William, Lowell Gudmundson, and Mario Samper Kutschback. *Coffee, Society, and Power in Latin America.* Baltimore: Johns Hopkins University Press, 1995.

Sabloff, Jeremy A. *The New Archaeology and the Ancient Maya.* New York: Scientific American Library, 1994.

Schele, Linda, and David Freidel. *A Forest of Kings: The Untold Story of the Ancient Maya.* New York: Quill, 1990.

Schele, Linda, and Peter Mathews. *The Code of Kings: The Language of Seven Sacred Maya Temples and Tombs.* New York: Scribner, 1998.

Schele, Linda, and Mary Ellen Miller. *The Blood of Kings: Dynasty and Ritual in Maya Art.* Preface by Michael D. Coe. London: Thames and Hudson, 1992.

Schlesinger, Stephen, and Stephen Kinzer. *Bitter Fruit: The Untold Story of the American Coup in Guatemala.* 1982. New York: Anchor, 1990.

Schwartz, Norman B. *Forest Society: A Social History of Petén, Guatemala.* Philadelphia: University of Pennsylvania Press, 1990.

Scroggs, William Oscar. *Filibusters and Financiers: The Story of William Walker and His Associates.* New York: Macmillan, 1916.

Setzekorn, William David. *Formerly British Honduras: A Profile of the New Nation of Belize.* Athens: Ohio University Press, 1981.

Sharer, Robert J. *The Ancient Maya.* 5th ed. Stanford: Stanford University Press, 1994.

Simpson, Lesley Byrd. *The Encomienda in New Spain: The Beginning of Spanish Mexico.* Berkeley: University of California Press, 1966.

State Department, Bureau of Public Affairs. "Background Notes: Belize, August 1987." Washington, D.C.: GPO, 1987.

Stephens, John Lloyd. *Incidents of Travel in Central America, Chiapas and Yucatan.* 2 vols. 1841. Reprint with Publisher's Note from 1854 ed. New York: Dover, 1969.

———. *Incidents of Travel in Yucatan.* 2 vols. 1843. New York: Dover, 1963.

Stuart, George E. "Yucatán's Mysterious Hill Cities." *National Geographic,* April 2002: 54–69.

Sutherland, Anne. *The Making of Belize: Globalization in the Margins.* Westport, Conn.: Bergin and Garvey, 1998.

Thompson, J. Eric S. *The Rise and Fall of Maya Civilization.* Norman: University of Oklahoma Press, 1954.

Ucles, Mario Lungo. *El Salvador in the Eighties: Counterinsurgency and Revolution.* Philadelphia: Temple University Press, 1996.

Vanden, Harry E., and Gary Prevost. *Democracy and Socialism in Sandinista Nicaragua.* Boulder, Colo.: Lynne Rienner, 1993.

von Hagen, Victor Wolfgang. *Frederick Catherwood.* Oxford University Press, 1950.

———. *Maya Explorer, John Lloyd Stephens and the Lost Cites of Central America and Yucatán.* 1947. San Francisco: Chronicle Books, 1990.

Wasserstrom, William. "Van Wyck Brooks." In *The Makers of American Thought: An Introduction to Seven American Writers,"* edited by Ralph Ross. Minneapolis: University of Minnesota Press, 1974.

Webster, David. *The Fall of the Ancient Maya: Solving the Mystery of the Maya Collapse.* London: Thames and Hudson, 2002.

Williams, Philip J., and Knut Walter. *Militarization and Demilitarization in El Salvador's Transition to Democracy.* Pittsburgh: University of Pittsburgh Press, 1997.

Woodward, Ralph Lee, Jr. *Central America: A Nation Divided.* New York: Oxford University Press, 1999.

Index